Version 5.0

EXPLORING MICROSOFT® EXCEL

Robert T. Grauer

Maryann Barber

University of Miami

Prentice Hall, Englewood Cliffs, New Jersey 07632

Library of Congress Cataloging in Publication Data

Grauer, Robert T. [date]
    Exploring Microsoft Excel, version 5.0 / Robert T. Grauer,
    Maryann Barber.
    p. cm.
    Includes index.
    ISBN 0-13-079534-8
    1. Excel for Windows. 2. Business—Computer programs.
    3. Electronic spreadsheets. I. Barber, Maryann M. II. Title.
HF5548.4.L67G73 1994
650'.0258'5369—dc20   94
                                      CIP

Microsoft is a registered trademark and Windows is
a trademark of Microsoft Corporation.

Acquisitions editor: P. J. Boardman
Editorial / production supervisor: Greg Hubit Bookworks
Interior and cover design: Suzanne Behnke
Production coordinator: Patrice Fraccio
Managing editor: Maureen Wilson
Developmental editor: Harriet Serenkin
Editorial assistants: Renée Pelletier / Dolores Kenny

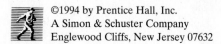

©1994 by Prentice Hall, Inc.
A Simon & Schuster Company
Englewood Cliffs, New Jersey 07632

Printed in the United States of America
10   9   8   7

ISBN 0-13-079534-8

Prentice Hall International (UK) Limited, *London*
Prentice Hall of Australia Pty. Limited, *Sydney*
Prentice Hall of Canada Inc., *Toronto*
Prentice Hall Hispanoamericano, S.A., *Mexico*
Prentice Hall of India Private Limited, *New Delhi*
Prentice Hall of Japan, Inc., *Tokyo*
Simon & Schuster Asia Pte. Ltd., *Singapore*
Editora Prentice Hall do Brasil, Ltda., *Rio de Janeiro*

Contents

3

Spreadsheets in Decision Making: What If?   81

4

Graphs and Charts: Delivering a Message   125

5

List and Data Management: Converting Data to Information   179

Appendix A: Toolbars   228

Index   235

Preface

Exploring Microsoft Excel 5.0 is one of several books (modules) in the Prentice Hall *Exploring Windows* series. Other modules include *Word for Windows 6.0, Microsoft Access 2.0, PowerPoint 4.0, WordPerfect for Windows 6.0, Lotus for Windows 4.0,* and an introductory module, *Exploring Windows 3.1*. The books are independent of one another but possess a common design, pedagogy, and writing style intended to serve the application courses in both two- and four-year schools.

Each book in the series is suitable on a stand-alone basis for any course that teaches a specific application; alternatively, several modules can be bound together for a single course that teaches multiple applications. The initial component, *Exploring Windows 3.1,* assumes no previous knowledge and includes an introductory section for the individual who has never used a computer.

The *Exploring Windows* series will appeal to students in a variety of disciplines including business, liberal arts, and the sciences. Each module has a consistent presentation that stresses the benefits of the Windows environment, especially the common user interface that performs the same task in identical fashion across applications. Each module emphasizes the benefits of multitasking, demonstrates the ability to share data between applications, and stresses the extensive on-line help facility to facilitate learning. Students are taught concepts, not just keystrokes or mouse clicks, with hands-on exercises in every chapter providing the necessary practice to master the material.

The *Exploring Windows* series is different from other books, both in its scope as well as the way in which material is presented. Students learn by doing. Concepts are stressed and memorization is minimized. Shortcuts and other important Windows information are consistently highlighted in the many boxed tips that appear throughout the series. Every chapter contains at least two directed exercises at the computer, but equally important are the less structured end-of-chapter problems that not only review the information but extend it as well. The end-of-chapter material is a distinguishing feature of the entire series, an integral part of the learning process, and a powerful motivational tool for students to learn and explore.

FEATURES AND BENEFITS

- *Exploring Microsoft Excel* presents concepts as well as keystrokes and mouse clicks, so that students learn the theory behind the applications. They are not just taught what to do but are provided with the rationale for why they are doing it, enabling them to extend the information to additional learning on their own.
- No previous knowledge is assumed on the part of the reader as a fast-paced introduction brings the reader or new user up to speed immediately.
- Practical information, beyond application-specific material, appears throughout the series. Students are cautioned about computer viruses and taught the importance of adequate backup. The *Exploring Windows* module, for example, teaches students to extend the warranty of a new computer and points out the advantages of a mail-order purchase.

- Problem solving and troubleshooting are stressed throughout the series. The authors are constantly anticipating mistakes that students may make and tell the reader how to recover from problems that invariably occur.
- Tips, tips, and more tips present application shortcuts in every chapter. Windows is designed for the mouse, but experienced users gravitate toward keyboard shortcuts once they have mastered basic skills. The series presents different ways to accomplish a given task, but in a logical and relaxed fashion.
- A unique Buying Guide in the introductory module presents a thorough introduction to PC hardware from the viewpoint of purchasing a computer. Students learn the subtleties in selecting a configuration—for example, how the resolution of a monitor affects its size, the advantages of a local bus, and the Intel CPU processor index.

ACKNOWLEDGMENTS

We want to thank the many individuals who helped bring this project to its successful conclusion. We are especially grateful to our editor at Prentice Hall, P. J. Boardman, without whom the series would not have been possible, and to Harriet Serenkin, the developmental editor, whose vision helped shape the project. Gretchen Marx of Saint Joseph College produced an outstanding set of Instructor Manuals. Greg Hubit was in charge of production. Deborah Emry, our marketing manager at Prentice Hall, developed the innovative campaign that helped make the series a success. Delores Kenny helped coordinate all phases of the project.

We also want to acknowledge our reviewers, who through their comments and constructive criticism made this a far better book.

Lynne Band, Middlesex Community College
Stuart P. Brian, Holy Family College
Kimberly Chambers, Scottsdale Community College
Alok Charturvedi, Purdue University
Jerry Chin, Southwest Missouri State University
Dean Combellick, Scottsdale Community College
Cody Copeland, Johnson County Community College
Paul E. Daurelle, Western Piedmont Community College
David Douglas, University of Arkansas
Raymond Frost, Central Connecticut State University
James Gips, Boston College
Vernon Griffin, Austin Community College
Wanda D. Heller, Seminole Community College
Bonnie Homan, San Francisco State University
Ernie Ivey, Polk Community College
Mike Kelly, Community College of Rhode Island
Jane King, Everett Community College
John Lesson, University of Central Florida
Alan Moltz, Naugatuck Valley Technical Community College
Nancy Monthofen, Scottsdale Community College
Delores Pusins, Hillsborough Community College
Gale E. Rand, College Misericordia
David Rinehard, Lansing Community College
Marilyn Salas, Scottsdale Community College
John Shepherd, Duquesne University
Sally Visci, Lorain County Community College
David Weiner, University of San Francisco
Connie Wells, Georgia State University
Jack Zeller, Kirkwood Community College

A final word of thanks to the unnamed students at the University of Miami who make it all worthwhile. And, most of all, thanks to you, our readers, for choosing this book. Please feel free to contact us with any comments and suggestions. We can be reached most easily on the Internet.

Robert T. Grauer
RGRAUER@UMIAMI.MIAMI.EDU

Maryann Barber
MBARBER@UMIAMI.MIAMI.EDU

INTERNATIONALIZE YOUR EDUCATION!!

Join International Business Seminars on
an Overseas Adventure

EARN COLLEGE CREDIT
GAIN INTERNATIONAL EXPERTISE
INTERACT WITH TOP-LEVEL EXECUTIVES
VISIT THE WORLD'S GREATEST CITIES
May 30, 1994–June 23, 1994

VISIT ORGANIZATIONS SUCH AS: Procter & Gamble Italia, NATO,
The European Parliament, Elektra Breganz, Philip Morris, Allianz Insurance,
Deutsche Aerospace, Digital Equipment, Coca-Cola, G.E. International,
Ernst & Young, Esso Italiana, Guccio Gucci, Targetti Lighting,
University of Innsbruck & British Bankers Association.

PRENTICE HALL INTERNATIONAL BUSINESS SCHOLARSHIP 1994

Prentice Hall and International Business Seminars have joined forces to create a scholarship for students to study and travel in Europe in the summer of 1994. We believe that in today's global business environment students should be exposed to as many different cultures as possible. Although many campuses reflect diversity in both their students and faculty, nothing can replace the educational value of learning about a continent, country, or city firsthand.

Each professor may sponsor one student to apply for the scholarship by writing a letter of recommendation and providing the student the application guidelines below.

You can receive more information on the PH Business Scholarship and/or additional travel programs with International Business Seminars by contacting your local Prentice Hall representative or International Business Seminars, P.O. Box 30279, Mesa, Arizona 85275, Telephone: (602) 830-0902; Fax: (602) 924-0527.

Introduction to Microsoft Excel: What Is a Spreadsheet?

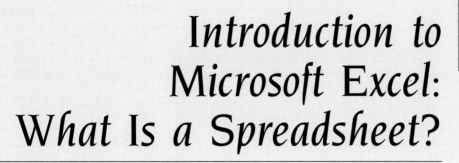

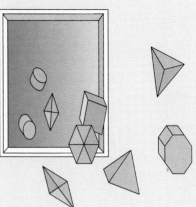

After reading this chapter you will be able to:

1. Explain the concept of a common user interface and its advantage in learning a new application.

2. Describe the basic mouse operations; use a mouse and/or the equivalent keyboard shortcuts to select commands from a pull-down menu.

3. Discuss the function of a dialog box; describe the different types of dialog boxes and the various ways in which information is supplied.

4. Access the on-line help facility and explain its various capabilities.

5. Describe a spreadsheet and suggest several potential applications; explain how the rows and columns of a spreadsheet are identified, and how its cells are labeled.

6. Distinguish between a formula and a constant; explain the use of a predefined function within a formula.

7. Open an Excel workbook; add and delete rows and columns of a worksheet; save and print the modified worksheet.

8. Distinguish between a pull-down menu, a shortcut menu, and a toolbar; describe how the TipWizard is intended to make you more proficient in Excel.

OVERVIEW

This chapter provides a broad-based introduction to spreadsheets and Microsoft Excel. It begins, however, with a discussion of basic Windows concepts, applicable to Windows applications in general, and to Microsoft Excel in particular. The emphasis is on the common user interface and consistent command structure that facilitates learning within the Windows environment. Indeed, you may already know much of this material, but that is precisely the point. Once you know one Windows application, it is that much easier to learn the next.

The second half of the chapter introduces the spreadsheet, the microcomputer application most widely used by managers and executives. Our intent is to show the wide diversity of business and other uses to which the spreadsheet model can be applied. For one example, we draw an analogy between the spreadsheet and the accountant's ledger. For a second example, we create an instructor's grade book.

The chapter covers the fundamentals of spreadsheets as implemented in Excel, which uses the term *worksheet* rather than *spreadsheet*. It discusses how the rows and columns of an Excel worksheet are labeled, the difference between a formula and a constant, and the ability of a worksheet to recalculate itself after a change is made.

The two hands-on exercises in the chapter enable you to apply all of the material at the computer, and are indispensable to the learn-by-doing philosophy we follow throughout the text.

THE WINDOWS DESKTOP

The *desktop* is the centerpiece of Microsoft Windows and is analogous to the desk on which you work. There are physical objects on your real desk and there are *windows* (framed rectangular areas) and *icons* (pictorial symbols) displayed on the Windows desktop. The components of a window are explained within the context of Figure 1.1, which contains the opening Windows screen on our computer.

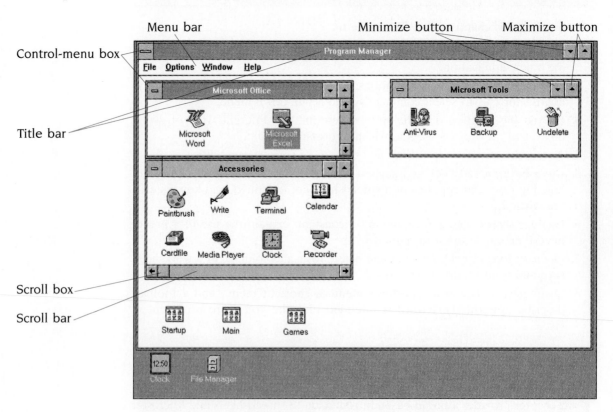

FIGURE 1.1 The Windows Desktop

Your desktop may be different from ours, just as your real desk is arranged differently from those of your friends. You can expect, however, to see a window titled Program Manager. You may or may not see other windows within Program Manager such as the Accessories, Microsoft Tools, and Microsoft Office windows shown in Figure 1.1.

Program Manager is crucial to the operation of Windows. It starts automatically when Windows is loaded and it remains active the entire time you are working in Windows. Closing Program Manager closes Windows. Program Manager is in essence an organizational tool that places applications in groups (e.g., Microsoft Office), then displays those groups as windows or group icons.

Regardless of the windows that are open on your desktop, every window contains the same basic elements: a title bar, control-menu box, and buttons to minimize and to maximize or restore the window. The ***title bar*** displays the name of the window—for example, Microsoft Office in Figure 1.1. The ***control-menu box*** accesses a pull-down menu that lets you select operations relevant to the window. The ***maximize button*** enlarges the window so that it takes the entire desktop. The ***minimize button*** reduces a window to an icon (but keeps the program active in memory). A ***restore button*** (a double arrow not shown in Figure 1.1) appears after a window has been maximized and returns the window to its previous size (the size before it was maximized).

Other elements that may or may not be present include a horizontal and/or vertical scroll bar and a menu bar. A horizontal (vertical) ***scroll bar*** will appear at the bottom (right) border of a window when the contents of the window are not completely visible. The ***scroll box*** appears within the scroll bar to facilitate moving within the window. A ***menu bar*** is found in the window for Program Manager, but not in the other windows. This is because Program Manager is a different kind of window, an application window rather than a document window.

An ***application window*** contains a program (application). A ***document window*** holds data for a program and is contained within an application window. The distinction between application and document windows is made clearer when we realize that Program Manager is a program and requires access to commands contained in pull-down menus located on the menu bar.

MICROSOFT TOOLS

The Microsoft Tools group is created automatically when you install (or upgrade to) MS-DOS 6.0. The name of each icon (Antivirus, Backup, and Undelete) is indicative of its function, and each program is an important tool in safeguarding your data. The Antivirus program allows you to scan disks for known viruses (and remove them when found). The Backup utility copies files from the hard disk to one or more floppy disk(s) in case of hard disk failure. The Undelete program allows you to recover files that you accidentally erased from a disk.

Common User Interface

One of the most significant benefits of the Windows environment is the ***common user interface,*** which provides a sense of familiarity when you begin to learn a new application. All applications work basically the same way. Thus, if you already know one Windows application, even one as simple as the Paintbrush accessory, it will be that much easier to learn Microsoft Excel. In similar fashion, it will take you less time to learn Word for Windows once you know Excel, because both applications share a common menu structure with consistent ways to select commands from those menus.

Consider, for example, Figures 1.2a and 1.2b, containing windows for Excel and Word, respectively. The applications are very different, yet the windows have many characteristics in common. You might even say that they have more similarities than differences, a remarkable statement considering the programs accom-

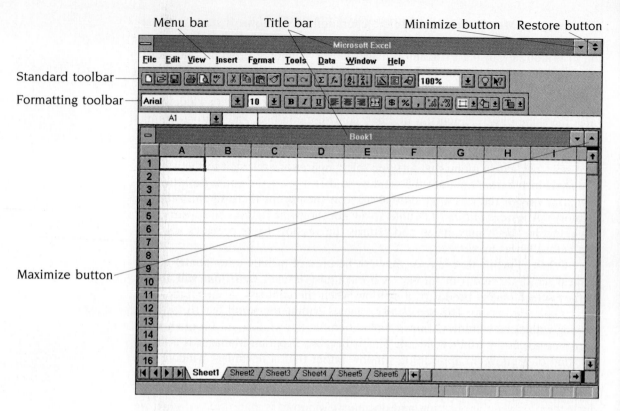

(a) Microsoft Excel 5.0

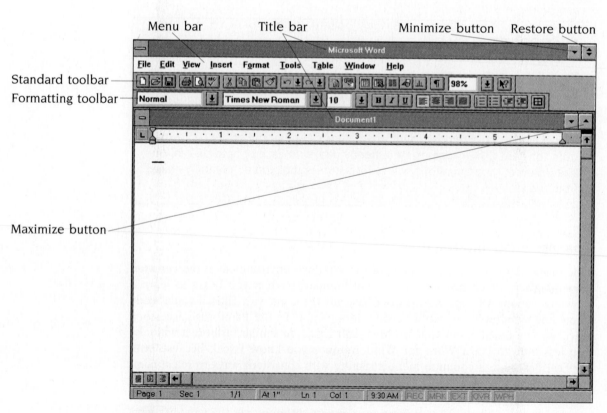

(b) Microsoft Word for Windows 6.0

FIGURE 1.2 The Common User Interface

plish very different tasks. A document window (Book1) is contained in the application window for Excel. In similar fashion, a document window (Document1) is present within the application window for Word.

The application windows for Excel and Word contain the same elements as any other application window: a title bar, menu bar, and control-menu box; and minimize and maximize or restore buttons. The menu bars are almost identical; that is, the File, Edit, View, Insert, Format, Tools, Window, and Help menus are present in both applications. The only difference between the menu bars is that Excel has a Data menu, whereas Word has a Table menu.

The commands within the menus are also consistent in both applications. The File menu contains the commands to open and close a file. The Edit menu contains the commands to cut, copy, and paste text; and so on. The means for accessing the pull-down menus are also consistent; that is, click the menu name (see mouse basics later in the chapter) or press the Alt key plus the underlined letter of the menu name—for example, Alt+F to pull down the File menu.

The application windows for Excel and Word also contain toolbars that provide alternate ways (shortcuts) to execute common commands. The **Standard toolbar** contains buttons (icons) for basic commands such as opening and closing a file or printing a document. The **Formatting toolbar** enables you to change fonts and justification, and to implement boldface, italics, or underlining. **Toolbars** are discussed further on page 22.

THE EXCEL WORKBOOK

An Excel **workbook** is the electronic equivalent of the three-ring binder. A workbook contains one or more worksheets (or chart sheets), each of which is identified by a **tab** at the bottom of the workbook. The worksheets in a workbook are normally related to one another; for example, each worksheet may contain the sales for a specific division within a company. The advantage of a workbook is that all of its worksheets are stored in a single file, which is accessed as a unit.

WORKING IN WINDOWS

The next several pages take you through the basic operations common to Windows applications in general, and to Excel in particular. You may already be familiar with much of this material, in which case you are already benefitting from the common user interface. We begin with the mouse and describe how it is used to access pull-down menus and to supply information in dialog boxes. We also emphasize the on-line help facility, which is present in every Windows application.

The Mouse

The mouse (or trackball) is essential to Microsoft Excel as it is to all other Windows applications, and you must be comfortable with its four basic actions:

- ➤ To *point* to an item, move the mouse pointer to the item.
- ➤ To *click* an item, point to it, then press and release the left mouse button. You can also click the right mouse button to display a shortcut menu as described on page 28.
- ➤ To *double click* an item, point to it, then click the left mouse button twice in succession.

➤ To *drag* an item, move the pointer to the item, then press and hold the left button while you move the item to a new position.

The mouse is a pointing device—move the mouse on your desk and the *mouse pointer,* typically a small arrowhead, moves on the monitor. The mouse pointer assumes different shapes according to the nature of the current action. You will see a double arrow when you change the size of a window, an I-beam to insert text, a hand to jump from one help topic to the next, or a circle with a line through it to indicate that an attempted action is invalid.

The mouse pointer will also change to an hourglass to indicate Excel is processing your most recent command, and that no further commands may be issued until the action is completed. The more powerful your computer, the less frequently the hourglass will appear. Conversely, the less powerful your system, the more you will see the hourglass.

A right-handed person will hold the mouse in his or her right hand and click the left button, whereas a left-handed individual may want to hold the mouse in the left hand and click the right button. If this sounds complicated, it's not, and you can master the mouse with the on-line tutorial provided in Windows (see step 2 in the hands-on exercise on page 16).

MOUSE TIP FOR LEFTIES

Customize the mouse to reverse the actions of the left and right buttons. Double click the Main group icon in Program Manager to open the group, then double click the Control Panel icon. Double click the Mouse icon, click the Swap Left/Right buttons check box, then click OK.

Excel is designed for a mouse, but it provides keyboard equivalents for almost every command, with toolbars offering still other ways to accomplish the most frequent operations. You may (at first) wonder why there are so many different ways to do the same thing, but you will come to recognize the many options as part of Excel's charm. The most appropriate technique depends on personal preference, as well as the specific situation.

If, for example, your hands are already on the keyboard, it is faster to use the keyboard equivalent. Other times, your hand will be on the mouse and that will be the fastest way. It is not necessary to memorize anything, nor should you even try; just be flexible and willing to experiment. The more you do, the easier it will be!

MOUSE TIP: PICK UP THE MOUSE

It seems that you always run out of room on your real desk just when you need to move the mouse a little further. The solution is to pick up the mouse and move it closer to you—the pointer will stay in its present position on the screen, but when you put the mouse down, you will have more room on your desk in which to work.

Pull-down Menus

Pull-down menus, such as those in Figure 1.3, are essential to all Windows applications. A pull-down menu is accessed by clicking the menu name (within the menu bar) or by pressing the Alt key plus the underlined letter in the menu name—for example, Alt+H to pull down the Help menu.

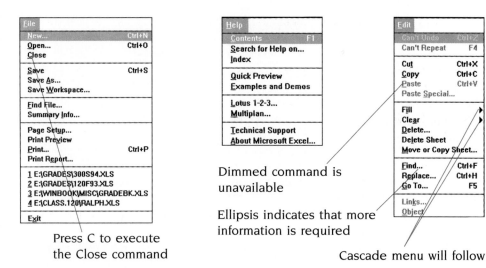

Press C to execute
the Close command

Dimmed command is
unavailable

Ellipsis indicates that more
information is required

Cascade menu will follow

FIGURE 1.3 Pull-down Menus

Menu options (commands) are executed by clicking the command once the menu has been pulled down or by pressing the underlined letter (e.g., press C to execute the Close command in the File menu). You can also bypass the menu entirely if you know the equivalent keystrokes shown to the right of the command in the menu (e.g., Ctrl+X, Ctrl+C, and Ctrl+V in the Edit menu to cut, copy, and paste text, respectively). A *dimmed command* (e.g., the Paste command within the Edit menu) indicates that command is not currently executable; that is, some additional action has to be taken for the command to become available.

An arrowhead after a command indicates a *cascade menu* will follow with additional menu options. For example, clicking either the Fill or Clear command in the Edit menu produces a secondary menu from which a command must be selected.

Other commands are followed by an *ellipsis* (. . .) to indicate that more information is required to execute the command; for example, selection of the Find command in the Edit menu requires the user to specify the text to be found. The additional information is entered into a dialog box, which appears immediately after the command has been selected.

Dialog Boxes

A *dialog box* appears when additional information is needed to execute a command—that is, whenever a menu option is followed by an ellipsis. There are many different ways to supply that information, which in turn leads to different types of dialog boxes as shown in Figure 1.4.

Check boxes are used when multiple options can be in effect at the same time. The Toolbars dialog box in Figure 1.4a, for example, uses check boxes to specify the toolbars that are to be displayed. The Standard and Formatting boxes are both checked, and hence both toolbars will be displayed. The check boxes at the bottom of the dialog box indicate that Color Toolbars are to be used and that ToolTips are to be shown. The individual options are selected (or cleared) by clicking on the appropriate check box.

Option buttons indicate mutually exclusive choices, one of which must be chosen. Portrait orientation is selected in the Page Setup dialog box in Figure 1.4b, which automatically deselects Landscape orientation; that is, clicking the Portrait option button automatically clears the Landscape button. The Page Setup dialog box also illustrates the use of a *tabbed dialog box,* in which one dialog box provides multiple sets of options, with each set of options on a separate tab. Clicking a tab brings that set of options to the front of the dialog box.

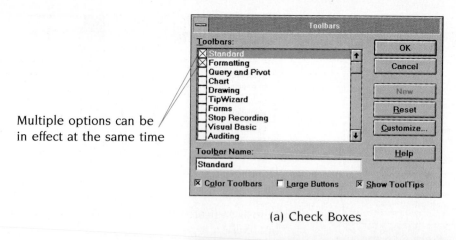

Multiple options can be in effect at the same time

(a) Check Boxes

Tab

Mutually exclusive options

(b) Option Buttons

Text box requires that specific data be entered

Command buttons

(c) Text Boxes

FIGURE 1.4   Dialog Boxes

A *text box* indicates that specific data is required such as the search and replace character strings in Figure 1.4c. Some text boxes are initially empty and display a flashing vertical bar to mark the insertion point for the text you enter. Other text boxes will already contain an entry, in which case you can click anywhere in the box to establish the insertion point and then edit the entry.

An *open list box,* such as the list of file names in Figure 1.4d, displays the available choices, any of which is selected by clicking the desired item. A *drop-down list box,* such as the list of available drives or file types, conserves space by showing only the current selection; click on the arrow of a drop-down list box to produce a list of available options.

All of the dialog boxes in Figure 1.4 contain one or more *command buttons* to initiate an action. The function of a command button is generally apparent from its name. The Help button produces a context-sensitive help screen. The Cancel button returns to the previous screen with no action taken. The OK command button accepts the information and closes the dialog box.

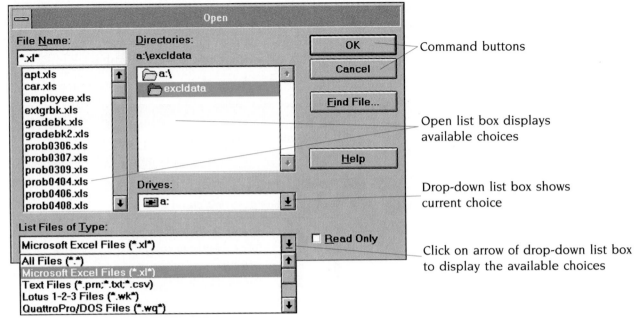

(d) List Boxes

FIGURE 1.4 Dialog Boxes (continued)

On-line Help

Excel provides extensive *on-line help,* which is accessed by pulling down the *Help menu.* The Excel Help menu was shown earlier in Figure 1.3 and contains the following choices:

Contents	Displays a list of help topics
Search for Help on . . .	Searches for help on a specific subject
Index	An alphabetical index of all Help topics
Quick Preview	Highlights new features in Excel 5.0 and suggests tips for Lotus users converting to Microsoft Excel
Examples and Demos	Demonstrates major features in Microsoft Excel
Lotus 1-2-3 . . .	Detailed help in converting from Lotus to Excel
Technical Support	Describes the different types of technical support available
About Microsoft Excel . . .	Indicates the specific release of Excel you are using

The Contents command displays the window of Figure 1.5a and provides access to all elements within the Help Facility. A Help window contains all of the elements found in any other application window: a title bar, minimize and maximize or restore buttons, a control-menu box, and optionally, a vertical or horizontal scroll bar. There is also a menu bar with commands available through the indicated pull-down menus.

The command buttons near the top of the help window enable you to move around more easily; that is, you can click a button to perform the indicated function. The Contents button returns to the screen in Figure 1.5a from elsewhere within Help. The Search button produces the screen of Figure 1.5b and allows you to look for information on a specific topic. Type a key word in the text box and the corresponding term will be selected in the adjacent list box. Double click the highlighted item to produce a list of available topics in the lower list box. Double click the topic you want (or select the topic and click the Go To command button) to see the actual help text, such as the screen shown in Figure 1.5c.

The Back button returns directly to the previous help topic. The History button is more general as it displays a list of all topics selected within the current session and makes it easy to return to any of the previous topics. The Index button produces a window with an alphabetic index of the Help topics.

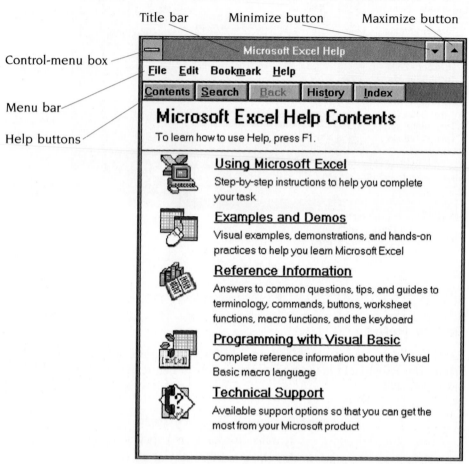

(a) Contents Command

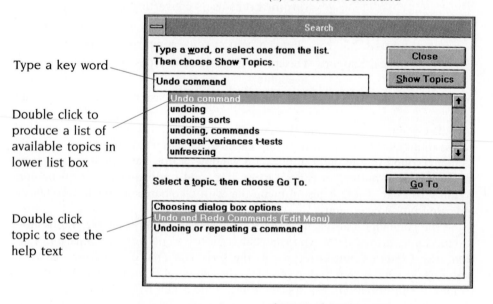

(b) Search Command

FIGURE 1.5 On-line Help

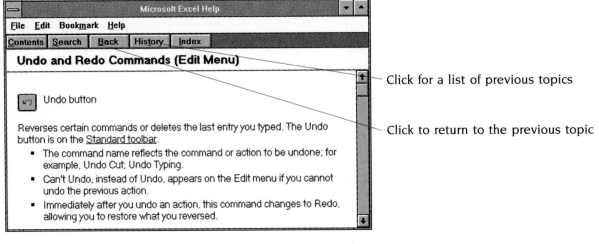

(c) Help Text

FIGURE 1.5 On-line Help (continued)

INTRODUCTION TO SPREADSHEETS

A *spreadsheet* is the computerized equivalent of an accountant's ledger. As with the ledger, it consists of a grid of rows and columns that enables you to organize data in a readily understandable format. Figures 1.6a and 1.6b show the same information displayed in ledger and spreadsheet format, respectively.

"What is the big deal?", you might ask. The big deal is that after you change an entry (or entries), the spreadsheet will, automatically and almost instantly, recompute the entire spreadsheet. Consider, for example, the profit projection spreadsheet shown in Figure 1.6b. As the spreadsheet is presently constructed, the unit price is $20, producing gross sales of $24,000 and a net profit of $4,800. If the unit price is increased to $22 per unit, the spreadsheet recomputes every formula, adjusting the values of gross sales and net profit. The modified spreadsheet of Figure 1.6c appears automatically on your monitor.

		1	2	3	4	Prepared by Approved by	Initials Date
	Profit Production					5	6
1	Unit Price		20				1
2	Unit Sales		1,200				2
3	Gross Sales		24,000				3
4							4
5	Costs						5
6	Production		10,000				6
7	Distribution		1,200				7
8	Marketing		5,000				8
9	Overhead		3,000				9
10							10
11	Total Cost		19,200				11
12							12
13	Net Profit		4,800				13

(a) The Accountant's Ledger

FIGURE 1.6 The Accountant's Ledger

	A	B
1	Profit Projection	
2		
3	Unit Price	$20
4	Unit Sales	1,200
5	Gross Sales	$24,000
6		
7	Cost	
8	Production	$10,000
9	Distribution	$1,200
10	Marketing	$5,000
11	Overhead	$3,000
12	Total Costs	$19,200
13		
14	Net Profits	$4,800

(b) Original Spreadsheet

	A	B
1	Profit Projection	
2		
3	Unit Price	$22
4	Unit Sales	1,200
5	Gross Sales	$26,400
6		
7	Cost	
8	Production	$10,000
9	Distribution	$1,200
10	Marketing	$5,000
11	Overhead	$3,000
12	Total Costs	$19,200
13		
14	Net Profits	$7,200

Increase Unit Price

Values are automatically adjusted

(c) Modified Spreadsheet

FIGURE 1.6 The Accountant's Ledger (continued)

With a bottle of white-out or a good eraser the same changes could also be made to the ledger. But imagine for a moment a ledger with hundreds of entries, many of which depend on the entry you wish to change. You can appreciate the time required to make all the necessary changes to the ledger by hand. However, the same spreadsheet, with hundreds of entries, will be recomputed automatically by the computer. And the computer will not make mistakes. Herein lies the advantage of a spreadsheet: the ability to make (or consider making) changes, and to have the computer carry out the recalculation faster and more accurately than could be accomplished manually.

The Professor's Grade Book

A second example of a spreadsheet, one with which you can easily identify, is that of a professor's grade book. The grades are recorded by hand in a notebook, which is nothing more than a different kind of accountant's ledger. Figure 1.7 contains both manual and spreadsheet versions of a grade book.

Figure 1.7a shows a handwritten grade book as it has been done since the days of the little red schoolhouse. For the sake of simplicity, only five students are shown, each with three grades. The professor has computed class averages for each exam, as well as a semester average for every student, in which the final counts *twice* as much as either test; for example, Adams's average is equal to: $(100+90+81+81)/4 = 88$.

Figure 1.7b shows the grade book as it might appear in a spreadsheet, and is essentially unchanged from Figure 1.7a. Walker's grade on the final exam in Figure 1.7b is 90, giving him a semester average of 85 and producing a class average on the final of 75.2. Now consider Figure 1.7c, in which the grade on Walker's final has been changed to 100, causing the class average on the final to go from 75.2 to 77.2, and Walker's semester average to change from 85 to 90. As with the profit projection, a change to any entry within the grade book automatically recalculates all dependent values as well. Hence, when Walker's final exam was regraded, all dependent values (the class average for the final as well as Walker's semester average) were recomputed.

As simple as the idea of a spreadsheet may seem, it provided the first major reason for managers to have a personal computer on their desks. Essentially, anything that can be done with a pencil, a pad of paper, and a calculator can be done faster and far more accurately with a spreadsheet.

	Test1	Test2	Final	Wgt Avg*
Adams	100	90	81	88
Baker	90	76	87	85
Glassman	90	78	78	81
Moldof	60	60	40	50
Walker	80	80	90	85
Class Average	84.0	76.8	75.2	

*Note: Final counts double

(a) The Professor's Grade Book

	A	B	C	D	E
1	Student	Test 1	Test 2	Final	Wgt Avg
2					
3	Adams	100	90	81	88.0
4	Baker	90	76	87	85.0
5	Glassman	90	78	78	81.0
6	Moldof	60	60	40	50.0
7	Walker	80	80	90	85.0
8					
9	Class Avg	84.0	76.8	75.2	

(b) Original Grades

	A	B	C	D	E
1	Student	Test 1	Test 2	Final	Wgt Avg
2					
3	Adams	100	90	81	88.0
4	Baker	90	76	87	85.0
5	Glassman	90	78	78	81.0
6	Moldof	60	60	40	50.0
7	Walker	80	80	100	90.0
8					
9	Class Avg	84.0	76.8	77.2	

Grade changed to 100

Values are automatically adjusted

(c) Modified Spreadsheet

FIGURE 1.7 The Professor's Grade Book

Row and Column Headings

A spreadsheet is divided into rows and columns, with each row and column assigned a heading. Rows are given numeric headings ranging from 1 to a maximum of 16,384. Columns are assigned alphabetic headings from column A to Z, then continue from AA to AZ and then from BA to BZ and so on, until the last of 256 columns is reached.

The intersection of a row and column forms a ***cell,*** with the number of cells in a spreadsheet equal to the number of rows times the number of columns. The professor's grade book in Figure 1.7, for example, has 5 columns labeled A through E, 9 rows numbered from 1 to 9, and a total of 45 cells. Each cell has a unique ***cell reference;*** for example, the cell at the intersection of column A and row 9 is known as cell A9. The column heading always precedes the row heading in the cell reference.

Formulas and Constants

Figure 1.8 shows an alternate view of the spreadsheet for the professor's grade book, which displays the *cell contents* rather than the computed values. This figure displays the formulas and constants that were entered into the individual cells that give the spreadsheet its ability to recalculate all values whenever any entry changes.

Constant →

Function →

	A	B	C	D	E
1	Student	Test 1	Test 2	Final	Wgt Avg
2					
3	Adams	100	90	81	=(B3+C3+2*D3)/4
4	Baker	90	76	87	=(B4+C4+2*D4)/4
5	Glassman	90	78	78	=(B5+C5+2*D5)/4
6	Moldof	60	60	40	=(B6+C6+2*D6)/4
7	Walker	80	80	90	=(B7+C7+2*D7)/4
8					
9	Class Avg	=AVERAGE(B3:B7)	=AVERAGE(C3:C7)	=AVERAGE(D3:D7)	

FIGURE 1.8   The Professor's Grade Book (cell formulas)   Formula

A *constant* is an entry that does not change. It may be a number such as a student's grade on an exam, or it may be descriptive text (a label) such as a student's name. A *formula* is a combination of numeric constants, cell references, arithmetic operators, and/or functions, that displays the result of a calculation. Every cell in a spreadsheet contains either a formula or a constant.

A formula always begins with an equal sign; a constant does not. Consider, for example, the formula in cell E3, =(B3+C3+2*D3)/4, which computes Adams's weighted average for the semester. The formula is built in accordance with the professor's rules for computing a student's weighted average, which counts the final twice as much as either exam. (The symbols +, −, *, /, and ^ indicate addition, subtraction, multiplication, division, and exponentiation, respectively. It follows the normal rules for arithmetic precedence. Any expression in parentheses is evaluated first. Exponentiation is done next, then multiplication or division in left to right order, then addition or subtraction also in left-to-right order.)

The formula in cell E3 takes the grade on the first exam (in cell B3), plus the grade on the second exam (in cell C3), plus two times the grade on the final (found in cell D3), and divides the result by four. The fact that we enter a formula for the weighted average rather than a constant means that should any of the individual grades change, all dependent results will also change. This in essence is the basic principle behind the spreadsheet and explains why when one number changes, various other numbers throughout the spreadsheet change as well.

A formula may also include a *function,* or predefined computational task, such as the AVERAGE function in cells B9, C9, and D9. The function in cell B9, for example, =AVERAGE(B3:B7), is interpreted to mean the average of all cells starting at B3 and ending at B7; that is, the average of cells B3, B4, B5, B6, and B7. You can appreciate that functions are often easier to use than the corresponding formulas, especially with larger spreadsheets (and classes with many students).

MICROSOFT EXCEL

Figure 1.9 displays the professor's grade book as it is implemented in Microsoft Excel. Excel shares the common user interface present in all other Windows applications.

You should recognize several familiar elements: the desktop, minimize and restore buttons, a menu bar, horizontal and vertical scroll bars, and a control-menu box.

The desktop in Figure 1.9 contains an application window for Excel. It also contains a document window within Excel for a specific workbook. Both windows have been maximized, with the title bar of the workbook (GRADEBK.XLS) merged into the title bar of the application window. The terminology is important and we distinguish among spreadsheet, worksheet, and workbook. Excel refers to a spreadsheet as a *worksheet.* Spreadsheet is a generic term. Workbook and worksheet are unique to Excel. An Excel workbook contains one or more worksheets. The professor's gradebook is in Sheet1 of the GRADEBK.XLS workbook as indicated by the tabs at the bottom of the workbook.

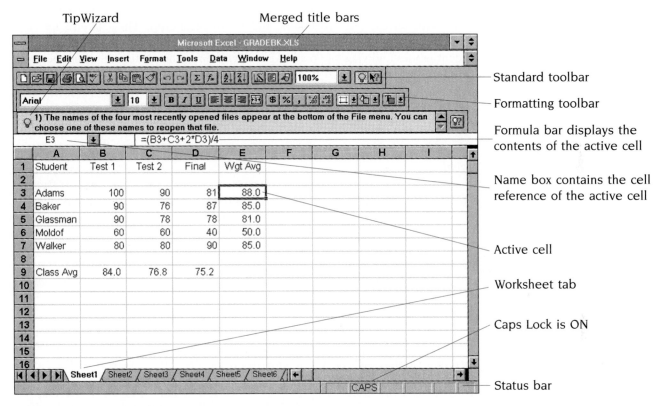

FIGURE 1.9 Microsoft Excel

Figure 1.9 resembles the grade book shown earlier, but it includes several other elements that enable you to create and/or edit the worksheet. The heavy border around cell E3 indicates that it (cell E3) is the *active cell,* and that any actions taken at this point will affect the contents of cell E3. The active cell can be changed by clicking a different cell, or by using the arrow keys to move to a different cell.

The displayed value in cell E3 is 88.0, but as indicated earlier, the cell contains a formula to compute the weighted average rather than containing the number itself. The contents of the active cell, =(B3+C3+2*D3)/4, are displayed in the *formula bar* near the top of the worksheet. The cell reference for the active cell, cell E3 in Figure 1.9, appears in the *Name box* at the left of the formula bar.

Several other elements of Figure 1.9 bear mention. The Standard and Formatting toolbars are displayed below the menu bar and contain icons that provide immediate access to common commands. The TipWizard (see page 22) appears immediately under the toolbars and offers suggestions to make you work more efficiently.

The **status bar** at the bottom of the worksheet keeps you informed of what is happening as you work within Excel. It displays information about a selected command or an operation in progress. It also shows the status of the keyboard toggle switches such as the Caps Lock key, which has been toggled on in the figure.

LEARNING BY DOING

We come now to the first of two hands-on exercises that implement our learn-by-doing philosophy. The initial exercise shows you how to load Windows and practice with the mouse, then directs you to load Microsoft Excel and retrieve the professor's grade book from the data disk provided by your instructor. The data disk expedites the way in which you learn, especially at the beginning, as you can experiment with an existing workbook and its worksheet(s). The exercise has you explore the various elements on the screen, then directs you to change individual student grades and view the resulting recalculation. The exercise also instructs you to print the worksheet and to save the changes you make.

Hands-On Exercise 1:

Introduction to Microsoft Excel

Objective To load Windows and Microsoft Excel; to retrieve and print an existing worksheet. The exercise introduces you to the data disk and reviews basic Windows operations: pull-down menus, dialog boxes, and the use of a mouse.

Step 1: Load Windows
➤ Type **WIN,** then press the **enter key** to load Windows if it is not already loaded. The appearance of your desktop will be different from ours, but it should resemble Figure 1.1 at the beginning of the chapter.
➤ You will most likely see a window containing Program Manager, but if not, you should see an icon titled Program Manager near the bottom of the screen; double click on this icon to open the Program Manager window.

DOUBLE CLICKING FOR BEGINNERS

If you are having trouble double clicking, it is because you are not clicking quickly enough, or more likely, because you are moving the mouse (however slightly) between clicks. Relax, hold the mouse firmly in place, and try again.

Step 2: Master the mouse
➤ A mouse is essential to the operation of Microsoft Excel as it is to all other Windows applications. The easiest way to practice is with the mouse tutorial found in the Help menu of Windows itself.
➤ Pull down the **Help menu.** Click **Windows Tutorial.** Type **M** to begin, then follow the on-screen instructions.
➤ Exit the tutorial when you are finished.

Step 3: Install the data disk

➤ Do this step *only* if you have your own computer and want to copy the files from the data disk to the hard drive. Place the data disk in drive A (or whatever drive is appropriate).

➤ Pull down the **File menu.** Click **Run.** Type **A:INSTALL C** in the text box. Click **OK.** (The drive letters in the command, A and C, are both variable. If, for example, the data disk were in drive B and you wanted to copy its files to drive D, you would type the command **B:INSTALL D.**)

➤ Follow the on-screen instructions to install the data disk.

Step 4: Load Microsoft Excel

➤ Double click the icon for the group containing Microsoft Excel if that group is not already open.

➤ Double click the program icon for **Microsoft Excel.**

➤ Click the **maximize button** (if necessary) so that the application window containing Microsoft Excel fills the entire screen.

➤ Click the **maximize button** in the document window (if necessary) to produce a screen similar to Figure 1.10a. (You will not see the Open dialog box until you complete step 5.)

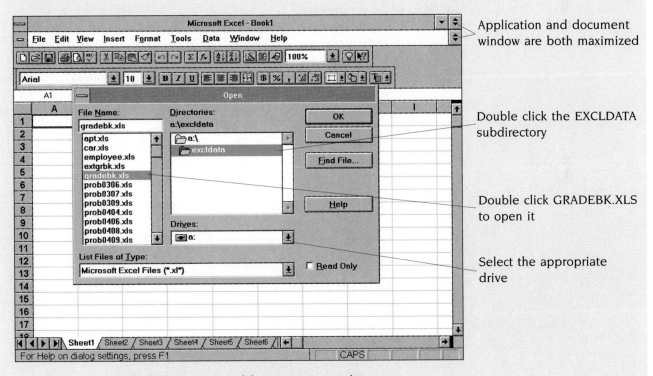

(a) Retrieving a Spreadsheet (steps 4 and 5)

FIGURE 1.10 Hands-on Exercise 1

Step 5: Open the workbook

➤ Pull down the **File menu.** Click **Open** to produce a dialog box similar to the one in Figure 1.10a.

➤ Click the appropriate drive, drive C or drive A.

➤ Double click the root directory (a:\ or c:\) in the Directories list box to display the subdirectories on the selected drive.
➤ Double click the **EXCLDATA** directory to make it the active directory.
➤ Double click **GRADEBK.XLS** to open the workbook for this exercise.

ABOUT MICROSOFT EXCEL

About Microsoft Excel on the Help menu displays information about the specific release of Excel, including the product serial number. Execution of the command produces a dialog box with a System Information command button; click the button to learn about the hardware installed on your system, including the amount of memory and available space on the hard drive.

Step 6: The active cell and formula bar
➤ Click in cell **B3,** the cell containing Adams's grade on the first test.
➤ Cell B3 is now the active cell and is surrounded by a heavy border. The Name box indicates the active cell; the contents of the active cell are displayed in the formula bar.
➤ Click in cell **B4** (or press the **down arrow key**) to make it the active cell. The Name box indicates cell B4, while the formula bar indicates a grade of 90.
➤ Click in cell **E3,** the cell containing the formula to compute Adams's weighted average. The worksheet displays the computed average of 88, but the formula bar displays the formula, =(B3+C3+2*D3)/4, to compute that average.
➤ Continue to change the active cell (with the mouse or arrow keys) and notice how the display in the Name box and formula bar change to reflect the active cell.

THE UNDO COMMAND

The Undo command reverses the effect of the most recent operation and is invaluable at any time, but especially when you are learning. Pull down the Edit menu and click Undo (or click the Undo icon on the Standard toolbar) to cancel the effects of the preceding command. Use the Undo command whenever something happens to your worksheet that is different from what you intended.

Step 7: Experiment (what if?)
➤ Let's assume that an error was made in recording Baker's grade on the second test.
➤ Click in cell **C4,** the cell containing this particular grade.
➤ Enter a corrected value of **86** (instead of the previous entry of 76). Press **enter** (or click in another cell).
➤ The effects of this change ripple through the worksheet, automatically changing the computed value for Baker's average in cell E4 to 87.5. The class average on the second test in cell C9 changes to 78.8.

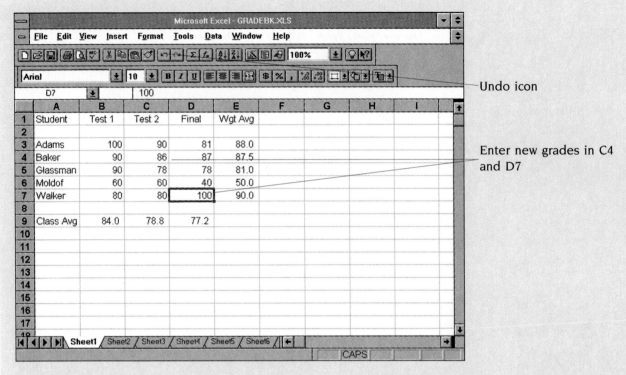

Undo icon

Enter new grades in C4 and D7

(b) What If (step 7)

FIGURE 1.10 Hands-on Exercise I (continued)

➤ Change Walker's grade on the final from 90 to **100.** Press **enter** (or click in another cell). Walker's average in cell E7 changes to 90.0, while the class average in cell D9 changes to 77.2.

➤ Your worksheet should match Figure 1.10b.

Step 8: Save the modified worksheet

➤ It is very, very important to save your work periodically during a session.

➤ Pull down the **File menu.** Click **Save** to save the changes (or, alternatively, click the **Save icon,** the third icon from the left, on the Standard toolbar).

Step 9: Print the worksheet

➤ Pull down the **File menu.** Click **Print** to produce a dialog box requesting information about the Print command as shown in Figure 1.10c.

➤ Click the **OK** command button to accept the default options and print the worksheet. You can also click the **printer icon** on the Standard toolbar to print the worksheet immediately and bypass the associated dialog box.

SAVE YOUR WORK

We cannot overemphasize the importance of periodically saving a worksheet, so if something goes wrong, you won't lose everything. Nothing is more frustrating than to lose two hours of effort, due to an unexpected problem in Windows or to a temporary loss of power. Save your work frequently, at least once every 15 minutes. Click the Save icon on the Standard toolbar or pull down the File menu and click Save. Do it!

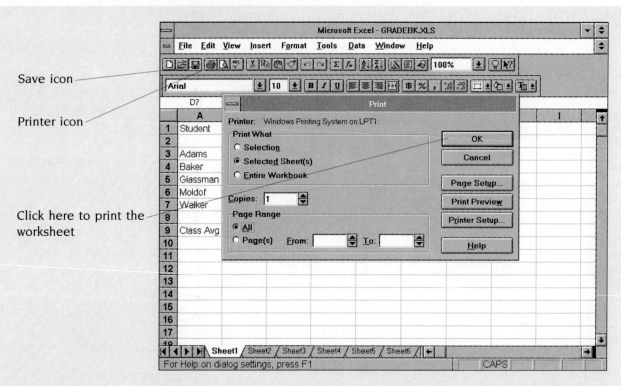

Save icon

Printer icon

Click here to print the
worksheet

(c) Print the Spreadsheet (step 9)

FIGURE 1.10 Hands-on Exercise 1 (continued)

EXECUTE COMMANDS QUICKLY

The quickest way to select a command from a pull-down menu is to point
to the menu name, then drag the pointer (i.e., press and hold the left
mouse button) to the desired command, and release the mouse. The command is executed when you release the button.

Step 10: Exit Excel and Windows

➤ Pull down the **File menu.** Click **Exit** to close Excel and return to Program
Manager.

➤ Pull down the **File menu** in Program Manager. Click **Exit Windows.** You will
see an informational message indicating that you are leaving Windows. Click
the **OK** command button to exit.

MODIFYING THE WORKSHEET

We trust that you completed the hands-on exercise without difficulty and that you
are more confident in your ability than when you first began. The exercise was
not complicated, but it did accomplish several objectives and set the stage for a
second exercise, which follows shortly.

Consider now Figure 1.11, which contains a modified version of the professor's grade book. Figure 1.11a shows the grade book at the end of the first hands-
on exercise and reflects the changes made to the grades for Baker and Walker.

	A	B	C	D	E
1	Student	Test 1	Test 2	Final	Wgt Avg
2					
3	Adams	100	90	81	88.0
4	Baker	90	86	87	87.5
5	Glassman	90	78	78	81.0
6	Moldof	60	60	40	50.0
7	Walker	80	80	100	90.0
8					
9	Class Avg	84.0	78.8	77.2	

Formula references cells B3, C3, and D3

Function references rows 3–7

(a) After Hands-on Exercise 1

New column added for the student's major

	A	B	C	D	E	F
1	Student	Major	Test 1	Test 2	Final	Wgt Avg
2						
3	Adams	CIS	100	90	81	88.0
4	Baker	MKT	90	86	87	87.5
5	Coulter	ACC	85	95	100	95.0
6	Davis	FIN	75	75	85	80.0
7	Glassman	CIS	90	78	78	81.0
8	Walker	CIS	80	80	100	90.0
9						
10	Class Avg		86.7	84.0	88.5	

New students added to the class; Moldof deleted from the class

Formula now references cells C3, D3, and E3 as a result of inserted column

Function now averages grades in rows 3–8 as a result of inserted rows

(b) After Hands-on Exercise 2

FIGURE 1.11 The Modified Grade Book

Figure 1.11b shows the worksheet as it will appear at the end of the second exercise. Several changes bear mention:

1. One student has dropped the class and two other students have been added. Moldof appeared in the original worksheet in Figure 1.11a, but has somehow managed to withdraw; Coulter and Davis did not appear in the original grade book but have been added to the worksheet in Figure 1.11b.

2. A new column, containing the student's major, has been added for every student.

The implementation of these changes is accomplished through a combination of the Insert and Delete commands that enable you to add and/or remove rows or columns as necessary. The important thing to realize is that cell references in existing formulas are adjusted *automatically* to account for the changes brought about by the addition (deletion) of rows and columns.

Consider, once again, the formula to compute Adams's weighted average, which is contained in cell E3 of the original grade book, but in cell F3 in the modified grade book. The original formula in Figure 1.11a referenced cells B3, C3, and D3 to obtain the grades on test 1, test 2, and the final. The revised formula in Figure 1.11b reflects the fact that a new column has been inserted, and references cells C3, D3, and E3. The change in the formula is made automatically by Excel without any action on the part of the user (other than to insert the new column).

In similar fashion, the formulas to compute the class averages appear in row 9 of the original worksheet and reflect the entries in rows 3 through 7. The revised worksheet has a net increase of one student, which automatically moves the formulas containing the AVERAGE function to row 10. It also adjusts the AVERAGE function to use values from rows 3 through 8 to accommodate the additional student.

Required Commands

The **Row** and **Column commands** in the **Insert menu** add new row(s) and column(s) to an existing worksheet. Excel automatically adjusts any cell reference in existing formulas to account for the additional rows or columns. If, for example, cell B6 contained the formula =B2+B3 and a new row were inserted between rows 2 and 3, the formula in cell B6 would move to B7 and become =B2+B4.

The **Delete command** in the Edit menu removes existing row(s) or column(s) from a worksheet. Cell references are adjusted automatically to account for the deleted elements. If, for example, cell B6 contained the formula =B2+B3 and row 1 were deleted, the formula in cell B6 would move to cell B5 and become =B1+B2.

The hands-on exercise that follows requires the Open and Save commands found in the File menu. The **Open command** brings a workbook (containing one or more worksheets) from disk into memory. The **Save command** copies the workbook in memory to disk. The **Save As command** saves the workbook under a different name, and is useful when you want to retain a copy of the original workbook (and its worksheets) prior to making changes. The initial execution of the Save command (as well as every execution of the Save As command) requires you to enter a file name from one to eight characters; the extension XLS is assigned automatically.

TOOLBARS

As we have already indicated, Excel provides several different ways to accomplish the same task. Commands may be accessed from a pull-down menu, from a shortcut menu, and/or through keyboard equivalents. Commands can also be executed from one of several toolbars, and since toolbars remain visible throughout a session, this is a technique worth pursuing.

The Standard and Formatting toolbars appear by default and contain most of the basic commands you will need. The icons may at first appear overwhelming, but you will be surprised at how quickly you learn to use them. The easiest way to master the toolbars is to view the icons in groups according to their general function, as shown in Figure 1.12.

Remember, too, there is absolutely no need to memorize the function of the individual buttons (nor should you even try). That will come with time. Indeed, if you use another Microsoft application such as Word for Windows, you already recognize many of the icons on the Standard and Formatting toolbars. Most individuals start by using the pull-down menus, then look for shortcuts along the way. The following exercise describes both techniques and lets you choose the one you prefer. Additional information on customizing toolbars is presented in Chapter 2.

THE TIPWIZARD

The **TipWizard** greets you with a *tip-of-the-day* every time you start Excel but that is only one of its capabilities. The true purpose of the TipWizard is to introduce you to new features by suggesting more efficient ways to accomplish the tasks you are doing.

The TipWizard monitors your work and offers advice throughout a session. The TipWizard button on the Standard toolbar "lights up" whenever there is a suggestion. (Click the button to display the TipWizard; click the button a second time to close it.) You can read the suggestions as they occur and/or review them at the end of a session. You needn't always follow the advice of the TipWizard (at

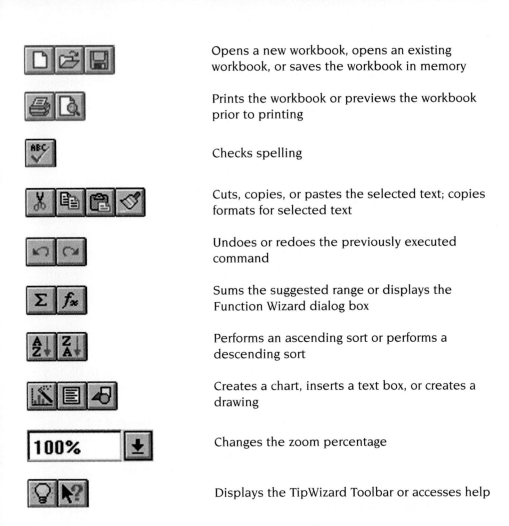

Opens a new workbook, opens an existing workbook, or saves the workbook in memory

Prints the workbook or previews the workbook prior to printing

Checks spelling

Cuts, copies, or pastes the selected text; copies formats for selected text

Undoes or redoes the previously executed command

Sums the suggested range or displays the Function Wizard dialog box

Performs an ascending sort or performs a descending sort

Creates a chart, inserts a text box, or creates a drawing

Changes the zoom percentage

Displays the TipWizard Toolbar or accesses help

(a) The Standard Toolbar

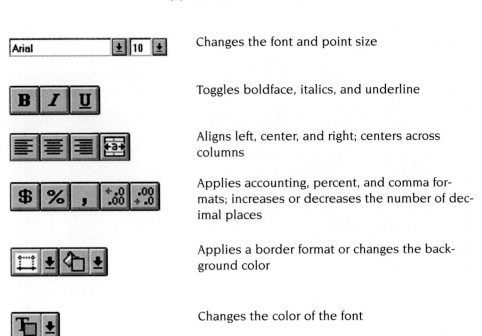

Changes the font and point size

Toggles boldface, italics, and underline

Aligns left, center, and right; centers across columns

Applies accounting, percent, and comma formats; increases or decreases the number of decimal places

Applies a border format or changes the background color

Changes the color of the font

(b) The Formatting Toolbar

FIGURE 1.12 Toolbars

first you may not even understand all of its suggestions), but over time it will make you much more proficient.

The TipWizard will not repeat a tip from one session to the next unless it is specifically reset as described in step 1 of the following exercise. This is especially important in a laboratory situation when you are sharing the same computer with other students.

HANDS-ON EXERCISE 2:

Modifying a Worksheet

Objective To open an existing workbook, to insert and delete rows and columns of a worksheet; to save the revised workbook; to use the TipWizard, Undo command, and on-line help. Use Figure 1.13 as a guide in doing the exercise.

Step 1: Tip of the day
➤ Load Microsoft Excel as described in the previous exercise.
➤ If necessary, click the **TipWizard button** on the Standard toolbar to display the tip of the day as shown in Figure 1.13a. Do not be concerned if your tip is different from ours.
➤ Pull down the **Tools menu,** click **Options,** then click the **General tab** to display the dialog box in Figure 1.13a.
➤ Click the check box to Reset TipWizard. Click **OK.** The contents of the Tip-Wizard box change to indicate that you have reset the TipWizard and that the tips may repeat.
➤ Click the **TipWizard button** a second time to close the TipWizard box.

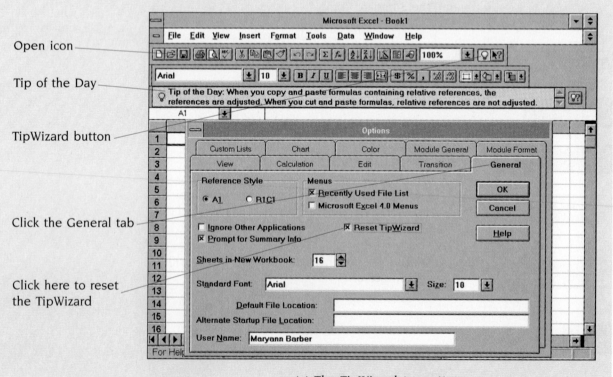

(a) The TipWizard (step 1)

FIGURE 1.13 Hands-on Exercise 2

CHANGING TOOLBARS

You can display (or hide) a toolbar with a shortcut menu provided at least one toolbar is visible. Point to any toolbar, click the right mouse button to display the Toolbar shortcut menu, then click the individual toolbars on or off as appropriate. If you do not see any toolbars, pull down the View menu, click Toolbars to display a dialog box listing the available toolbars, check the toolbars you want displayed, and click OK.

Step 2: Open the workbook
- ➤ Pull down the **File menu** and click **Open** (or click the **open icon** on the Standard toolbar) to produce a dialog box in which you specify the name of a file to open.
- ➤ Click the arrow for the Drives drop-down list box. Click the appropriate drive, drive C or drive A, depending on whether you installed the data disk. Double click the root directory (a:\ or c:\) in the Directories list box to display the subdirectories on the selected drive.
- ➤ Double click the **EXCLDATA** directory to make it the active directory. Double click **GRADEBK.XLS** to open the workbook from the first exercise.

Step 3: The Save As command
- ➤ Pull down the **File menu.** Click **Save As** to produce the dialog box of Figure 1.13b, which requests the name of the file.
- ➤ Type **GRADEBK2** as the name of the file (the XLS extension is added automatically). Press the **enter key.** Click the **Cancel command button** (or press the **Esc key**) if you are prompted for summary information.
- ➤ There are now two identical copies of the file on disk—GRADEBK.XLS, which we supplied, and GRADEBK2.XLS, which you just created. The title bar of the document window reflects the latter name.

SUMMARY INFORMATION

Excel maintains summary information on each workbook that is intended to help you find files more quickly. This is indeed a powerful capability, but it is typically not used by beginners. To suppress the prompt for summary information, pull down the Tools menu, click Options, click the General tab, then clear the box to Prompt for Summary Info.

Step 4: Delete a row
- ➤ Click any cell in **row 6** (the row you will delete). Pull down the **Edit menu.** Click **Delete** to produce the dialog box in Figure 1.13c. Click **Entire Row.** Click **OK** to delete row 6.
- ➤ Moldof has disappeared from the grade book, and the class averages (now in row 8) have been updated automatically.

Step 5: The Undo command
- ➤ Pull down the **Edit menu** and click **Undo Delete** (or click the Undo icon on the Standard toolbar) to reverse the preceding command and put Moldof back in the worksheet.
- ➤ Click any cell in row 6, and this time delete Moldof for good.

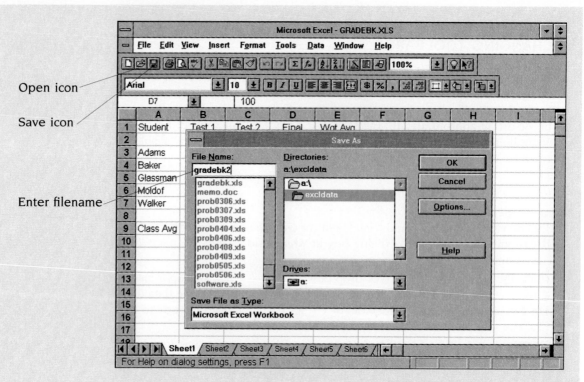

(b) The Save As command (step 3)

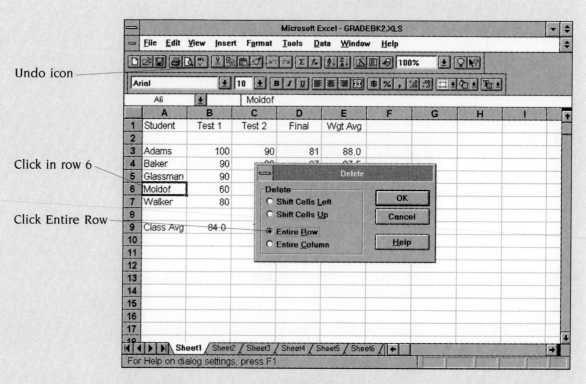

(c) Deleting a Row (step 4)

FIGURE 1.13 Hands-on Exercise 2 (continued)

TOOLBAR HELP

Point to any button on any toolbar and Excel displays the name of the toolbar button, which is indicative of its function. If pointing to a button has no effect, pull down the View menu, click Toolbars, and check the box to Show ToolTips.

Step 6: Insert a row

➤ Click any cell in **row 5** (the row containing Glassman's grades).

➤ Pull down the **Insert menu.** Click **Rows** to add a new row above the current row. Row 5 is now blank (it is the newly inserted row) and Glassman (who was in row 5) is now in row 6.

➤ Enter the data for the new student in row 5 as shown in Figure 1.13d:

—Click in cell **A5.** Type **Coulter.** Press the **right arrow key** or click in cell B5.

—Type **85.** Press the **right arrow key** or click in cell C5.

—Type **95.** Press the **right arrow key** or click in cell D5.

—Type **100.** Press the **right arrow key** or click in cell E5.

—Enter the formula to compute the weighted average, **=(B5+C5+2*D5)/4;** be sure to begin the formula with an equal sign. Press **enter.**

➤ Click the **Save icon** on the Standard toolbar or pull down the **File menu** and click **Save** to save the changes made to this point.

Save icon   Undo icon

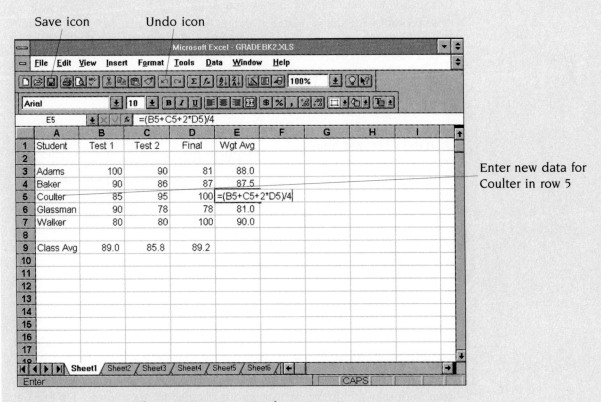

Enter new data for Coulter in row 5

(d) Inserting a New Student (step 6)

FIGURE 1.13 Hands-on Exercise 2 (continued)

ERASING VERSUS DELETING

The Edit Delete command deletes the selected cell, row, or column from the worksheet. It is very different from the Edit Clear command, which erases the contents (and/or formatting) of the selected cells, but does not delete the cells from the worksheet. The Edit Delete command causes Excel to adjust cell references throughout the worksheet. The Edit Clear command does not adjust cell references.

Step 7: Use a shortcut menu

➤ Point to the **row heading** for row 6 (which now contains Glassman's grades). Click the **right mouse button** to produce the shortcut menu in Figure 1.13e.

➤ Click **Insert** to add a new row 6, which causes Glassman to move to row 7.

➤ Click in cell **A6.** Type **Davis.** Enter Davis's grades in the appropriate cells (75, 75, and 85 in cells B6, C6, and D6, respectively).

➤ Click in cell **E6.** Enter the formula to compute the weighted average, **=(B6+C6+2*D6)/4.** Press **enter.**

➤ Save the workbook.

Step 8: Add a column

➤ Click any cell in **column B.** Pull down the **Insert menu.** Click **Columns** to insert a new column.

➤ Column B is now blank (it is the new column) and all existing columns have been moved to the right; that is, the grades for Test 1 are now in column C, the grades for Test 2 in column D, and so on.

➤ The formulas for the weighted averages have been adjusted to accommodate the additional column; for example, the entry in cell F3 is now =(C3+D3+2*E3)/4.

➤ Click in cell **B1.** Type **Major.** Click in cell **B3.** Enter the students' majors as shown in Figure 1.13f.

SHORTCUT MENUS

Shortcut menus provide an alternate way to execute commands. Point to any cell, or to any row or column heading, then click the right mouse button to display a shortcut menu with commands appropriate to the item you are pointing to. Point to a command, then click the left mouse button to execute the command from the shortcut menu. Press the Esc key or click outside the menu to close the menu without executing a command.

THE HELP BUTTON

Click the Help button on the Standard toolbar (the mouse pointer changes to include a large question mark), then click any other toolbar icon to display a help screen with information about that button. Double click the Help button to produce the Search dialog box normally accessed through the Help menu.

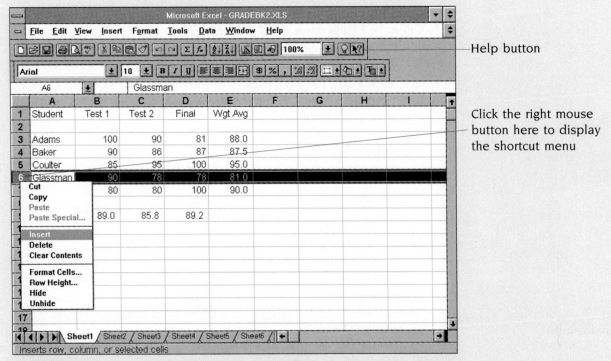

Help button

Click the right mouse button here to display the shortcut menu

(e) Shortcut Menu (step 7)

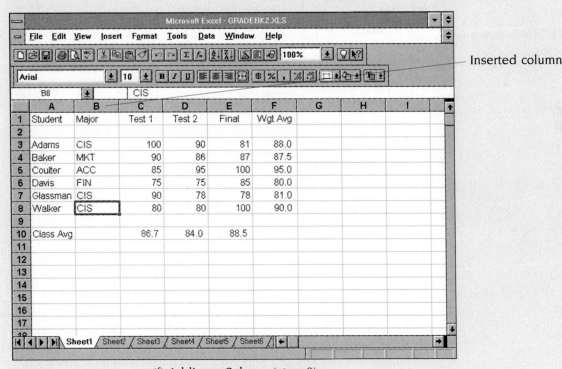

Inserted column

(f) Adding a Column (step 8)

FIGURE 1.13   Hands-on Exercise 2 (continued)

Step 10: The Standard toolbar

➤ Click the **Save icon** on the Standard toolbar to save the workbook.

➤ Click the **Print icon** on the Standard toolbar to print the worksheet.

➤ Click the **TipWizard icon** to open the TipWizard box.

Step 11: On-line help

➤ Pull down the **Help menu.** Click **Search for Help on.** Type **TipWizard** in the text box as shown in Figure 1.13g.

➤ Double click **TipWizard** in the upper list box.

➤ Double click **Using the TipWizard** in the lower list box. Read the How To help screen with information on the TipWizard. Click the **Close command button** when you are finished.

➤ Double click the **control-menu box** in the help screen to exit Help and return to the worksheet.

➤ Pull down the **File menu.** Click **Exit** to leave Excel.

TipWizard icon

TipWizard box

Type keyword

Double click to see topics in lower list box

Double click to see help text

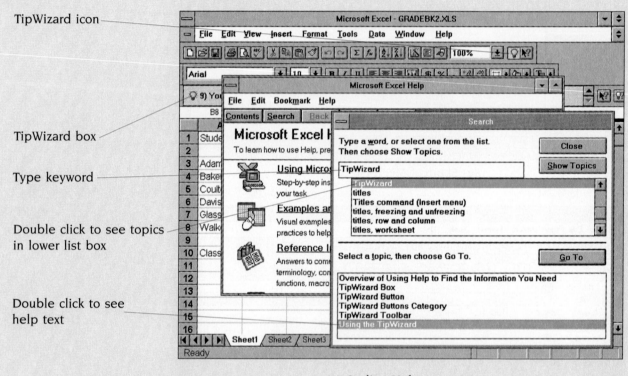

(g) On-line Help (step 11)

FIGURE 1.13   Hands-on Exercise 2 (continued)

SUMMARY

The common user interface ensures that all Windows applications are similar in appearance and work basically the same way, with common conventions and a consistent menu structure. It provides you with an intuitive understanding of any application, even before you begin to use it, and means that once you learn one application, it is that much easier to learn the next.

The mouse is essential to Microsoft Excel as it is to all other Windows applications, but keyboard equivalents are provided for virtually all operations. Toolbars and shortcut menus provide other ways to execute common commands. On-line help provides detailed information about all aspects of Microsoft Excel.

A spreadsheet is the computerized equivalent of an accountant's ledger. It is divided into rows and columns, with each row and column assigned a heading. The intersection of a row and column forms a cell.

Spreadsheet is a generic term. Workbook and worksheet are Excel specific. An Excel workbook contains one or more worksheets.

Every cell in a worksheet (spreadsheet) contains either a formula or a constant. A formula begins with an equal sign, a constant does not. A constant is an entry that does not change and may be numeric or descriptive text. A formula is a combination of numeric constants, cell references, arithmetic operators, and/or functions that produce a new value from existing values.

The Insert and Delete commands add or remove rows or columns as necessary. The Open command brings a workbook from disk into memory; the Save command copies the workbook in memory to disk.

 ## Key Words and Concepts

Active cell	Ellipsis	Restore button
Application window	File Menu	Row command
Cascade menu	Formatting toolbar	Save command
Cell	Formula	Save As command
Cell contents	Formula bar	Scroll bar
Cell reference	Function	Scroll box
Check box	Help menu	Shortcut menu
Click	Icon	Spreadsheet
Column command	Insert menu	Standard toolbar
Command button	Maximize button	Status bar
Common user interface	Menu bar	Tab
Constant	Minimize button	Tabbed dialog box
Control-menu box	Mouse pointer	Text box
Delete command	Name box	TipWizard
Desktop	On-line help	Title bar
Dialog box	Open command	Toolbar
Dimmed command	Open list box	Undo command
Document window	Option button	Value
Double click	Point	Window
Drag	Print command	Workbook
Drop-down list box	Program Manager	Worksheet
Edit menu	Pull-down menu	

 ## Multiple Choice

1. Which of the following will execute a command from a pull-down menu?
   (a) Clicking on the command once the menu has been pulled down
   (b) Typing the underlined letter in the command
   (c) Both (a) and (b)
   (d) Neither (a) nor (b)

2. The File Open command:
   (a) Brings a workbook from disk into memory
   (b) Brings a workbook from disk into memory, then erases the workbook on disk

(c) Stores the workbook in memory on disk

(d) Stores the workbook in memory on disk, then erases the workbook from memory

3. The File Save command:
   (a) Brings a workbook from disk into memory
   (b) Brings a workbook from disk into memory, then erases the workbook on disk
   (c) Stores the workbook in memory on disk
   (d) Stores the workbook in memory on disk, then erases the workbook from memory

4. What is the significance of three dots next to a menu option?
   (a) The option is not accessible
   (b) A dialog box will appear if the option is selected
   (c) A help window will appear if the option is selected
   (d) There are no equivalent keystrokes for the particular option

5. What is the significance of a menu option that appears faded (dimmed)?
   (a) The option is not currently accessible
   (b) A dialog box will appear if the option is selected
   (c) A help window will appear if the option is selected
   (d) There are no equivalent keystrokes for the particular option

6. Which of the following elements may be found within a help window?
   (a) Title bar, menu bar, and control-menu box
   (b) Minimize, maximize, and/or a restore button
   (c) Vertical and/or horizontal scroll bars
   (d) All of the above

7. Which of the following is true regarding a dialog box?
   (a) Option buttons indicate mutually exclusive choices
   (b) Check boxes imply that multiple options may be selected
   (c) Both (a) and (b)
   (d) Neither (a) nor (b)

8. Which of the following are found in the application windows for both Excel and Word for Windows?
   (a) The Standard and Formatting toolbars
   (b) The File, Edit, and Help menus
   (c) Both (a) and (b) above
   (d) Neither (a) nor (b)

9. In the absence of parentheses, the order of operation is:
   (a) Exponentiation, addition or subtraction, multiplication or division
   (b) Addition or subtraction, multiplication or division, exponentiation
   (c) Multiplication or division, exponentiation, addition or subtraction
   (d) Exponentiation, multiplication or division, addition or subtraction

10. The entry =AVERAGE(A4:A6):
    (a) Is invalid because the cells are not contiguous
    (b) Computes the average of cells A4 and A6
    (c) Computes the average of cells A4, A5, and A6
    (d) None of the above

11. A right-handed person will normally:
- (a) Click the right and left mouse buttons to access a pull-down menu and shortcut menu, respectively
- (b) Click the left and right mouse buttons to access a pull-down menu and shortcut menu, respectively
- (c) Click the left mouse button to access both a pull-down menu and a short-cut menu
- (d) Click the right mouse button to access both a pull-down menu and a shortcut menu

12. What is the effect of typing F5+F6 into a cell *without* a beginning equal sign?
- (a) The entry is equivalent to the formula =F5+F6
- (b) The cell will display the contents of cell F5 plus cell F6
- (c) The entry will be treated as a constant and display the literal value F5+F6
- (d) The entry will be rejected by Excel, which will signal an error message

13. A worksheet is superior to manual calculation because:
- (a) The worksheet computes its entries faster
- (b) The worksheet computes its results more accurately
- (c) The worksheet recalculates its results whenever cell contents are changed
- (d) All the above

14. The cell at the intersection of the second column and third row has the cell reference:
- (a) B3
- (b) 3B
- (c) C2
- (d) 2C

15. Which of the following is true?
- (a) A worksheet contains one or more workbooks
- (b) A workbook contains one or more worksheets
- (c) A spreadsheet contains one or more worksheets
- (d) A worksheet contains one or more spreadsheets

ANSWERS

1. c	**6.** d.	**11.** b
2. a	**7.** c.	**12.** c
3. c	**8.** c.	**13.** d
4. b	**9.** d.	**14.** a
5. a	**10.** c.	**15.** b

EXPLORING EXCEL

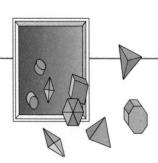

1. Use Figure 1.14 to identify the elements of a Microsoft Excel screen by matching each element with the appropriate letter.

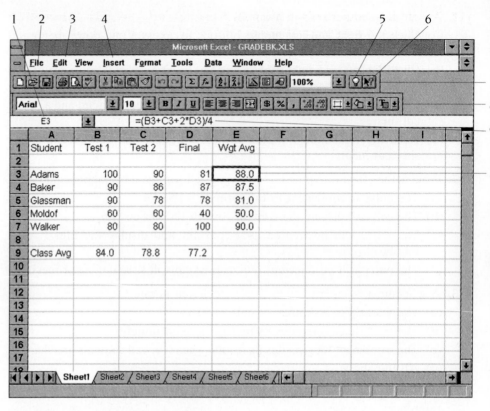

FIGURE 1.14 Screen for Problem 1

___ Formatting toolbar

___ Active cell

___ Contains the Delete command to remove rows from the worksheet

___ Help button

___ TipWizard icon

___ Standard toolbar

___ Contains the Open and Save commands

___ Name box

___ Formula bar

___ Contains the commands to add rows and columns to the worksheet

2. The common user interface: Answer the following with respect to Figures 1.2a and 1.2b that appeared earlier in the chapter.

   a. Which pull-down menus are common to both Excel and Word?

   b. How do you access the Edit menu in Excel? in Word?

   c. How do you open a file in Microsoft Excel? Do you think the same command will work in Microsoft Word as well?

   d. Which icons correspond to the Open and Save commands in the Excel toolbar? Which icons correspond to the Open and Save commands in the Microsoft Word toolbar?

   e. Which icons will boldface, italicize, and underline a selected item in Excel and Word? Are these icons descriptive of the tasks they perform?

   f. What do your answers to parts a through e tell you about the advantages of a common user interface?

3. Troubleshooting: The informational messages in Figure 1.15 appeared (or could have appeared) in response to various commands issued during the chapter.

    a. The message in Figure 1.15a is produced when the user exits Excel, but only under a specific circumstance. When will that message be produced? When would No be an appropriate response to this message?

    b. The message in Figure 1.15b appeared in response to a File Open command in conjunction with the files shown earlier in Figure 1.10a. What is the most likely corrective action?

    c. The message in Figure 1.15c also appears in response to a File Open command. What corrective action needs to be taken?

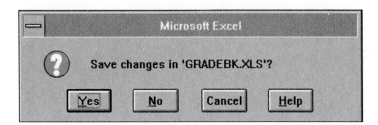

(a) Informational Message 1

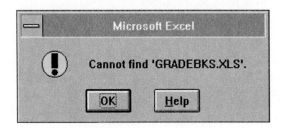

(b) Informational Message 2

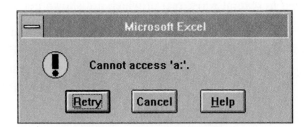

(c) Informational Message 3

FIGURE 1.15 Informational Messages for Problem 3

4. Exploring help: Answer the following with respect to Figure 1.16:

    a. What is the significance of the scroll box that appears within the scroll bar?

    b. What happens if you click on the down (up) arrow within the scroll bar?

    c. What happens if you press the maximize button? Might this action eliminate the need to scroll within the help window?

    d. How do you print the help topic shown in the window?

    e. Which entries in the help screen are underlined? Is there a difference between a dotted and a solid underline?

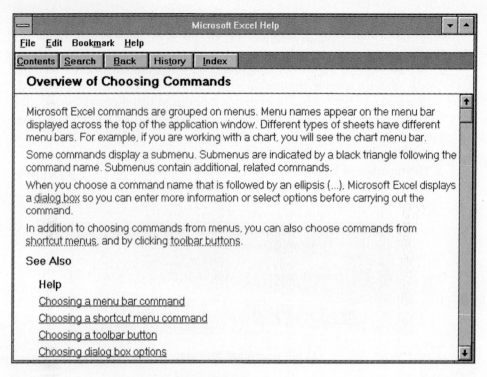

FIGURE 1.16   Help Screen for Problem 4

5. Design a worksheet that would be useful to you. You might want to consider applications such as an annual budget, the cost of a stereo or computer system, the number of calories you consume (burn) in a day, calculation of federal income tax, and so on. The applications are limited only by your imagination.

6. Figure 1.17 contains a simple worksheet showing the earnings for Widgets of America, before and after taxes. The cell values in cells B6, B7, and B9 may be produced in several ways, two of which are shown below. For example:

	Method 1	Method 2
Cell B6	10000−4000	=B3−B4
Cell B7	.30*6000	=.30*B6
Cell B9	6000−1800	=B6−B7

Which is the better method, and why?

	A	B
1	Widgets of America	
2		
3	Revenue	10000
4	Expenses	4000
5		
6	Earnings before taxes	6000
7	Taxes	1800
8		
9	Earnings after taxes	4200

FIGURE 1.17   Spreadsheet for Problem 6

7. Answer the following with respect to the screen in Figure 1.18, which depicts the use of a worksheet in a simplified calculation for income tax.

   a. Is the application window for Excel maximized?

   b. Is the document window containing the worksheet maximized?

   c. What is the active cell?

   d. What are the contents of the active cell?

   e. Assume that the income in cell B2 changes to $125,000. What other numbers will change automatically?

   f. Assume that an additional deduction for local income taxes of $3,000 is entered between rows 9 and 10. Which formula (if any) has to be explicitly changed to accommodate the new deduction?

   g. Which formula(s) will change automatically after the row containing the additional deduction has been added to the worksheet?

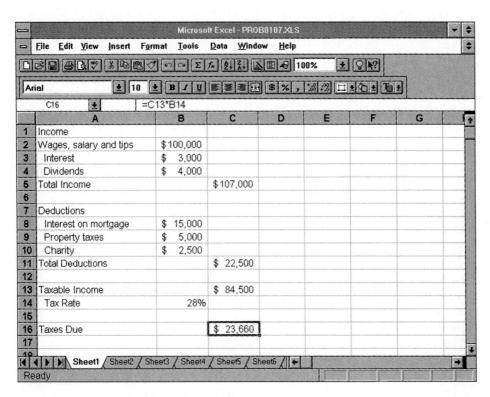

FIGURE 1.18 Spreadsheet for Problem 7

8. Return to the grade book at the end of the second hands-on exercise and implement the following changes:

   a. The professor has decided to weigh test 1, test 2, and the final equally, rather than counting the final as two exams.

   b. A new student, Milgrom, must be entered on the roster with grades of 88, 80, and 84, respectively.

   c. Baker is to be dropped from the class roll.

   d. Enter the label, *Grading Assistant*, followed by your name somewhere in the worksheet.

   e. Print the worksheet after all modifications have been made and submit it to your instructor.

9. Figure 1.19 contains a simple profit projection in the form of a worksheet that you are to implement in Microsoft Excel. *Be sure to enter formulas* *rather than numbers where appropriate—for example, in the cells containing gross income, total material cost, total labor cost, total cost, and gross profit.*

a. Add your name somewhere in the worksheet and identify yourself as a financial planner. Print the worksheet as it appears in Figure 1.19, then implement the following modifications.

b. Change the selling price in cell B4 to 6, which should automatically change several other numbers in the worksheet—for example, the gross income in cell B5.

c. Add an overhead expense in cell B12 of $1000 (enter an appropriate label in cell A12), then change the formula in cell B13 to accommodate the additional expense.

d. Assume a tax rate of 30 percent. Enter the formula to compute the anticipated tax in row 16 and the after-tax profit in row 17.

e. Assume that the numbers in column B are for 1994. Create a corresponding forecast for 1995 in column C. Assume the number of units sold will be 10 percent higher, and that the selling price and all other costs increase by 8 percent.

f. Add column D for 1996, using the same anticipated rates of change.

g. Print the worksheet a second time after completing the modifications in parts b through f. Submit both versions of the printed worksheet (in part a and part g) to your instructor.

	A	B
1		
2	Income	
3	Number of units	1,500
4	Selling price	$ 8
5	Gross Income	$12,000
6		
7	Expenses	
8	Material cost per unit	$ 4
9	Total material cost	$ 6,000
10	Labor cost per unit	$ 1
11	Total labor cost	$ 1,500
12		
13	Total cost	$ 7,500
14		
15	Gross Profit	$ 4,500

FIGURE 1.19   Spreadsheet for Problem 9

10. Create a worksheet that shows your income and expenses for a typical month according to the format in Figure 1.20. Enter your budget rather than ours.

a. Enter your name in cell A1.

b. Enter the text Monthly Income in cell A3 and the corresponding amount in cell B3.

c. Enter the text Monthly Expenses in A5.

d. Enter at least 5 different expenses in consecutive rows, beginning in A6, and enter the corresponding amounts in column B.

e. Enter the text Total Expenses in the row immediately below your last expense item. Enter the formula to compute the total in the corresponding cell in column B.

	A	B
1	Maryann Barber's Budget	
2		
3	Monthly Income	1000
4		
5	Monthly Expenses	
6	Food	250
7	Rent	350
8	Utilities	100
9	Phone	20
10	Gas	40
11	Total expenses:	760
12		
13	What's left for fun	240

FIGURE 1.20 Spreadsheet for Problem 10

f. Skip one blank row and then enter the text What's left for fun in column A. Enter the formula to compute how much money you have left at the end of the month in column B.

g. Insert a new row eight. Add an additional expense that you left out, entering the text in A8 and the amount in B8. Does the formula for total expenses reflect the additional expense? If not, change the formula so that it does.

h. Change the amount of your monthly income to reflect the fact that you now have a part-time work/study position. Do you now have more money left at the end of the month? Did the formula indicating the amount left recompute automatically to reflect the increased income in cell A3?

i. Why did the formula in step g not reflect the change made, while the formula in step h did reflect the change made?

 Case Studies

Buying a Computer

You have decided to buy a PC and have settled on a minimum configuration consisting of an entry-level 80486, with 4MB of RAM, and a 100MB hard disk. You would like a modem if it fits into the budget, and you need a printer. You also need software: DOS, Windows, a Windows-based word processor, and a Windows-based spreadsheet. You can spend up to $2,500 and hope that, at today's prices, you can find a system that goes beyond your minimum requirements—for example, a system with a faster processor, 8MB of RAM, and a 200MB hard disk. We suggest you shop around and look for educational discounts on software and/or a suite of applications to save money.

Create a spreadsheet based on real data that presents several alternatives. Show different configurations from the same vendor and/or comparable systems from different vendors. Include the vendor's telephone number with their estimate. Bring the spreadsheet to class together with the supporting documentation in the form of printed advertisements.

Portfolio Management

A spreadsheet is an ideal vehicle to track the progress of your investments. You need to maintain the name of the company, the number of shares purchased, the date of the purchase, and the purchase price. You can then enter the current price and see immediately the potential gain or loss on each investment as well as the current value of the portfolio. Retrieve the STOCKS.XLS workbook from the data disk, enter the closing prices of the listed investments, and compute the current value of the portfolio.

Accuracy Counts

The UNDERBID.XLS workbook on the data disk was the last assignment completed by your predecessor prior to his unfortunate dismissal. The worksheet contains a significant error, which caused your company to underbid a contract and assume a subsequent loss of $100,000. As you look for the error, don't be distracted by the attractive formatting. The shading, lines, and other touches are nice, but accuracy is more important than anything else. Write a memo to your instructor describing the nature of the error. Include suggestions in the memo on how to avoid mistakes of this nature in the future.

Planning for Disaster

This case has nothing to do with spreadsheets per se, but it is perhaps the most important case of all, as it deals with the question of backup. Do you have a backup strategy? Do you even know what a backup strategy is? You had better learn, because sooner or later you will wish you had one. You will erase a file, be unable to read from a floppy disk, or worse yet suffer a hardware failure in which you are unable to access the hard drive. The problem always seems to occur the night before an assignment is due. The ultimate disaster is the disappearance of your computer, by theft or natural disaster (e.g., Hurricane Andrew, the floods in the Midwest, or the Los Angeles earthquake). Describe in 250 words or fewer the backup strategy you plan to implement in conjunction with your work in this class.

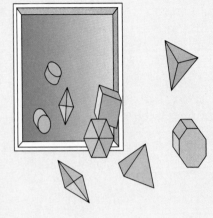

2

Gaining Proficiency: Copying, Moving, and Formatting

After reading this chapter you will be able to:

1. Explain the importance of isolating assumptions within a worksheet.
2. Define a cell range; select and deselect ranges within a worksheet.
3. Copy and/or move cells within a worksheet; differentiate among relative, absolute, and mixed addresses.
4. Format a worksheet to include boldface, italics, shading, and borders; change the font and/or alignment of a selected entry.
5. Change the width of a column; explain what happens if a column is too narrow to display the computed result.
6. Print a worksheet two ways: to show the computed values or cell formulas.
7. Use the Page Setup command to print a worksheet with or without gridlines and/or row and column headings; preview a worksheet before printing.
8. Use the Formatting toolbar.

OVERVIEW

This chapter continues the grade book example of Chapter 1. It is perhaps the most important chapter in the entire text as it describes the basic commands to create a worksheet. We begin with the definition of a cell range and the commands to build a worksheet without regard to its appearance. We focus on the Copy command and the difference between relative and absolute addresses. We stress the importance of isolating the assumptions within a worksheet so that alternative strategies may be easily evaluated.

The second half of the chapter presents formatting commands to improve the appearance of a worksheet after it has been created. You will be pleased with the dramatic impact you can achieve with a few simple commands, but we emphasize that *accuracy in a worksheet is much more important than appearance.*

The two hands-on exercises are absolutely critical if you are to master the material. As you do the exercises, you will realize that there are many different ways to accomplish the same task. Our approach is to present the most basic way first and the shortcuts later. You will like the shortcuts better, but you may not remember them and hence you need to understand the underlying concepts. You can always find the necessary command from the appropriate menu, and if you don't know which menu, you can always look to on-line help.

A BETTER GRADE BOOK

Figure 2.1 contains a much improved version of the professor's grade book. The most obvious difference is in the appearance of the worksheet, as a variety of formatting commands have been used to make it more attractive. The exam scores and weighted averages are centered under the appropriate headings. Boldface and italics are used for emphasis. Shading is used to highlight different areas of the worksheet. The title has been centered over the worksheet.

Title added

Shading, bold, and italics used for emphasis

Values are centered

Exam weights are indicated

	A	B	C	D	E
1	*CIS 120 - Spring 1994*				
2					
3	*Student*	*Test 1*	*Test 2*	*Final*	*Average*
4	Costa, Frank	70	80	90	82.5
5	Ford, Judd	70	65	80	73.8
6	Grauer, Jessica	90	80	98	91.5
7	Kinzer, Jessica	80	78	98	88.5
8	Krein, Darren	85	70	95	86.3
9	Moldof, Adam	75	75	80	77.5
10					
11	*Class Averages*	*78.3*	*74.7*	*90.2*	
12					
13	*Exam Weights*	*25%*	*25%*	*50%*	

FIGURE 2.1   A Better Grade Book

The most *significant* difference, however, is that the weight of each exam is indicated within the worksheet, and the formulas to compute the student averages are based on these values. In other words the professor can change the contents of the cells containing the exam weights, and see immediately the effect on the student averages.

This is one of the most important concepts in the development of a worksheet and enables the professor to explore alternative grading strategies. The professor may notice, for example, that the class did significantly better on the final than on either of the first two exams. He or she may decide to give the class a break and increase the weight of the final relative to the other tests. What if the professor increases the weight of the final to 60% and decreases the weight of the other tests? What if he or she decides that the final should count 70%? The effect of these changes can be seen immediately by entering the new exam weights in the appropriate cells at the bottom of the worksheet.

CELL FORMULAS

A worksheet should always be printed twice, once to show the computed results, and once to show the cell formulas. To display cell formulas, pull down the Tools menu, click Options, click the View tab, then check the box for formulas. Use the Page Setup command to specify cell gridlines and row and column headings, then click the Print command button to print.

CELL RANGES

Every command in Excel operates on a rectangular group of cells known as a *range*. A range may be as small as a single cell or as large as the entire worksheet. It may consist of a row or part of a row, a column or part of a column, or multiple rows and columns. The cells within a range are specified by indicating the diagonally opposite corners, typically the upper-left and lower-right corners of the rectangle. For example, cells A1 through E13 (A1:E13) indicate the active area of the worksheet in Figure 2.1.

The easiest way to select a range is by dragging the mouse; that is, click at the beginning of the range, press and hold the left mouse button as you move to the end of the range, then release the mouse. Once selected, the range is highlighted and its cells are affected by any subsequent command. The range remains selected until another range is defined or until you click another cell anywhere on the worksheet.

COPY COMMAND

The *Copy command* duplicates the contents of a cell, or range of cells, and saves you from having to enter the contents of every cell individually. It is much easier, for example, to enter the formula to compute the test average once, and copy it to obtain the average for the remaining tests, rather than explicitly entering the formula for every test.

Figure 2.2 illustrates how the copy command can be used to duplicate the formula to compute the class average. The cell that you are copying from, cell B11, is called the *source range.* The cells that you are copying to, cells C11 to D11, are the *destination* (or target) *range.* The formula is not copied exactly, but is adjusted as it is copied, to compute the average for the respective test.

	A	B	C	D	E
1			*CIS 120 - Spring 1994*		
2					
3	*Student*	*Test 1*	*Test 2*	*Test 3*	*Average*
4	Costa, Frank	70	80	90	=$B13*B4+$C$13*C4+$D$13*D4
5	Ford, Judd	70	65	80	=$B13*B5+$C$13*C5+$D$13*D5
6	Grauer, Jessica	90	80	98	=$B13*B6+$C$13*C6+$D$13*D6
7	Kinzer, Jessica	80	78	98	=$B13*B7+$C$13*C7+$D$13*D7
8	Krein, Darren	85	70	95	=$B13*B8+$C$13*C8+$D$13*D8
9	Moldof, Adam	75	75	80	=$B13*B9+$C$13*C9+$D$13*D9
10					
11	*Class Averages*	=AVERAGE(B4:B9)	=AVERAGE(C4:C9)	=AVERAGE(D4:D9)	
12					
13	*Exam Weights*	25%	25%	50%	

Absolute reference

Relative reference

Source range (B11)   Destination range (C11:D11)

FIGURE 2.2 A Copy Command

The formula (function) to compute the average on the first test was entered into cell B11 as =AVERAGE(B4:B9). This formula references the cell seven rows above the cell containing the formula (i.e., cell B4 is seven rows above cell B11) as well as cell B9, which is two rows above the formula. When the formula in cell B11 is copied to C11, it is adjusted so that the cells referenced in cell C11 are in the same relative position as those referenced by the formula in cell B11—that is, seven and two rows above the formula itself. Thus the formula in cell C11 becomes =AVERAGE(C4:C9), and in similar fashion, the formula in cell D11 becomes =AVERAGE(D4:D9).

Figure 2.2 also illustrates how the Copy command is used to copy the formula for a student's weighted average, from cell E4 (the source range) to cells E5 through E9 (the destination range). This is slightly more complicated than the previous example, because the formula is based on a student's grades, which vary from one student to the next, and on the exam weights, which do not. The cells referring to the student's grades should adjust as the formula is copied, but the addresses referencing the weights should not.

The distinction between cell references that remain constant versus cell addresses that change is made through a dollar sign. An **absolute reference** remains constant throughout the copy operation and is specified with a dollar sign in front of the column and row designation—for example, $B$13. A **relative reference,** on the other hand, changes during a copy operation and is specified without dollar signs—for example, B4. (A **mixed reference** uses a single dollar sign to make the row relative and the column absolute—for example, $A5—or vice versa, to make the row absolute and the column relative as in A$5. Mixed references are not discussed further.)

Consider, for example, the formula to compute a student's weighted average as it appears in cell E4 of Figure 2.2:

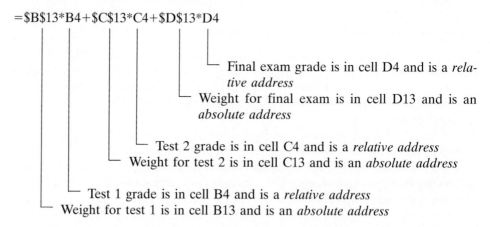

=$B$13*B4+$C$13*C4+$D$13*D4

Final exam grade is in cell D4 and is a *relative address*

Weight for final exam is in cell D13 and is an *absolute address*

Test 2 grade is in cell C4 and is a *relative address*

Weight for test 2 is in cell C13 and is an *absolute address*

Test 1 grade is in cell B4 and is a *relative address*

Weight for test 1 is in cell B13 and is an *absolute address*

The formula in cell E4 uses a combination of relative and absolute addresses to compute the student's weighted average. Relative addresses are used for the exam grades (found in cells B4, C4, and D4) and change automatically when the formula is copied to the other rows. Absolute addresses are used for the exam weights (found in cells B13, C13, and D13) and remain constant from student to student.

The copy operation is implemented by using the Windows clipboard and a combination of the **Copy** and **Paste commands** from the Edit menu. The contents of the source range are copied to the **clipboard,** from where they are pasted to the destination range. The contents of the clipboard are replaced with each subsequent Copy command, but are unaffected by the Paste command. Thus you can execute the Paste command several times in succession, to paste the contents of the clipboard to multiple locations.

MOVE COMMAND

The **Move command** is not used in the grade book, but its presentation is essential for the sake of completeness. The Move command transfers the contents of a cell (or range of cells) from one location to another. After the move is completed, the cells where the move originated (that is, the source range) are empty. This is in contrast to the Copy command, by which the entries remain in the source range and are duplicated in the destination range.

A simple move operation is depicted in Figure 2.3a, in which the contents of cell A3 are moved to cell C3, with the formula in cell C3 unchanged after the move. In other words, the Move command simply picks up the contents of cell

A3 (to add the values in cells A1 and A2), and puts it down in cell C3. The source range, cell A3, is empty after the Move command has been executed.

	A	B	C
1	5		
2	2		
3	=A1+A2		

	A	B	C	
1	5			← Source range is empty
2	2			
3			=A1+A2	← Formula is unchanged

(a) Example 1 (only cell A3 is moved)

FIGURE 2.3 The Move Command

Figure 2.3b depicts a situation wherein the formula itself remains in the same cell, but one of the values it references is moved to a new location; that is, the entry in A1 is moved to C1. The formula in cell A3 is adjusted to follow the moved entry to its new location; that is, the formula is now =C1+A2.

	A	B	C
1	5		
2	2		
3	=A1+A2		

	A	B	C	
1			5	
2	2			
3	=C1+A2			← Cell reference adjusted to follow moved entry

(b) Example 2 (only cell A1 is moved)

FIGURE 2.3 The Move Command (continued)

The situation is different in Figure 2.3c as the contents of all three cells—A1, A2, and A3—are moved. After the move has taken place, cells C1 and C2 contain the 5 and the 2, respectively, with the formula in cell C3 adjusted to reflect the movement of the contents of cells A1 and A2. Once again the source range (column A) is empty after the move is completed.

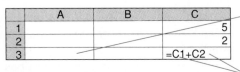

	A	B	C
1	5		
2	2		
3	=A1+A2		

	A	B	C	
1			5	← Source range is empty
2			2	
3			=C1+C2	← Cell references adjusted to follow moved entries

(c) Example 3 (all three cells in column A are moved)

FIGURE 2.3 The Move Command (continued)

Figure 2.3d contains an additional formula in cell B1, which is *dependent* on cell A3, which in turn is moved to cell C3. The formula in cell C3 is unchanged after the move because *only* the formula was moved, *not* the values it referenced. The formula in cell B1 changes (even though the contents of cell B1 were not moved) because cell B1 refers to an entry (A3) that was transferred to a new location (C3).

	A	B	C
1	5	=A3*4	
2	2		
3	=A1+A2		

	A	B	C	
1	5	=C3*4		← Formula references value in A3 / Cell reference adjusted to follow moved entry
2	2			
3			=A1+A2	← Formula is unchanged

(d) Example 4 (dependent cells)

FIGURE 2.3 The Move Command (continued)

Figure 2.3e shows that the specification of an absolute address has no meaning in a Move command. Absolute addresses are treated exactly the same as relative addresses and are adjusted as necessary to reflect the move operation. The example combines Figures 2.3b and 2.3c and shows that all of the absolute references were changed to reflect the entries that moved.

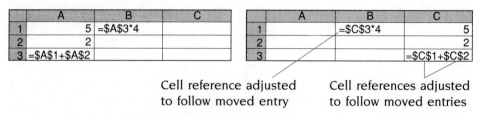

(e) Example 5 (absolute cell addresses)

FIGURE 2.3   The Move Command (continued)

The Move command is a convenient way to improve the appearance of a worksheet after it has been developed. It is subtle in its operation, and we suggest you think twice before moving cell entries because of the complexities involved.

The move operation is implemented by using the Windows clipboard and a combination of the *Cut* and *Paste* commands from the Edit menu. The contents of the source range are transferred to the clipboard, from where they are pasted to the destination range. (The contents of the clipboard are erased by the Paste command when the Paste command follows a Cut command.)

LEARNING BY DOING

As we have already indicated, there are many different ways to accomplish the same task. You can execute commands by using a pull-down menu, a shortcut menu, a toolbar, or the keyboard. In the following exercise we emphasize pull-down menus (the most basic technique) but suggest various shortcuts as appropriate. We also direct you to reset the TipWizard so that Excel can monitor your actions and offer additional suggestions.

Realize, however, that while the shortcuts are interesting, it is far more important to focus on the underlying concepts in the exercise, rather than specific key strokes or mouse clicks. The professor's grade book was developed to emphasize the difference between relative and absolute cell references. The grade book also illustrates the importance of isolating assumptions so that alternative strategies (e.g., different exam weights) can be considered.

HANDS-ON EXERCISE 1:

Creating a Worksheet

Objective To build the worksheet of Figure 2.1 without regard to its appearance; to create a formula containing relative and absolute references; to use the Copy command within a worksheet. Use Figure 2.4 as a guide in doing the exercise.

Step 1: Load Excel

➤ Load Excel as you did in the previous chapter.

➤ If necessary, click the **TipWizard icon** on the Standard toolbar to open the TipWizard box and display the tip of the day.

➤ Pull down the **Tools menu,** click **Options,** and click the **General tab.** Click the check box to **Reset TipWizard,** then click **OK.** The contents of the Tip-Wizard box change to indicate that you have reset the TipWizard and that the tips may repeat.

Step 2: Enter the column headings

➤ Click in cell **A1.** Enter the title of the worksheet, **CIS120 - Spring 1994** as in Figure 2.4a.

➤ Press the **down arrow key** twice to move to cell **A3.** Type **Student.**

➤ Press the **right arrow key** to move to cell **B3.** Type **Test 1.**

➤ Press the **right arrow key** to move to cell **C3.** Type **Test 2.** Type **Final** in cell **D3** and **Average** in cell **E3.**

Step 3: Save the workbook

➤ Pull down the **File menu** and click **Save** (or click the **Save icon** on the Standard toolbar).

➤ If you have not changed the default directory:
— Click drive A or drive C as appropriate.
— Double click the **EXCLDATA** directory to make it the active directory.

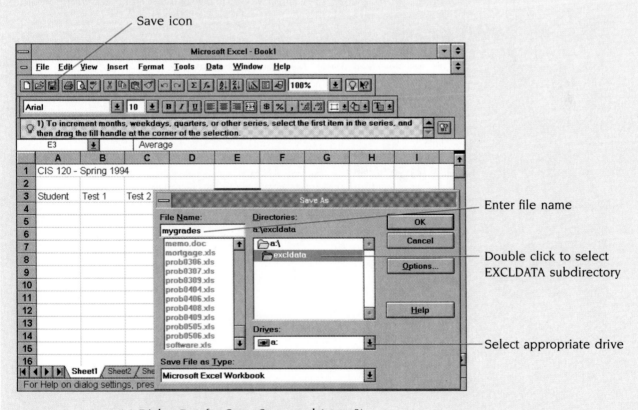

(a) Dialog Box for Save Command (step 3)

FIGURE 2.4 Hands-on Exercise I

➤ Click in the File Name text box. Type **MYGRADES** as the name of the workbook as shown in Figure 2.4a. Click **OK** (or press **enter**). Click the **Cancel command button** (or press the **Esc key**) if you are prompted for summary information.

CHANGE THE DEFAULT DIRECTORY

The *default directory* is the directory Excel uses to retrieve (save) a workbook unless it is otherwise instructed. To change the default directory, pull down the Tools menu, click Options, and click the General tab. Type the name of the new directory (e.g., C:\EXCLDATA) in the Default File Location text box, then click OK. The next time you access the File menu, the default directory will reflect the change.

Step 4: Enter the student data and literal information

➤ Click in cell **A4** and type **Costa, Frank.**

➤ Move across row 4 and enter Frank's grades on the two tests and the final. Use Figure 2.4b as a guide. Do *not* enter Frank's average in cell E4 as that will be entered as a formula in step 4.

➤ Do *not* be concerned that you cannot see Frank's entire name because the default width of column A is not yet wide enough to display the entire name.

Do not enter the average —

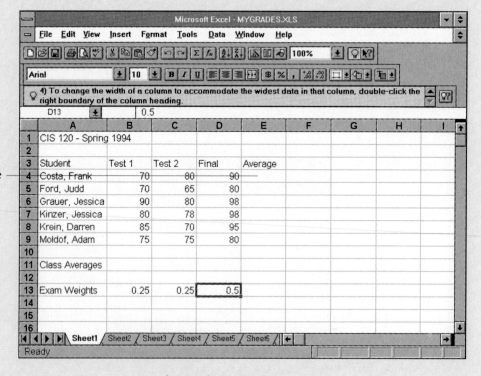

(b) Grade Book after Step 5

FIGURE 2.4 Hands-on Exercise 1 (continued)

➤ Enter the names and grades for the other students in rows 5 through 9. Do *not* enter their averages.

➤ Complete the entries in column A by typing **Class Averages** and **Exam Weights** in cells **A11** and **A13,** respectively.

➤ Save the workbook.

Step 5: Enter the exam weights
➤ Click in cell **B13** and enter **.25,** the weight for the first exam.

➤ Press the **right arrow key** to move to cell **C13** and enter **.25,** the weight for the second exam.

➤ Press the **right arrow key** to move to cell **D13** and enter **.5,** the weight for the final. Do *not* be concerned that the exam weights do not appear as percentages; they will be formatted in the second exercise later in the chapter.

➤ The worksheet should match Figure 2.4b except that column A is too narrow to display the entire name of each student.

Step 6: Compute the weighted average for the first student
➤ Click in cell **E4** and type the formula **=$B$13*B4+$C$13*C4+$D$13*D4** to compute the weighted average for the first student. Press the **enter key** when you have completed the formula.

➤ Check that the displayed value in cell E4 is 82.5, which indicates you entered the formula correctly.

➤ Save the workbook.

CORRECTING MISTAKES

The fastest way to change the contents of an existing cell is to double click in the cell and then make the changes directly in the cell rather than on the formula bar. Use the mouse or arrow keys to position yourself at the point of correction. Press the Ins key to toggle between insertion and replacement and/or use the Del key to delete a character. Press the Home and End keys to move to the first and last characters, respectively.

Step 7: Copy the weighted average
➤ Check that cell **E4,** the source range for the Copy command, is still selected.

➤ Pull down the **Edit menu** as in Figure 2.4c.

➤ Click **Copy**; a flashing border (the *marquee*) will surround cell E4, indicating that its contents have been copied to the clipboard.

➤ Click cell **E5.** Drag the mouse over cells **E5** through **E9** to select the destination range as in Figure 2.4d.

➤ Pull down the **Edit menu** and click **Paste** to copy the contents of the clipboard to the destination range. You should see the weighted averages for the other students in cells E5 through E9.

➤ Press **Esc** to remove the marquee surrounding cell E4.

➤ Click anywhere in the worksheet to deselect cells E5 through E9.

➤ Save the workbook.

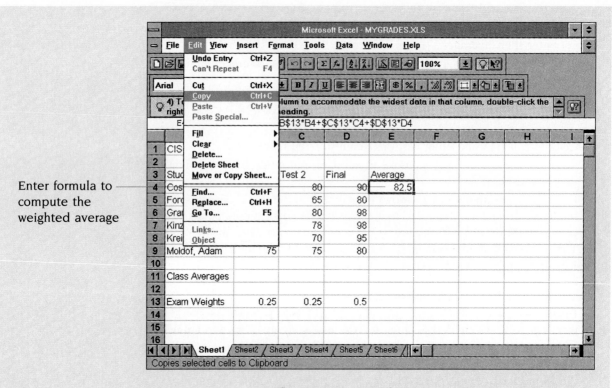

Enter formula to
compute the
weighted average

(c) The Copy Command (steps 6 and 7)

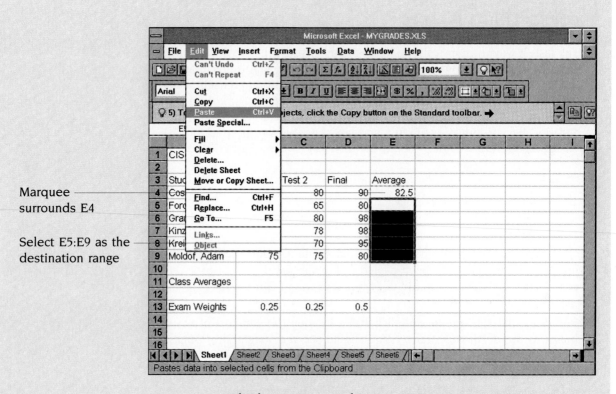

Marquee
surrounds E4

Select E5:E9 as the
destination range

(d) The Marquee and Destination Range (step 7)

FIGURE 2.4   Hands-on Exercise 1 (continued)

CUT, COPY, AND PASTE

Ctrl+X, Ctrl+C, and Ctrl+V are keyboard equivalents to cut, copy, and paste, respectively, and apply to Excel, Word for Windows, and Windows applications in general. (The keystrokes are easier to remember when you realize that the operative letters X, C, and V are next to each other at the bottom left side of the keyboard.) Alternatively, you can use the Cut, Copy, and Paste icons on the Standard toolbar, which are also found on the Standard toolbar in Word for Windows.

Step 8: Compute the class averages

➤ Click in cell **B11** and type the formula **=AVERAGE(B4:B9)** to compute the class average on the first test. Press the **enter key** when you have completed the formula.

➤ Click in cell B11, then click the **right mouse button** to produce the shortcut menu in Figure 2.4e. Click **Copy**, which produces the marquee around cell B11.

➤ Click cell **C11.** Drag the mouse over cells **C11** and **D11,** the destination range for the Copy command.

➤ Click the **Paste icon** on the Standard toolbar to copy the contents of the clipboard to the destination range.

➤ Press **Esc** to remove the marquee. Click anywhere in the worksheet to deselect cells C11 through D11.

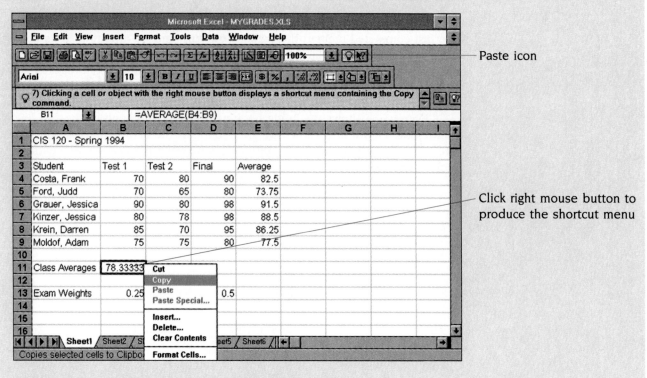

(e) Shortcut Menu (step 8)

FIGURE 2.4 Hands-on Exercise 1 (continued)

To define a range with the keyboard, move to the first cell in the range—that is, the cell in the upper left corner. Press and hold the Shift key as you use the arrow keys to extend the selection over the remaining cells in the range.

Step 9: What if? Change the exam weights
- Change the entries in cells **B13** and **C13** to **.20** and the entry in cell **D13** to **.60.** The weighted average for every student changes automatically; for example, Costa and Moldof change to 84 and 78, respectively.
- The professor decides this does not make a significant difference and goes back to the original weights; reenter .25, .25, and .50 in cells B13, C13, and D13, respectively.

Step 10: Save the completed workbook
- Click the **Save icon** on the Standard toolbar to save the workbook.
- Exit Excel if you are not ready to begin the next exercise.

FORMATTING

The professor's grade book is developed in two stages as in Figure 2.5. The exercise just completed created the grade book, but paid no attention to its appearance. It had you enter the data for every student, develop the formulas to compute the semester average for every student based on exam weights at the bottom of the worksheet, and finally, develop the formulas to compute the class averages for each exam.

Figure 2.5a shows the grade book as it exists at the end of the first hands-on exercise. Figure 2.5b shows the grade book at the end of the second exercise after it has been formatted. The differences between the two are due entirely to formatting. Consider:

- The exam weights are formatted as percentages in Figure 2.5b as opposed to decimals in Figure 2.5a.
- The class and student averages are displayed with a single decimal point in Figure 2.5b as opposed to a variable number of decimal places in Figure 2.5a.
- Boldface and italics are used for emphasis as are shading and borders.
- Exam grades and computed averages are centered under their respective headings.
- The worksheet title is centered across all five columns.
- The width of column A has been increased so that the students' names are completely visible.

The next several pages describe how to format the gradebook and make it more attractive. You should not, however, lose sight of accuracy. Be sure a worksheet is correct before you focus on its appearance.

	A	B	C	D	E
1	CIS 120 - Spring 1994				
2					
3	Student	Test 1	Test 2	Final	Average
4	Costa, Fra	70	80	90	82.5
5	Ford, Judd	70	65	80	73.75
6	Grauer, Je	90	80	98	91.5
7	Kinzer, Je	80	78	98	88.5
8	Krein, Dar	85	70	95	86.25
9	Moldof, Ac	75	75	80	77.5
10					
11	Class Ave	78.333	74.667	90.167	
12					
13	Exam Wei	0.25	.025	0.5	

(a) At the End of Exercise 1

Column A is wider

	A	B	C	D	E
1	*CIS 120 - Spring 1994*				
2					
3	*Student*	*Test 1*	*Test 2*	*Final*	*Average*
4	Costa, Frank	70	80	90	82.5
5	Ford, Judd	70	65	80	73.8
6	Grauer, Jessica	90	80	98	91.5
7	Kinzer, Jessica	80	78	98	88.5
8	Krein, Darren	85	70	95	86.3
9	Moldof, Adam	75	75	80	77.5
10					
11	*Class Averages*	*78.3*	*74.7*	*90.2*	
12					
13	*Exam Weights*	*25%*	*25%*	*50%*	

Title is centered over spreadsheet

Shading, bold, and italics are used for emphasis

Averages are displayed with one decimal place

Exam weights are formatted as percentages

(b) At the End of Exercise 2

FIGURE 2.5 Developing the Grade Book

THE FORMATTING TOOLBAR

The Formatting toolbar is the fastest way to implement most formatting operations. There are buttons for boldface, italics, and underlining; justification (including centering across columns); accounting, percent, and comma formats; as well as icons to increase or decrease the number of decimal places. There are also several list boxes that enable you to choose the font, point size, and font color, as well as the type of border and shading.

Column Widths

A column is often too narrow to display the contents of one or more cells in that column. The action taken by Excel depends on whether the cell contains a text or numeric entry, and if it is a text entry, on whether or not the adjacent cell is empty.

The student names in Figure 2.5a, for example, are partially hidden because column A is too narrow to display the entire name. Cells A4 through A9 contain the complete names of each student, but because the adjacent cells in column B contain data, the entries in column A are truncated (cut off) at the cell width. The situation is different for the worksheet title in cell A1. This time the adjacent cell (cell B1) is empty, so that the contents of cell A1 overflow into that cell and are completely visible.

Numbers are treated differently from text and do not depend on the contents of the adjacent cell. Excel displays a series of number signs (######) when a cell containing a numeric entry is too narrow to display the entry in its current format. You can correct the problem by changing the format of the number (e.g., display the number with fewer decimal places). You can also increase the cell width by using the *Column command* in the *Format menu.*

Row Heights

The row height changes automatically as the *font* size is increased. Row 1 in Figure 2.5b, for example, has a greater height than the other rows to accommodate the larger font size in the title of the worksheet. The row height can also be changed manually through the *Row command* in the Format menu.

FORMAT CELLS COMMAND

The *Format Cells command* controls the formatting for Numbers, Alignment, Fonts, Borders, and Patterns (color). Execution of the command produces a tabbed dialog box in which you choose the particular formatting category, then enter the desired options. (Almost every formatting option can also be specified from the *Formatting toolbar.*)

All formatting is done within the context of select-then-do. You select the cells to which the formatting is to apply, then you execute the Format Cells command or click the appropriate icon.

FORMATS VERSUS VALUES

Changing the format of a number changes the way the number is displayed but does *not* change its value. If, for example, you entered 1.2345 into a cell but displayed the number as 1.23, the actual value (1.2345) would be used in all calculations involving that cell.

Numeric Formats

General format is the default format for numeric entries and displays a number according to the way it was originally entered. Numbers are shown as integers (e.g., 123), decimal fractions (e.g, 1.23), or in scientific notation (e.g., 1.23E+10) if the number is larger than the width of the cell or if it exceeds 11 digits. You can also display any number in one of several built-in formats as shown in Figure 2.6a:

➤ *Number format* displays a number with or without commas, and with any number of decimal places.

➤ *Accounting format* displays negative values in parentheses, displays zero values as hyphens, and positions the dollar sign at the left of the cell.

➤ *Date format* applies to any value entered as a date as described in Chapter 3. The date may be displayed in many different formats, such as 3/16/94 or 16-Mar-94.

➤ *Time format* applies to any value entered as a time as described in Chapter 3. The time may be displayed in a variety of formats—for example, 10:50 PM or the equivalent 22:50 (military time).

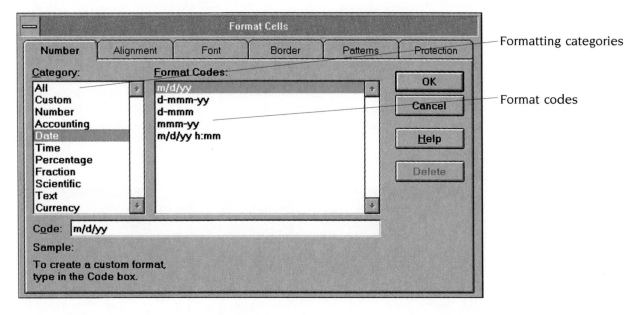

(a) The Number Tab

FIGURE 2.6   The Format Cells Command

➤ *Percentage format* causes the number to be multiplied by 100 for display purposes only; a percent sign is included, and any number of decimal places can be specified.

➤ *Fraction format* displays a number as a fraction and is appropriate when there is no exact decimal equivalent—for example, 1/3.

➤ *Scientific format* displays a number as a decimal fraction followed by a whole-number exponent of 10; for example, the number 12345 would appear as 1.2345E+04. The exponent, +04 in the example, is the number of places the decimal point is moved to the right or left (if the exponent is negative). Very small numbers have negative exponents; for example, the entry .0000012 would be displayed as 1.2E−06. Scientific notation is used only with very large or very small numbers and is generally not used in a business environment.

➤ *Text format* left justifies the entry and is useful for numerical values that are treated as text, such as zip codes or phone numbers.

➤ *Currency format* displays the value with a $, with commas as appropriate, and with any number of decimal places.

Each formatting category contains its own set of format codes (e.g., five codes in the Date category in Figure 2.6a) that provide additional flexibility within the category. Additional information on formatting codes can be obtained by using on-line help.

DATES VERSUS FRACTIONS

A fraction may be entered directly into a cell by preceding the fraction with an equal sign—for example, =1/3. Omission of the equal sign causes Excel to treat the entry as a date; that is, 1/3 will be stored as January 3 (of the current year).

Alignment

The contents of a cell may be aligned horizontally and/or vertically as indicated by the dialog box of Figure 2.6b. The options for horizontal alignment include left (the default for text), center, right (the default for numbers), and full justification. You can also center an entry across a range of selected cells as in the grade book of Figure 2.5b, which centered the title in cell A1 across columns A through E. The Fill option duplicates the characters in the cell across the entire width of that cell.

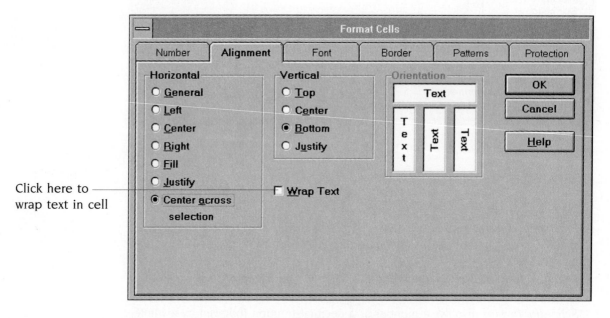

Click here to wrap text in cell

(b) The Alignment Tab

FIGURE 2.6   The Format Cells Command (continued)

Vertical alignment is important only if the row height is changed and the characters are smaller than the height of the row. Entries may be vertically aligned at the top, center, or bottom (the default) of a cell.

It is also possible to wrap the text within a cell to emulate the word wrap capability of a word processor. And finally, you can achieve some very interesting effects by choosing from one of the four orientations within the alignment window.

Fonts

Windows 3.1 supports a font technology known as *TrueType.* TrueType fonts are installed automatically with Windows and are available from any application. You can use the same fonts in Excel as you do in Word for Windows. In addition, True-Type fonts are scalable, allowing you to select any *point size* from 4 to 127 points (there are 72 points to the inch). And finally, TrueType fonts are truly WYSIWYG (What You See Is What You Get), meaning that the worksheet you see on the monitor will match the worksheet produced by the printer.

Windows includes a limited number of TrueType fonts—Arial, Times New Roman, Courier New, Symbol, and Wingdings—which offer sufficient variety to produce some truly impressive worksheets. (Additional fonts are available from Microsoft and/or other vendors.)

Any entry in a worksheet may be displayed in any font, style, or point size as indicated by the dialog box of Figure 2.6c. The example shows Arial, Bold Italic, and 14 points, and corresponds to the selection for the worksheet title in the improved grade book. You can even select a different color, but you will need a color monitor and/or color printer to see the effect.

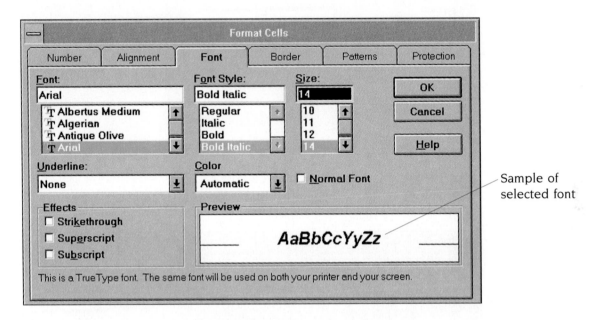

(c) The Font Tab

FIGURE 2.6 The Format Cells Command (continued)

Borders, Patterns, and Shading

The *Border tab* in Figure 2.6d enables you to create a border around a cell (or cells) for additional emphasis. You can outline the entire selection, or you can choose the specific side or sides as indicated in the figure; for example, thicker lines on the bottom and right sides produce a drop shadow, which is very effective. You can also specify a different color for the border, but you will need a color monitor (and printer) to see the effect.

The *Patterns tab* in Figure 2.6e lets you choose a different color to shade the cell and further emphasize its contents. The Pattern list box lets you select an alternate pattern such as dots or slanted lines.

VARIATIONS IN PRINTING

The final way to control the appearance of a worksheet is through printing. You can print a worksheet with or without row and column headings, and with or without the cell *gridlines.* These and other options are controlled by the Page Setup command. You can also view a worksheet prior to printing through the Print Preview command. Both commands are executed from the File menu.

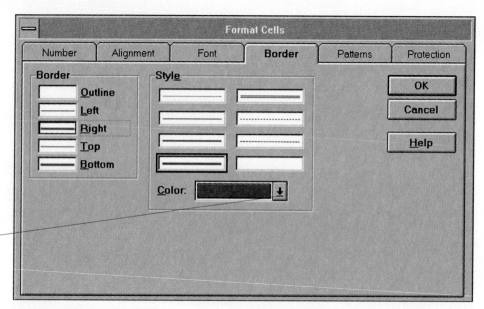

Select border color

(d) The Border Tab

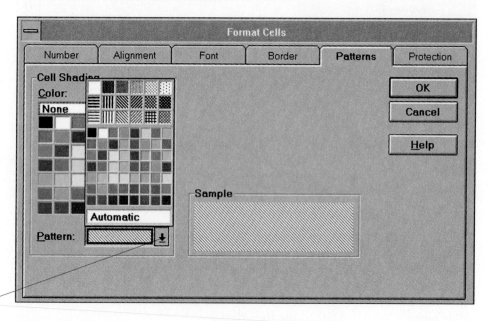

Click here to produce
display of sample
patterns and colors

(e) The Patterns Tab

FIGURE 2.6   The Format Cells Command (continued)

The Page Setup Command

The ***Page Setup command*** gives you complete control of the printed worksheet.
Many of its options may not appear important now, but you will appreciate them
as you develop larger and more complicated worksheets later in the text.

The Page tab in Figure 2.7a determines the orientation and scaling of the
printed page. ***Portrait orientation*** ($8\frac{1}{2} \times 11$) prints vertically down the page.
Landscape orientation ($11 \times 8\frac{1}{2}$) prints horizontally across the page. The option

buttons imply mutually exclusive items, one of which *must* be selected; that is, a worksheet must be printed in either portrait *or* landscape orientation. Option buttons are also used to choose the scaling factor. You can reduce (enlarge) the output by a designated scaling factor *or* you can force the output to fit on a specified number of pages.

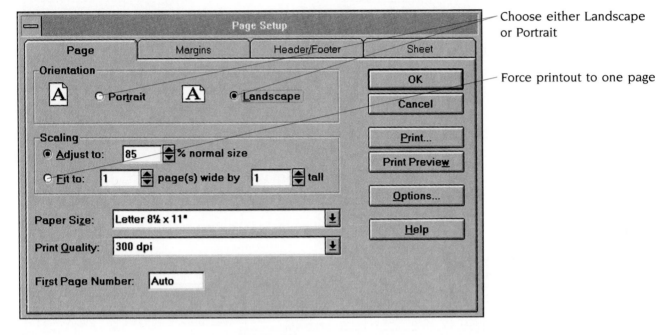

(a) The Page Tab

FIGURE 2.7   The Page Setup Command

The Margins tab in Figure 2.7b not only controls the margins, but will also center the worksheet horizontally and/or vertically. Check boxes are associated with the centering options and imply that multiple options can be chosen; for example, horizontally and vertically are both selected. The Margin tab also determines the distance of the header and footer from the edge of the page.

The Header/Footer tab in Figure 2.7c lets you create a ***header*** (and/or ***footer***) that appears at the top (and/or bottom) of every page. The pull-down list boxes let you choose from several preformatted entries, or alternatively, you can click the appropriate command button to customize either entry.

The Sheet tab in Figure 2.7d offers several additional options, the most important of which are Gridlines and Row and Column Headings. Information about the additional entries can be obtained by clicking the Help command button.

The Print Preview Command

The ***Print Preview command*** in the File menu (or the Print Preview command button in Figures 2.7a, 2.7b, and 2.7c) displays the worksheet as it will appear when printed. The command is invaluable and will save you considerable time as you don't have to rely on trial and error to obtain the perfect printout. The Print Preview command is illustrated in Figure 2.7e, which corresponds to the various settings in Figures 2.7a through 2.7d.

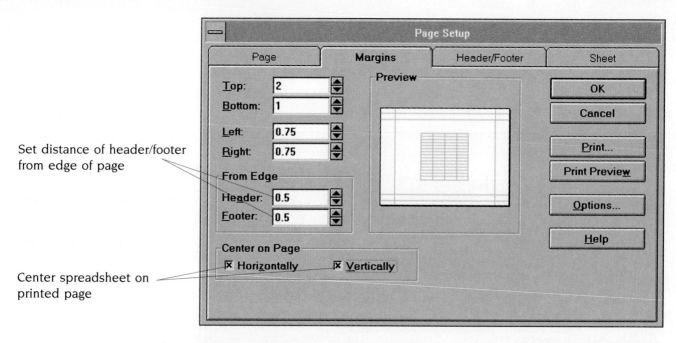

Set distance of header/footer
from edge of page

Center spreadsheet on
printed page

(b) The Margins Tab

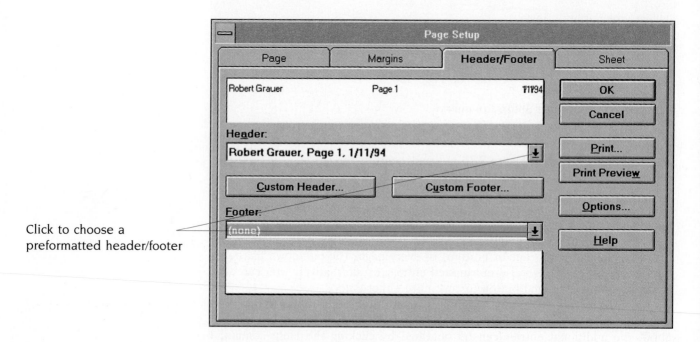

Click to choose a
preformatted header/footer

(c) The Header/Footer Tab

FIGURE 2.7 The Page Setup Command (continued)

The worksheet is printed horizontally across the page (landscape orientation in Figure 2.7a). It has been centered horizontally and vertically within the specified margins (Figure 2.7b). A custom header has been chosen and there is no footer (Figure 2.7c). Gridlines and row and column headings both appear (Figure 2.7d).

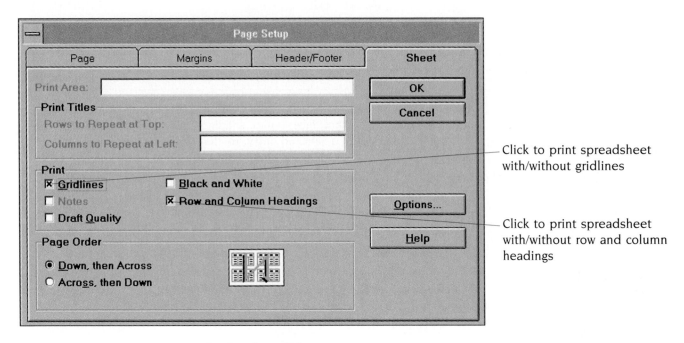

Click to print spreadsheet with/without gridlines

Click to print spreadsheet with/without row and column headings

(d) The Sheet Tab

Click here to return to worksheet

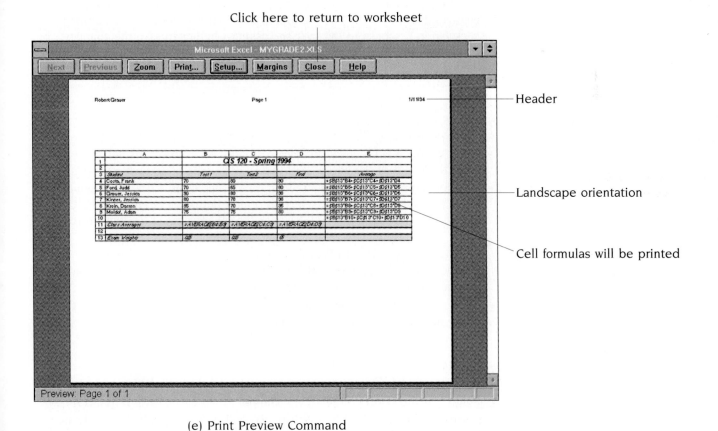

Header

Landscape orientation

Cell formulas will be printed

(e) Print Preview Command

FIGURE 2.7 The Page Setup Command (continued)

HANDS-ON EXERCISE 2:

Formatting a Worksheet

Objective To format a worksheet using both pull-down menus and the Formatting toolbar; to use boldface, italics, shading, and borders; to change the font and/or alignment of a selected entry; to change the width of a column; to print the cell contents as well as the computed values. Use Figure 2.8 as a guide in doing the exercise.

Step 1: Fonts
➤ Open the MYGRADES.XLS workbook from the first exercise.
➤ Click in cell **A1** to select the cell containing the title of the worksheet.
➤ Pull down the **Format** menu. Click **Cells.** If necessary, click the **Font tab.**
➤ Click **Arial** from the Font list box, **Bold Italic** from the Font Style box, and **14** from the Size box. Click the **OK** command button.

QUIT WITHOUT SAVING

There are times when you will edit a workbook beyond recognition and wish you had never started. The Undo command, useful as it is, reverses only the most recent operation and is of no use if you need to cancel all changes. Pull down the File menu and click on the Close command, then click No in response to the message asking whether to save the changes. Pull down the File menu, click Open to reopen the file, then begin all over.

Step 2: Alignment
➤ Click in cell **A1.** Drag the mouse over cells **A1** through **E1,** which represents the width of the entire worksheet.
➤ Pull down the **Format menu** a second time. Click **Cells.** Click the **Alignment tab.** Click the **Center across selection** option button as in Figure 2.8a. Click **OK** to center the entry in cell A1 over the selected range (cells A1 through E1).
➤ If necessary, click the TipWizard icon to open the TipWizard box; the TipWizard suggests that you click the Center Across Selection button on the Formatting toolbar as a more efficient way to center text.
➤ Click in cell **B3.** Drag the mouse over cells **B3** through **E13.** Click the **Centering icon** on the Formatting toolbar.

Step 3: Increase the width of column A
➤ Click in cell **A4.** Drag the mouse over cells **A4** through **A13.**
➤ Pull down the **Format menu,** click **Column,** then click **AutoFit Selection** as shown in Figure 2.8b. The width of the selected cells increases to accommodate the longest entry in the selected range.
➤ Click the **Save icon** on the Standard toolbar to save the workbook.

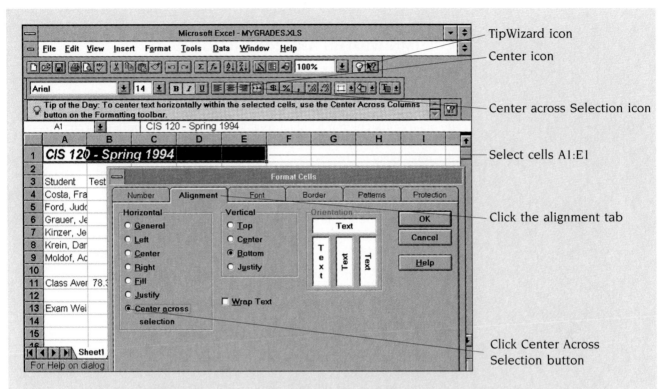

(a) Center across Columns (step 2)

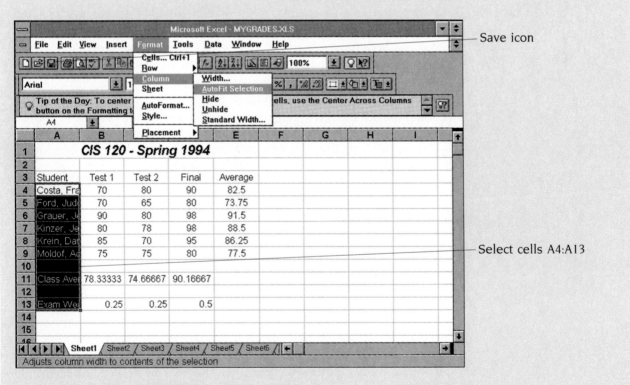

(b) Changing Column Widths (step 3)

FIGURE 2.8 Hands-on Exercise 2 (continued)

COLUMN WIDTHS AND ROW HEIGHTS

Drag the border between column labels to change the column width; for example, to increase (decrease) the width of column A, drag the border between column labels A and B to the right (left). Double click the right boundary of a column heading to change the column width to accommodate the widest entry in that column. Use the same technique to change the row heights.

Step 4: Format the exam weights (shortcut menu versus Formatting toolbar)

➤ Click in cell **B13.** Drag the mouse over cells **B13** through **D13.**

➤ Click the **right mouse button** to produce the shortcut menu in Figure 2.8c. Click **Format Cells** to produce the Format Cells dialog box.

➤ If necessary, click the **Number tab.** Click **Percentage** in the Category list box. Click **0%** in the Format Codes list box. Click the **OK** command button. The exam weights are now displayed with percent signs.

➤ Click the **Undo icon** on the Standard toolbar to cancel the formatting command.

➤ Click the **% icon** on the Formatting toolbar to reformat the exam weights as percentages.

Step 5: Noncontiguous ranges

➤ Select cells **B11** through **D11,** the cells that contain the class averages for the three exams.

➤ Press *and* hold the **Ctrl key** and click cell **E4.** Continue to press the Ctrl key and drag the mouse over cells **E4** through **E9.** Release the **Ctrl key.**

➤ You will see two noncontiguous (nonadjacent) ranges highlighted, cells B11:D11 and cells E4:E9 as in Figure 2.8d.

➤ Format the selected cells using either the Formatting toolbar or the Format menu.
  —To use the Formatting toolbar, click the icon on the toolbar to increase or reduce the number of decimal places as necessary.
  —To use the Format menu, pull down the **Format menu,** click **Cells,** click the **Number tab,** then click **Number** in the category list box. Click in the Code list box. Type **0.0** to display the numbers with a single decimal point. Click the **OK** command button.

AUTOMATIC FORMATTING

Excel converts any number entered with a dollar sign to currency format and any number entered with a percent sign to percentage format. The automatic formatting enables you to save a step by typing $100,000 or 7.5% directly into a cell, rather than entering 100000 or .075, and subsequently having to format the number

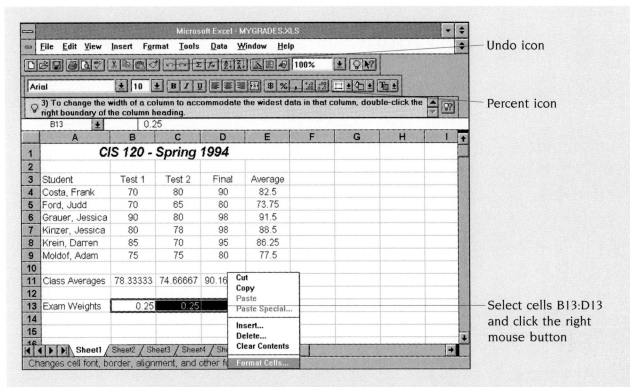

Undo icon

Percent icon

Select cells B13:D13 and click the right mouse button

(c) Format Exam Weights (step 4)

Increase decimals   Reduce decimals

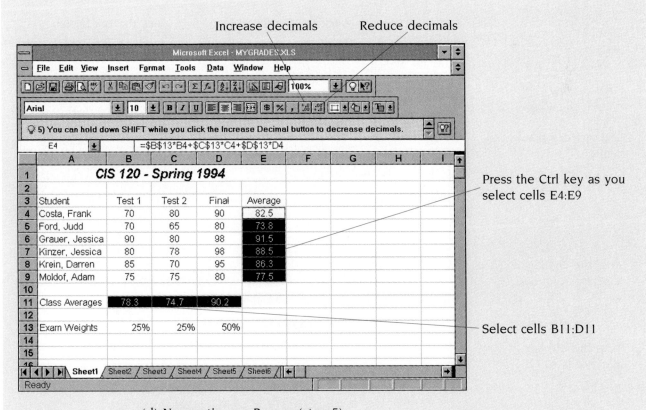

Press the Ctrl key as you select cells E4:E9

Select cells B11:D11

(d) Noncontiguous Ranges (step 5)

FIGURE 2.8 Hands-on Exercise 2 (continued)

THE FORMAT PAINTER

The **Format Painter** copies the formatting of the selected cell to other cells in the worksheet. Click the cell whose formatting you want to copy, then double click the Format Painter button on the Standard toolbar. The mouse pointer changes to a paintbrush to indicate that you can copy the current formatting; just drag the paintbrush over the additional cells, which will assume the identical formatting as the original cell. Repeat the painting process as often as necessary, then click the Format Painter icon a second time to return to normal editing.

Step 6: Borders

➤ Drag the mouse over cells **A3** through **E3.** Press *and* hold the **Ctrl key.** Drag the mouse over the range **A11:E11.** Continue to press the **Ctrl key.** Drag the mouse over the range **A13:E13.**

➤ Pull down the **Format menu** and click **Cells** (or click the **right mouse button** to produce a shortcut menu, then click **Format Cells**). Click the **Border tab** to access the dialog box in Figure 2.8e.

➤ Choose a line width from the Style options. Click the **Top** and **Bottom** boxes in the Border options. Click **OK** to exit the dialog box and return to the worksheet.

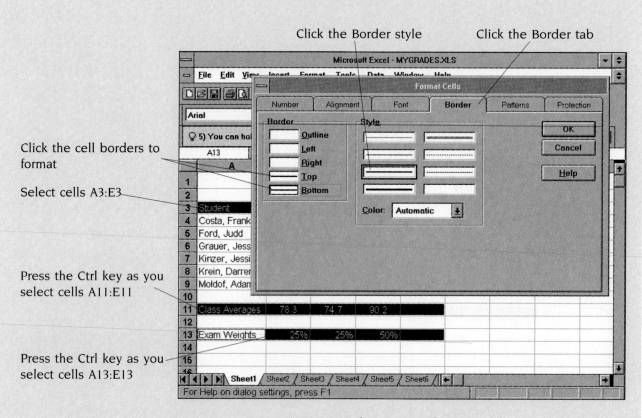

(e) Border Command (step 6)

FIGURE 2.8 Hands-on Exercise 2 (continued)

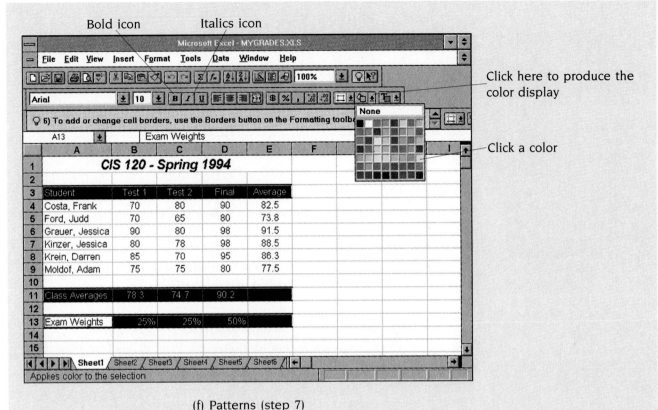

(f) Patterns (step 7)

FIGURE 2.8 Hands-on Exercise 2 (continued)

Step 7: Color

➤ Check that all three ranges are still selected (A3:E3, A11:E11, *and* A13:E13).

➤ Click the **down arrow** on the **Color button** on the Formatting toolbar. Click light grey (or whatever color appeals to you) as shown in Figure 2.8f.

➤ Click the **boldface** and **italics icons** on the Formatting toolbar. Click outside the selected cells to see the effects of the formatting change.

➤ Save the workbook.

SELECTING NONCONTIGUOUS RANGES

Dragging the mouse to select a range always produces some type of rectangle; it may be a single cell, a row or column, or a group of rows and columns. You can, however, select noncontiguous (nonadjacent) ranges by selecting the first range in the normal fashion, then pressing and holding the Ctrl key as you select the additional range(s). This is especially useful when the same command is to be applied to multiple ranges within a worksheet.

DESELECTING A RANGE

The effects of a formatting change are often difficult to see when the selected cells are highlighted. Thus, you may need to deselect the range by clicking elsewhere in the worksheet to see the results of a formatting command.

Step 8: The Print Preview command
➤ Pull down the **File menu.** Click **Print Preview** to see the worksheet prior to printing as in Figure 2.8g.
➤ Click the **Setup command button.**
— Click the **Margins tab** to display the dialog box shown in the figure. Check the box to center the worksheet horizontally.
— Click the **Sheet tab.** Check the boxes to include row and column headings and gridlines.
— Click **OK** to exit the Page Setup dialog box.
➤ Click the **Print command button** to display the Print dialog box, then click **OK** to print the worksheet.
➤ Save the workbook.

Click to display the Page Setup dialog box

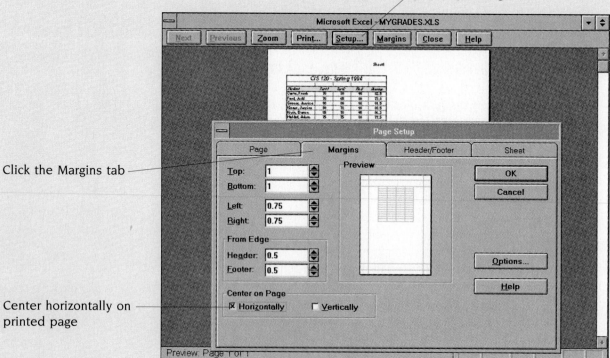

Click the Margins tab

Center horizontally on printed page

(g) Print Preview Command (step 8)

FIGURE 2.8   Hands-on Exercise 2 (continued)

KEYBOARD SHORTCUTS: THE DIALOG BOX

Press Tab or Shift+Tab to move forward (backward) between fields in a dialog box, or press the Alt key plus the underlined letter to move directly to an option. Use the space bar to toggle check boxes on or off and the up (down) arrow keys to move between options in a list box. Press enter to activate the highlighted command button or press Esc to exit the dialog box without accepting the changes.

Step 9: Print the cell formulas

➤ Pull down the **Tools menu.** Click **Options.** Click the **View tab.** Check the box for **Formulas.** Click **OK.** The worksheet should display the cell formulas.

➤ If necessary, click the arrow to the right of the horizontal scroll box so that column E, the column containing the cell formulas, comes into view. Double click the border between the column headings for columns E and F to increase the width of column E to accommodate the widest entry in the column.

➤ Pull down the **File menu** and click **Print Preview** (or click the **Print Preview icon** on the Standard toolbar).

➤ Click the **Setup command button** to display the Page Setup dialog box.
— Click the **Page tab.** Click the **Landscape** orientation button.
— Click the **Header/Footer tab.** Click the arrow on the Header list box. Scroll to the top of the list and click **None** to remove the header. Click the arrow on the Footer list box. Scroll to the top of the list and click **None** to remove the footer.
— Click **OK** to exit the Page Setup dialog box. Your monitor should match the display in Figure 2.8h.

➤ Save the workbook.

➤ Click the **Print command button** to display the Print dialog box, then click **OK** to print the worksheet.

➤ Exit Excel.

DISPLAY THE CELL FORMULAS

Press Ctrl+` (the single left quotation mark) to toggle between the cell formulas and computed results. (The left quotation mark is on the same key as the ~ at the upper left of the keyboard.)

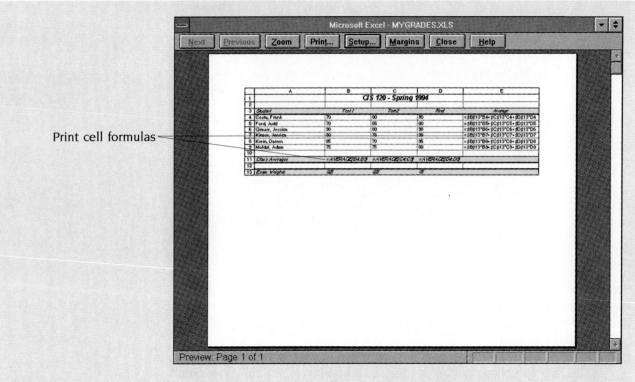

Print cell formulas

(h) Print Cell Formulas (step 9)

FIGURE 2.8 Hands-on Exercise 2 (continued)

A WORD OF CAUTION

The formatting capabilities within Excel make it all too easy to get caught up in the appearance of a worksheet without paying attention to its accuracy. Consider, for example, the grade book of Figure 2.9, which our professor uses in a different course. The grade book is beautifully formatted, *but its calculations are wrong.*

➤ Baker should have received an A rather than a B. His weighted average (the combination of the quiz average and final exam) was 87, and with two assignments, he should have had a final average of 91.

➤ Charles should have received a B rather than a C. True, he did not do any homework and he did do poorly on the final, but, with the semester quizzes and final exam counting equally, his weighted average should have been 80.

➤ Goodman should have received an A rather than a B. She aced both quizzes (she was excused from the first quiz) as well as the final, and in addition, she received a 4-point bonus for homework.

The errors in our example may be contrived, but they could occur. Consider:

➤ The professor decides at the last minute to assign a third homework but forgot to modify the formulas to include the additional column.

➤ The professor has another last-minute change of heart and decides to count the semester quizzes and final exam evenly. He was careless, however, when he developed the original worksheet, because the formulas to compute the weighted average specify constants (as in the worksheet of Chapter 1) rather than absolute references to the cells containing the exam weights.

	A	B	C	D	E	F	G	H	I	J	K	L
1						CIS 120 - Final Grade Book						
2												
3			Assignments			Quizzes			Quiz	Final	Wgt		Course
4	Name	#1	#2	#3	#1	#2	#3	Avg	Exam	Avg	Bonus	Grade
5	Baker		OK	OK	77	89	95	87	87	87	2	B
6	Charles				84	76	86	82	78	79	0	C
7	Goodman	OK	OK		Absent	95	94	63	95	85	4	B
8	Johnson	OK	OK		90	86	70	82	90	88	4	A
9	Jones		OK	OK	75	85	71	77	86	83	2	B
10	Irving	OK		OK	65	85	75	75	78	77	2	C
11	Lang		OK		84	88	83	85	94	91	2	A
12	London	OK	OK		72	69	75	72	82	79	4	B
13	Molgrom	OK	OK		100	65	90	85	100	96	4	A
14	Mills	OK	OK		75	85	80	80	65	70	4	C
15	Nelson				65	60	61	62	60	61	0	D
16												
17								Wgt				
18								Avg	Grade			
19		Grading Criteria							F			
20		Bonus for each homework			2			60	D			
21		Weight of semester quizzes			50%			70	C			
22		Weight of final exam			50%			80	B			
23								90	A			
24												
25												

Should be one grade higher

FIGURE 2.9 Style Over Substance

➤ The professor forgot that he had excused Goodman from the first quiz and hence did not adjust the formula to compute Goodman's average on the basis of two quizzes rather than three.

Our professor is only human, but he would have done well to print the cell formulas to audit the mechanics of the worksheet and double check its calculations. Suffice it to say that the accuracy of a worksheet is far more important than its appearance, and you are well advised to remember this as you create and/or use a worksheet. Ask yourself if any of the worksheets you have created contained an error, and if so, what the financial consequences would be if those worksheets were used for other than an academic exercise.

SUMMARY

All worksheet commands operate on a cell or group of cells known as a range. A range is selected by dragging the mouse to highlight the range; the range remains selected until another range is defined or you click another cell in the worksheet. Noncontiguous (nonadjacent) ranges may be selected with the Ctrl key.

The formulas in a cell or range of cells may be copied or moved anywhere within a worksheet. An absolute reference remains constant throughout a copy operation, whereas a relative address is adjusted for the new location. Absolute and relative references have no meaning in a move operation. The copy and move operations are implemented through the Copy and Paste commands, and the Cut and Paste commands, respectively.

Formatting is done within the context of select-then-do; that is, select the cell or range of cells, then execute the appropriate command. The Format Cells command controls the formatting for Numbers, Alignment, Font, Borders, and Patterns (colors). The Formatting toolbar simplifies the formatting process.

The Page Setup command provides complete control over the printed page, enabling you to print a worksheet with or without gridlines or row and column headings. The Page Setup command also controls margins, headers and footers, centering, and orientation. The Print Preview command shows the worksheet prior to printing.

A worksheet should always be printed twice, once with displayed values and once with cell formulas. The latter is an important tool in checking the accuracy of a worksheet, which is far more important than its appearance.

Key Words and Concepts

Absolute reference	Format Cells command	Paste command
Accounting format	Format menu	Patterns tab
Alignment	Format Painter	Percentage format
Border tab	Formatting toolbar	Point size
Cell formulas	Fraction format	Portrait orientation
Clipboard	General format	Print Preview command
Column command	Gridlines	Range
Copy command	Header	Relative reference
Currency format	Landscape orientation	Row command
Cut command	Marquee	Scientific format
Date format	Mixed reference	Source range
Default directory	Move command	Style
Destination range	Noncontiguous range	Text format
Font	Number format	Time format
Footer	Page Setup command	TrueType

Multiple Choice

1. Cell F6 contains the formula =AVERAGE(B6:D6). What will be the contents of cell F7 if the entry in cell F6 is *copied* to cell F7?
   (a) =AVERAGE(B6:D6)
   (b) =AVERAGE(B7:D7)
   (c) =AVERAGE($B$6:$D$6)
   (d) =AVERAGE($B$7:$D$7)

2. Cell F6 contains the formula =AVERAGE(B6:D6). What will be the contents of cell F7 if the entry in cell F6 is *moved* to cell F7?
   (a) =AVERAGE(B6:D6)
   (b) =AVERAGE(B7:D7)
   (c) =AVERAGE($B$6:$D$6)
   (d) =AVERAGE($B$7:$D$7)

3. A formula containing the entry $A$4 is copied to a cell one column over and two rows down. How will the entry appear in its new location?
   (a) Both the row and column will change
   (b) Neither the row nor column will change
   (c) The row will change but the column will remain the same
   (d) The column will change but the row will remain the same

4. Which of the following is true regarding a printed worksheet?
   (a) It may be printed with or without the row and column headings
   (b) It may be printed with or without the gridlines
   (c) Both (a) and (b) above
   (d) Neither (a) nor (b)

5. A cell range may consist of:
   (a) Part of one row and part of a different row
   (b) Part of one column and part of a different column
   (c) Both (a) and (b) above
   (d) Neither (a) nor (b)

6. Which command will take a cell, or group of cells, and duplicate them elsewhere in the worksheet, without changing the original cell references?
   (a) Copy command, provided relative addresses were specified
   (b) Copy command, provided absolute addresses were specified
   (c) Move command, provided relative addresses were specified
   (d) Move command, provided absolute addresses were specified

7. Which options are mutually exclusive in the Page Setup menu?
   (a) Portrait and landscape orientation
   (b) Cell gridlines and row and column headings
   (c) Headers and footers
   (d) Left and right margins

8. The Formatting toolbar contains icons to
   (a) Change to percent format
   (b) Increase or decrease the number of decimal places
   (c) Center an entry across columns
   (d) All of the above

9. Given that percentage format is in effect, and that the number .056 has been entered into the active cell, how will the contents of the cell appear?
   (a) .056
   (b) 5.6%
   (c) .056%
   (d) 56%

10. Which of the following entries is equivalent to the decimal number .2?
    (a) 1/5
    (b) =1/5
    (c) Both (a) and (b)
    (d) Neither (a) nor (b)

11. What is the effect of two successive Undo commands, one right after the other?
    (a) The situation is not possible because the Undo command is not available in Microsoft Excel
    (b) The situation is not possible because the Undo command cannot be executed twice in a row
    (c) The Undo commands cancel each other out; that is, the worksheet is as it was prior to the first Undo command
    (d) The last two commands prior to the first Undo command are reversed

12. Which menu contains the commands to preview the worksheet before printing, to save the workbook under a new name, and to exit Excel without saving the workbook at all?
    (a) File menu
    (b) Edit menu
    (c) Save menu
    (d) Print menu

13. Which of the following fonts are included in Windows?
    (a) Arial and Times New Roman
    (b) Courier New
    (c) Wingdings and Symbol
    (d) All of the above

14. A numerical entry may be
    (a) Displayed in boldface and/or italics
    (b) Left, centered, or right aligned in a cell
    (c) Displayed in any TrueType font in any available point size
    (d) All of the above

15. Which of the following is controlled by the Page Setup command?
    (a) Headers and footers
    (b) Margins
    (c) Orientation
    (d) All of the above

ANSWERS

1. b	**6.** b	**11.** c
2. a	**7.** a	**12.** a
3. b	**8.** d	**13.** d
4. c	**9.** b	**14.** d
5. c	**10.** b	**15.** d

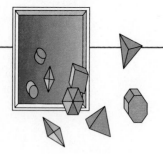

EXPLORING EXCEL

1. Use Figure 2.10 to match each action with its result; a given action may be used more than once, or not at all.

Action

a. Click at 12, then click at 1

b. Click at 19, then click at 1

c. Click at 13, drag to 14, click at 2

d. Click at 17, drag to 15, click at 2

e. Click at 18, drag to 16, click at 8

f. Click at 21, drag to 10, click at 7

g. Click at 21, then click at 4

h. Click at 20, drag to 11, click at 3

Result

____ Format the exam weights as percentages

____ Copy the formula to calculate the semester average for Frank Costa to the clipboard

____ Change the font size of the worksheet title

____ Paste the formula to calculate the semester average for the remaining students

____ Create a bottom border that separates the column titles from the students' names and grades

____ Copy the formula to calculate the average for Test 1 to the clipboard

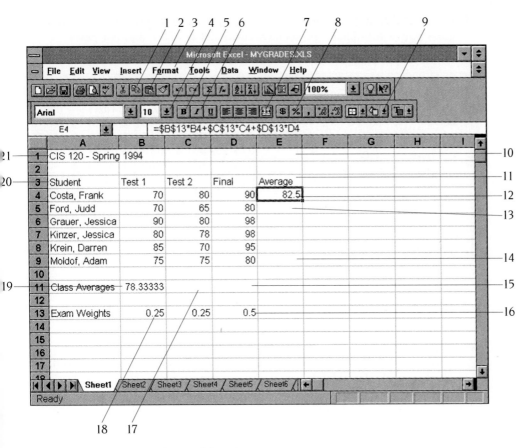

FIGURE 2.10 Screen for Problem 1

	Action	Result
i.	Click at 12, drag to 14, click at 9	___ Apply boldface and italic formatting to the worksheet title
j.	Click at 21, click at 5, click at 6	___ Paste the formula to calculate the test average for test 2 and the final
		___ Shade the student averages a light grey
		___ Center the worksheet title over the width of the worksheet

2. Figure 2.11 contains a worksheet in which the same number (1.2345) has been entered into every cell. The differences in appearance between the various cell entries are produced by different formats in the individual cells. Indicate the precise formatting for every cell.

	A	B	C	D
1	1	$1	123%	1E+00
2	1.23	$1.23	123.45%	1.23E+00
3	1.2345	$1.2345	123.4500%	1.2345E+00

FIGURE 2.11 Spreadsheet for Problem 2

3. Figure 2.12 contains a worksheet depicting simplified payroll calculations for gross pay, withholding tax, social security tax (FICA), and net pay.

	A	B	C	D	E	F	G	H
1	Employee	Hourly	Regular	Overtime	Gross	Withldg	Soc Sec	Net
2	Name	Wage	Hours	Hours	Pay	Tax	Tax	Pay
3	Adams	$ 8.00	40	3	$ 356.00	$ 99.68	$ 23.14	$ 233.18
4	Hall	$ 6.25	40	0	$ 250.00	$ 70.00	$ 16.25	$ 163.75
5	Costo	$ 9.50	25	0	$ 237.50	$ 66.50	$ 15.44	$ 155.56
6	Lee	$ 4.50	40	5	$ 213.75	$ 59.85	$ 13.89	$ 140.01
7	Arnold	$ 6.25	35	0	$ 218.75	$ 61.25	$ 14.22	$ 143.28
8	Vedo	$ 5.50	40	2	$ 236.50	$ 66.22	$ 15.37	$ 154.91
9								
10			Totals:		$1,512.50	$423.50	$98.31	$990.69
11								
12	Assumptions:							
13	Withholding Tax:		28.00%					
14	Social Security Tax:		6.50%					

FIGURE 2.12 Spreadsheet for Problem 3

a. What formula should be entered into cell E3 to compute an individual's gross pay? (An individual receives time and a half for overtime.)

b. What formula should be entered into cell F3 to compute the withholding tax?

c. What formula should be entered into cell G3 to compute the social security tax?

d. What formula should be entered into cell H3 to compute the net pay?

e. What formula should be entered into cell E10 to compute the total gross pay for the company? What formulas should be entered into cells F10 through H10 to compute the remaining totals?

4. Figure 2.13 contains two versions of a worksheet in which sales, costs, and profits are to be projected over a five-year horizon. The worksheets are only partially completed, and the intent in both is to copy the entries from year 2 (cells C2 through C4) to the remainder of the worksheet. As you can see, the first worksheet uses only relative references and the second uses only absolute references. Both worksheets are in error.

a. Show the erroneous entries that will result when column C is copied to columns D, E, and F for both worksheets.

b. What are the correct entries for column C so that the formulas will copy correctly?

	A	B	C	D	E	F
1		Year 1	Year 2	Year 3	Year 4	Year 5
2	Sales	1000	=B2+B2*C7			
3	Cost	800	=B3+B3*C8			
4	Profit	200	=C2-C3			
5						
6	Assumptions:					
7	Annual Sales Increase:		10%			
8	Annual Cost Increase:		8%			

(a) Error 1 (relative cell addresses)

FIGURE 2.13 Spreadsheet for Problem 4

	A	B	C	D	E	F
1		Year 1	Year 2	Year 3	Year 4	Year 5
2	Sales	1000	=$B$2+$B$2*$C$7			
3	Cost	800	=$B$3+$B$3*$C$8			
4	Profit	200	=$C$2-$C$3			
5						
6	Assumptions:					
7	Annual Sales Increase:		10%			
8	Annual Cost Increase:		8%			

(b) Error 2 (absolute cell addresses)

FIGURE 2.13 Spreadsheet for Problem 4 (continued)

5. Figure 2.14 shows how a worksheet can be used to prepare a sales invoice. What is your general impression of the worksheet? Is it formatted attractively? Is it accurate? Is the store receiving the correct amount; that is, is the subtotal shown on the invoice correct? Is Cori paying more or less than she should? Is the state getting the correct sales tax?

	A	B	C	D	E
1			**Kidlets Clothes**		
2			**Customer Invoice**		
3					
4	**Customer Name:**		Cori Rice		
5	**Address:**		7722 S.W. 142 Street		
6			Miami, Florida 33157		
7	**Phone:**		(305) 254-7111		
8					
9	**Item**		**Quantity**	**Cost**	**Total**
10	Reebok sneakers		1	$45.95	$45.95
11	Summer T-shirts		3	$19.99	$59.97
12	Barrettes		2	$6.00	$12.00
13	Shorts		3	$24.99	$74.97
14	**Subtotal**				**$117.92**
15	**Sales Tax**				**$76.65**
16	**Total**				**$194.57**

FIGURE 2.14 Spreadsheet for Problem 5

6. The worksheet in Figure 2.15 exists on the data disk as PROB0206.XLS. Complete the worksheet, following the steps below:

a. Click cell D6 and enter the formula to calculate the balance due on Kim Mallery's loan.

b. Copy the formula entered into D6 to the range D7:D11 to calculate the balance due for the other student loans.

c. Click cell B13 and enter the formula to calculate the total due for all student loans.

d. Copy the formula entered into B13 to the range C13:D13 to calculate the total amount paid and the total balance due.

e. Select the cells B6:D13 and format the numbers so that they display with dollar signs and commas, and no decimal places (e.g., $2,500).

f. Select the cells A1:D2 and center the titles across the width of the worksheet. With those cells still selected, change the font to 14 point Arial bold.

g. Select cells A5:D5 and create a bottom border to separate the headings from the data.

h. Save the workbook. Print the worksheet.

	A	B	C	D
1	UNCLE SAM'S LOANS, INC.			
2	College Loans for Good Students			
3				
4				
5	Customer	Amount Due	Amount Paid	Balance Due
6	Mallery, Kim	2500	31.66	
7	Camejo, Oscar	10000	126.67	
8	Rowe, Debbie-Ann	5000	63.33	
9	Bost, Tiffany	3500	44.33	
10	King, Beth Anne	12000	152.01	
11	Lali, Andrea	6000	76	
12				
13	Totals:			

FIGURE 2.15   Spreadsheet for Problem 6

7. Figure 2.16 contains a worksheet that was used to calculate the difference between the Asking Price and Selling Price on various real estate listings that were sold during June. It also contains the commission paid to the real estate agency as a result of selling those listings. Retrieve PROB0207.XLS from the data disk, then complete the worksheet following the steps outlined below:

	A	B	C	D	E	F
1	Coaches Realty - Sales for June					
2						
3			Asking	Selling		
4	Customer	Address	Price	Price	Difference	Commission
5	Landry	122 West 75 Terr.	450000	350000		
6	Spurrier	4567 S.W. 95 Street	750000	648500		
7	Shula	123 Alamo Road	350000	275000		
8	Lombardi	9000 Brickell Place	275000	250000		
9	Johnson	5596 Powerline Road	189000	189000		
10	Erickson	8900 N.W. 89 Street	456000	390000		
11	Bowden	75 Maynada Blvd	300000	265000		
12						
13		Totals:				
14						
15	Commission %:	0.035				

FIGURE 2.16   Spreadsheet for Problem 7

a. Click cell E5 and enter the formula to calculate the difference between the asking price and the selling price for the property belonging to Mr. Landry.

b. Click cell F5 and enter the formula to calculate the commission paid to the agency as a result of selling the property. (You will need to pay close attention to the difference between relative and absolute cell references so that the calculations will be correct when the formulas are copied to the other rows in the next step.)

c. Select cells E5:F5 and copy the formulas to E6:F11 to calculate the difference and commission for the rest of the properties.

d. Click cell C13 and enter the formula to calculate the total asking price, which is the sum of the asking prices for the individual listings in cells C5:C11.

e. Copy the formula in C13 to the range D13:F13 to calculate the other totals.

f. Select the range C5:F13 and format the numbers so that they display with dollar signs and commas, and no decimal places (e.g., $450,000).

g. Click cell B15 and format the number as a percentage.

h. Click cell A1 and center the title across the width of the worksheet. With the cell still selected, select cells A3:F4 as well and change the font to 12 point Arial bold italic.

i. Select cells A4:F4 and create a bottom border to separate the headings from the data.

j. Select cells F5:F11 and shade the commissions.

k. Save the workbook. Print the worksheet.

 Case Studies

Make an Impression

You do excellent work, but somehow you never get noticed. All of your worksheets are completely accurate and meet or exceed the requirements imposed by your supervisor. Something is still lacking, however, and the HELPME.XLS workbook on the data disk is typical of your work. A colleague took a look and said the problem is in formatting or the lack thereof. Let's see what you can do.

Establishing a Budget

You want to join a sorority and you really would like a car. Convince your parents that you can afford both by developing a detailed budget for your four years at school. Your worksheet should include all sources of income (scholarships, loans, summer jobs, work-study, etc.) as well as all expenses (tuition, books, room and board, and entertainment). Make the budget as realistic as possible by building in projected increases over the four-year period.

Your First Million

You have developed the perfect product and are seeking venture capital to go into immediate production. You have a firm order for 100,000 units in the first year at a selling price of $6.00 per unit. Both numbers are expected to increase 20 percent annually. You are able to rent a production facility for $50,000 a year for five years. The variable manufacturing cost is $1.50 per unit and is projected to increase at 10 percent a year. Administration and insurance costs another $25,000 a year and will increase at 5 percent annually. Develop a five-year financial forecast showing profits before and after taxes (assuming a tax rate of 36 percent).

Your worksheet should be completely flexible and capable of accommodating a change in any of the initial conditions or projected rates of increase, *without* having to edit or recopy any of the formulas. This will require you to isolate all of the assumptions (i.e., the initial conditions and rates of increase) in one area of the worksheet, and then reference these cells as absolute references when building the formulas. It's a challenging assignment, but then again you are going to make a lot of money.

Break-even Analysis

Widgets of America has developed the perfect product and is ready to go into production pending a review of a five-year break-even analysis. The manufacturing cost in the first year is $1.00 per unit and is estimated to increase at 5% annually. The projected selling price is $2.00 per unit and can increase at 10% annually. Overhead expenses are fixed at $100,000 per year over the life of the project. The advertising budget is $50,000 in the first year but will decrease 15% a year as the product gains acceptance. How many units have to be sold each year for the company to break even, given the current cost estimates and projected rates of increase?

As in the previous case, your worksheet should be completely flexible and capable of accommodating a change in any of the initial conditions or projected rates of increase. Be sure to isolate all of the assumptions (i.e., the initial conditions and rates of increase) in one area of the worksheet, and then reference these cells as absolute references when building the formulas.

Your Own Reference Manual

The clipboard is a temporary storage area available to all Windows applications. Selected text is cut or copied from one document into the clipboard, from where it can be pasted into another document altogether. Use on-line help to obtain detailed information on several topics in Excel, copy the information to the clipboard, then paste it into a new document, which will become your personal reference manual. To really do an outstanding job, you will have to format the reference manual after the information has been copied from the clipboard. Be sure to include a title page.

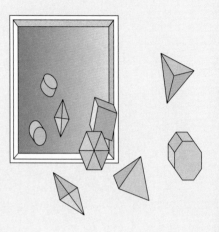

3

Spreadsheets in Decision Making: What If?

After reading this chapter you will be able to:

1. List the arguments of the PMT function and describe its use in financial decisions.

2. Use the Function Wizard to select a function, identify the function arguments, then enter the function into a worksheet.

3. Use the fill handle to copy a cell range to a range of adjacent cells.

4. Use pointing to create a cell formula; explain the advantage of pointing over typing in explicit cell references.

5. Use the AVERAGE, MAX, MIN, and COUNT functions in a worksheet.

6. Use the IF function to implement a decision; explain the table lookup function and how it is used in a worksheet.

7. Describe the DATE and TODAY functions; explain the use of date arithmetic.

8. Describe the additional measures needed to print large worksheets; explain how freezing panes may help in the development of a large worksheet.

9. Use the autofill capability to enter a series into a worksheet.

OVERVIEW

Excel is a truly fascinating program, but it is only a means to an end. A spreadsheet or worksheet is first and foremost a tool for decision making, and the objective of this chapter is to show you just how valuable that tool can be. We begin by presenting two worksheets that we think will be truly useful to you. The first evaluates the purchase of a car and helps you determine just how much car you can afford. The second will be of interest when you are looking for a mortgage to buy a home.

The chapter continues to develop your knowledge of Excel with emphasis on the predefined functions that are built into the program. We consider financial functions such as the PMT function to determine the monthly payment on a loan.

We introduce statistical functions (MAX, MIN, COUNT, and COUNTA), date functions (TODAY and DATE), and the IF and VLOOKUP functions to provide decision making within a worksheet.

The examples in the chapter review the important concept of relative and absolute cell references that was presented in the previous chapter. The hands-on exercises also introduce powerful shortcuts intended to make you more proficient in Excel; these are the fill handle to copy cells within a worksheet, pointing as a more accurate way to enter a formula, and autofill to enter a data series.

ANALYSIS OF A CAR LOAN

Figure 3.1 shows how a worksheet might be applied to the purchase of a car. In essence you need to know the monthly payment, which depends on the price of the car, the down payment, and the terms of the loan. In other words:

➤ Can you afford the monthly payment on the car of your choice?
➤ What if you settle for a less expensive car and receive a manufacturer's rebate?
➤ What if you work next summer to earn money for a down payment?
➤ What if you extend the life of the loan and receive a more favorable interest rate?

The answers to these and other questions determine whether you can afford a car, and if so, which car you will buy, and how you will pay for it. The decision is made easier by developing the worksheet in Figure 3.1, and then by changing the various parameters as indicated.

Figure 3.1a contains a ***template*** with text entries and cell formulas with formatting already applied, but *without* specific data. The template requires that you enter the price of the car, the manufacturer's rebate, the down payment, the interest rate, and the length of the loan. The worksheet uses these parameters to compute the monthly payment. (Implicit in this discussion is the existence of a PMT function within the worksheet program, which will be explained shortly.)

The availability of the worksheet lets you consider several alternatives, and therein lies its true value. You quickly realize that the purchase of a $14,999 car as shown in Figure 3.1b is prohibitive because the monthly payment is almost $500. Settling for a less expensive car and getting the manufacturer's rebate in Figure 3.1c helps somewhat, but the $413 payment is still too steep. Working next summer to earn an additional $3,000 for the down payment is a necessity (Figure 3.1d), and extending the loan to a fourth year at a lower interest rate makes the purchase possible (Figure 3.1e).

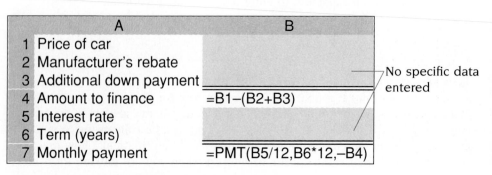

(a) The Template

FIGURE 3.1 "What If" Analysis on Car Loan

	A	B	
1	Price of car	$14,999	Data entered
2	Manufacturer's rebate		
3	Additional down payment		
4	Amount to finance	$14,999	
5	Interest rate	9%	
6	Term (years)	3	
7	Monthly payment	$476.96	

(b) Initial Parameters

	A	B	
1	Price of car	$13,999	Less expensive car
2	Manufacturer's rebate	$1,000	Rebate
3	Additional down payment	$0	
4	Amount to finance	$12,999	
5	Interest rate	9%	
6	Term (years)	3	
7	Monthly payment	$413.36	

(c) Less Expensive Car with Manufacturer's Rebate

	A	B	
1	Price of car	$13,999	
2	Manufacturer's rebate	$1,000	
3	Additional down payment	$3,000	Summer job
4	Amount to finance	$9,999	
5	Interest rate	9%	
6	Term (years)	3	
7	Monthly payment	$317.97	

(d) Summer Job

	A	B	
1	Price of car	$13,999	
2	Manufacturer's rebate	$1,000	
3	Additional down payment	$3,000	
4	Amount to finance	$9,999	
5	Interest rate	8%	Lower interest rate
6	Term (years)	4	More years
7	Monthly payment	$244.10	

(e) Longer Term and Better Rate

FIGURE 3.1 "What If" Analysis on Car Loan (continued)

PMT Function

A function is a predefined formula that accepts one or more **arguments** as input, performs the indicated calculation, then returns another value as output. The **PMT function** requires three arguments (the interest rate per period, the number of periods, and the amount of the loan), from which it computes the associated payment. Consider, for example, the PMT function as it might apply to Figure 3.1b:

=PMT(.09/12,36,Principal)

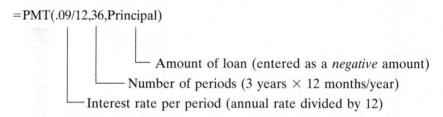

Amount of loan (entered as a *negative* amount)
Number of periods (3 years × 12 months/year)
Interest rate per period (annual rate divided by 12)

Instead of using specific values, however, the arguments in the PMT function are supplied as cell references, so that the computed payment can be based on values supplied by the user elsewhere in the worksheet. Thus, the PMT function is entered as =PMT(B5/12,B6*12,−B4) to reflect the terms of a specific loan whose arguments are in cells B4, B5, and B6. (The principal is entered as a negative amount because the money is lent to you.)

The analysis associated with Figure 3.1 shows how a worksheet is used in the decision-making process. A person defines a problem, then develops a worksheet that includes all of the associated parameters. He or she can then plug in specific numbers, changing one or more of the variables until a decision can be reached.

HOME MORTGAGES

The PMT function is incorporated into a second example using home mortgages, as shown in Figure 3.2. The worksheet lets you vary the amount of the loan and

	A	B	C	D
1	Amount Borrowed		$100,000	
2	Starting Interest		7.50%	
3				
4		Monthly Payment		
5	Interest	30 Years	15 Years	Difference
6	7.50%	$699.21	$927.01	$227.80
7	8.50%	$768.91	$984.74	$215.83
8	9.50%	$840.85	$1,044.22	$203.37
9	10.50%	$914.74	$1,105.40	$190.66
10	11.50%	$990.29	$1,168.19	$177.90
11	12.50%	$1,067.26	$1,232.52	$165.26

Difference in monthly payment between a 30-year and a 15-year loan

FIGURE 3.2   Variable Rate Mortgages

initial interest rate, then displays the associated monthly payment for a 30- and a 15-year mortgage, respectively.

The information provided by the worksheet is very different from what you might expect initially, but very informative in helping you decide which mortgage to take. Note, for example, that the difference in monthly payments for a $100,000 mortgage at 7.5% is only $227.80. Yes, this is a significant amount of money, but when viewed as a percentage of the total cost of a home (property taxes, maintenance, and so on), it becomes less significant.

Not convinced? Then consider the additional information presented in the worksheets of Figure 3.3. Figure 3.3a indicates the total interest over the life of a $100,000 loan at 7.5% is $151,717 for the 30-year mortgage. In other words, you will pay back the $100,000 in principal plus another $151,717 in interest if you select the longer term. The total interest for the 15-year loan is $66,862, which is less than half as much as for the 30-year loan.

If, like most people, you move before you pay off the mortgage, you will discover that almost all of the early payments in the 30-year loan go to interest rather than principal. The amortization schedule in Figure 3.3b shows that moving at the end of five years (60 months) pays off less than $6,000 of the principal versus almost $22,000 with the 15-year loan. (The latter number is not shown; that is, you have to change the term of the loan in cell C5 to see the amortization for the 15-year loan.)

	A	B	C	D	E
1	Amount Borrowed		$100,000		
2	Starting Interest		7.50%		
3					
4			30 Years		15 Years
5	Interest	Monthly Payment	Total Interest	Monthly Payment	Total Interest
6	7.50%	$699.21	$151,717	$927.01	$66,862
7	8.50%	$768.91	$176,809	$984.74	$77,253
8	9.50%	$840.85	$202,708	$1,044.22	$87,960
9	10.50%	$914.74	$229,306	$1,105.40	$98,972
10	11.50%	$990.29	$256,505	$1,168.19	$110,274
11	12.50%	$1,067.26	$284,213	$1,232.52	$121,854

Less interest is paid on a 15-year loan

(a) Total Interest

FIGURE 3.3   15- vs 30-year Mortgage

	A	B	C	D
1	Amortization Schedule			
2				
3	Principal		$100,000	
4	Annual Interest		7.50%	
5	Term (in years)		30	
6	Payment)		$699.21	
7				
8	Month	Toward Interest	Toward Principal	Balance
9				$100,000
10	1	$625.00	$74.21	$99,925.79
11	2	$624.54	$74.68	$99,851.11
12	3	$624.07	$75.15	$99,775.96
13	4	$623.60	$75.61	$99,700.35
14	5	$623.13	$76.09	$99,624.26
15	6	$622.65	$76.56	$99,547.70
	·	·	·	·
·	·	·	·	·
·	·	·	·	·
65	56	$594.67	$104.55	$95,042.20
66	57	$594.01	$105.20	$94,937.00
67	58	$593.36	$105.86	$94,831.14
68	59	$592.69	$106.52	$94,724.62
69	60	$592.03	$107.19	$94,617.44

5 years (60 months)

Less than $6,000 of the principal has been paid

(b) Amortization Schedule

FIGURE 3.3 15- vs 30-year Mortgage (continued)

Our objective is not to convince you of the merits of one loan over another, but to show you how useful a worksheet can be in the decision-making process. If you do eventually buy a home, and you select a 15-year mortgage, think of us.

Relative versus Absolute Addresses

Figure 3.4 displays the cell formulas for the mortgage analysis. All of the formulas are based on the amount borrowed and the starting interest, in cells C1 and C2, respectively. You can vary either or both of these parameters, and the worksheet will automatically recalculate the monthly payments.

The similarity in the formulas from one row to the next implies that the copy operation will be essential to the development of the worksheet. You must, however, remember the distinction between a *relative* and an ***absolute reference;*** that is, a cell reference that changes during a copy operation (relative) versus one that does not (absolute). Consider, for example, the PMT function as it appears in cell B6:

=PMT(A6/12,30*12,–$C$1)

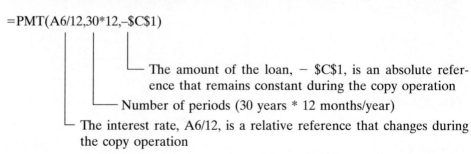

The amount of the loan, – $C$1, is an absolute reference that remains constant during the copy operation

Number of periods (30 years * 12 months/year)

The interest rate, A6/12, is a relative reference that changes during the copy operation

	A	B	C	D
1	Amount Borrowed		$100,000	
2	Starting Interest		7.50%	
3				
4		Monthly Payment		
5	Interest	30 Years	15 Years	Difference
6	=C2	=PMT(A6/12,30*12,–$C$1)	=PMT(A6/12,15*12,–$C$1)	=C6–B6
7	=A6+0.01	=PMT(A7/12,30*12,–$C$1)	=PMT(A7/12,15*12,–$C$1)	=C7–B7
8	=A7+0.01	=PMT(A8/12,30*12,–$C$1)	=PMT(A8/12,15*12,–$C$1)	=C8–B8
9	=A8+0.01	=PMT(A9/12,30*12,–$C$1)	=PMT(A9/12,15*12,–$C$1)	=C9–B9
10	=A9+0.01	=PMT(A10/12,30*12,–$C$1)	=PMT(A10/12,15*12,–$C$1)	=C10–B10
11	=A10+0.01	=PMT(A11/12,30*12,–$C$1)	=PMT(A11/12,15*12,–$C$1)	=C11–B11

FIGURE 3.4   Cell Formulas

The entry A6/12 (which is the first argument in the formula in cell B6) is interpreted to mean "divide the contents of the cell one column to the left by 12." Thus, when the PMT function in cell B6 is copied to cell B7, it (the copied formula) is adjusted to maintain this relationship and will contain the entry A7/12. The Copy command does not duplicate a relative address exactly, but adjusts it from row to row (or column to column) to maintain the relative relationship. The cell reference for the amount of the loan should not change, however, and is specified as an absolute address.

THE POWER OF EXCEL

You already know enough about Excel to develop the worksheet for the mortgage analysis. Excel is so powerful, however, and offers so many shortcuts, that we would be remiss not to show you alternative techniques. This section introduces the fill handle as a shortcut for copying cells, and pointing as a more accurate way to enter cell formulas. It also presents the Function Wizard, which helps you to enter the arguments in a function correctly. Don't overlook the boxed tip on the spell check, a feature we use all the time.

THE SPELL CHECK

Anyone familiar with a word processor takes the spell check for granted, but did you know the same capability exists within Excel? Pull down the Tools menu and click Spelling (or click the Spelling icon on the Standard toolbar), and let Excel do the rest.

The Fill Handle

The **fill handle** is a tiny black square that appears in the lower-right corner of the selected cells. It is the fastest way to copy a cell (or range of cells) to an *adjacent* cell (or range of cells). The process is quite easy and you get to practice in the exercise that follows shortly. In essence you:

➤ Select the cell or cells to be copied.
➤ Point to the fill handle for the selected cell(s), which changes the mouse pointer to a thin cross.
➤ Click and drag the fill handle over the destination range. A border appears to outline the destination range.
➤ Release the mouse to complete the copy operation.

Pointing

A cell address is entered into a formula by typing the reference explicitly (as we have done throughout the text) or by pointing. If you type the address, it is all too easy to make a mistake, such as typing A40 when you really mean A41. *Pointing* is more accurate as you use the mouse or cursor keys to reference the cell directly. The process is much easier than it sounds, and you get to practice in the hands-on exercise. In essence you:

➤ Select (click) the cell to contain the formula.
➤ Type an equal sign to begin entering the formula. The status bar indicates the *Enter mode,* which means that the formula bar is active as the formula is entered.
➤ Click the cell you want to reference in the formula (or use the cursor keys to move to the cell). A flashing box known as the *marquee* appears around the cell, the formula bar includes the cell reference, and the status bar indicates the *Point mode.*
➤ Type any arithmetic operator to place the cell reference in the formula and return to the Enter mode.
➤ Continue pointing to additional cells until you complete the formula.
➤ Press the enter key to complete the formula.

As with everything else, the more you practice, the easier it is. The hands-on exercise gives you ample opportunity to use what you have learned.

The Function Wizard

The *Function Wizard* helps you to select the appropriate function, then helps you to enter the correct arguments for that function into the worksheet. The functions in Excel are grouped into categories as shown in the open list box in the left of Figure 3.5a. Select the function category you want, then choose the function name from within that category. Click the Next command button to produce the dialog box in Figure 3.5b, in which you specify the arguments for the function.

The Function Wizard displays a text box for each argument, a description of each argument (as the text box is selected), and an indication of whether or not the argument is required. (Only the first three arguments are required in the PMT function.) Enter the value, cell reference, or formula for each argument by clicking in the text box and typing the entry, or by clicking the appropriate cell(s) in the worksheet.

Excel displays the calculated value for each argument immediately to the right of the argument. It also shows the computed value for the function as a whole at the top of the dialog box. All you need to do is click the Finish button to insert the function into the worksheet. The Function Wizard is illustrated in step 6 of the following exercise.

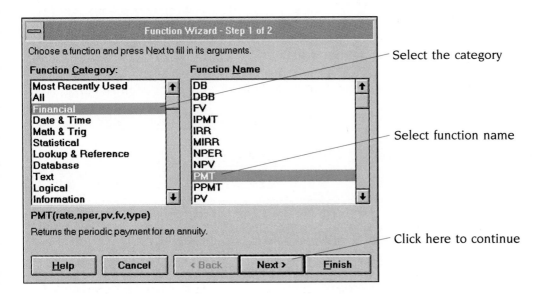

Select the category

Select function name

Click here to continue

(a) Step 1

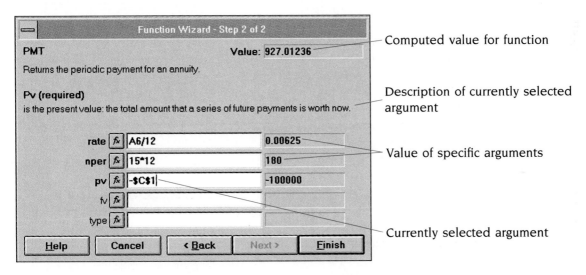

Computed value for function

Description of currently selected argument

Value of specific arguments

Currently selected argument

(b) Step 2

FIGURE 3.5   The Function Wizard

HANDS-ON EXERCISE 1:

Mortgage Analysis

Objective To develop the worksheet for the mortgage analysis; to use pointing to enter a formula and the fill handle to copy a formula. Use Figure 3.6 as a guide.

Step 1: Enter the descriptive labels

➤ Load Excel. Click in cell **A1.** Type **Amount Borrowed.** Click in cell **A2** (or press the **down arrow key**). Type **Starting Interest.**

➤ Click in cell **A4.** Type **Montly Payment.** (We deliberately misspelled "monthly" to illustrate the spell check in step 2.)

➤ Enter the remaining labels in cells A5 through D5 as shown in Figures 3.6a and 3.6b. Do not worry about formatting at this time as all formatting will be done at the end of the exercise.

➤ Save the workbook under the name **MORTGAGE.XLS.** Press **Esc** (or click the **Cancel command button**) if prompted for summary information.

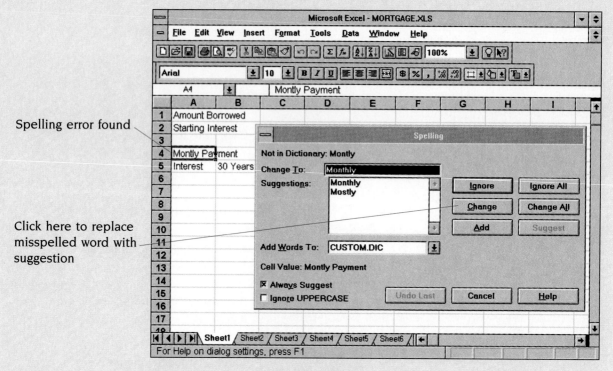

(a) The Spell Check (step 2)

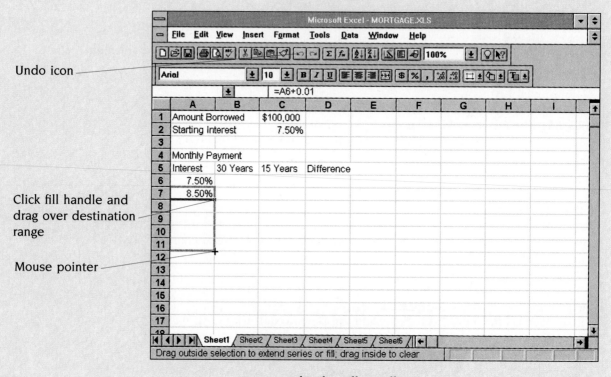

(b) The Fill Handle (step 4)

FIGURE 3.6   Hands-on Exercise 1

RESET THE TIPWIZARD

The TipWizard will not repeat a suggestion (from an earlier session) unless you reset it at the start of the new session. This is especially important in a laboratory situation where you are sharing a computer with many other students. Pull down the Tools menu, click Options, and click the General tab. Click the check box to Reset TipWizard, then click OK. If necessary, click the TipWizard icon on the Standard toolbar to open the TipWizard box, which will display suggestions as they occur throughout the session.

Step 2: The Spell Check
➤ Click in cell **A1** to begin the spell check at the beginning of the worksheet. Pull down the **Tools menu** and click **Spelling** (or click the Spelling icon on the Standard toolbar).
➤ Make corrections as necessary; for example, click the **Change command button** in the dialog box of Figure 3.6a to substitute the correct spelling.
➤ Continue checking the worksheet until you see the message indicating that the spell check is complete. Click **OK** when Excel indicates it has finished checking the entire worksheet.

Step 3: Enter the initial conditions
➤ Click in cell **C1.** Type **$100,000** (include the dollar sign and comma).
➤ Click in cell **C2.** Type **7.5%** (include the percent sign). Press **enter.**
➤ Save the workbook.

Step 4: Copy the column of interest rates (the fill handle)
➤ Click in cell **A6.** Type **=C2** to reference the starting interest rate in cell C2.
➤ Click in cell **A7.** Type the formula **=A6+.01** to increment the interest rate by one percent. Press **enter.**
➤ Click in cell **A7.** Point to the **fill handle** in the lower corner of cell A7. The mouse pointer changes to a thin cross.
➤ Drag the **fill handle** over cells **A8 through A11.** A border appears to indicate the destination range as in Figure 3.6b. Release the mouse to complete the copy operation. The formula and associated percentage format in cell A7 have been copied to cells A8 through A11.
➤ Click in Cell **C2.** Type **5%.** The entries in cells A6 through A11 change automatically. Click the **Undo icon** on the Standard toolbar to return to the original interest rate.
➤ Save the workbook.

THE EDIT CLEAR COMMAND

The Edit Clear command erases the contents of a cell and/or its formatting. Select the cell or cells to erase, pull down the Edit menu, click the Clear command, then click All, Formats, or Contents from the cascaded menu. Pressing the Del key is equivalent to executing the Edit Clear Contents command; that is, it clears the contents of a cell but not the formatting.

Step 5: Determine the 30-year payments

➤ Click in cell **B6.** Type the formula **=PMT(A6/12,30*12,−$C$1).** Press the **enter key.** Cell B6 should display $699.21.

➤ Click in cell **B6.** Point to the **fill handle** in the bottom-right corner of cell B6. The mouse pointer changes to a thin cross.

➤ Drag the **fill handle** over cells B7 through B11. A border appears to indicate the destination range. Release the mouse to complete the copy operation. The PMT function in cell B6 has been copied to cells B7 through B11; if you have done this step correctly, cell B11 will display $1,067.26.

➤ If you see a series of pound signs instead of numbers, it means that the cell (column) is too narrow to display the computed results in the selected format. Select the cell(s) containing the pound signs, pull down the **Format menu,** click **Column,** then click **AutoFit Selection** from the cascaded menu.

➤ Save the workbook.

MORE ABOUT THE FILL HANDLE

Use the fill handle as a shortcut for the Edit Clear command. To clear a cell, drag the fill handle to the top of the cell. To clear the contents *and* format, press and hold the Ctrl key as you drag the fill handle to the top of the cell. You can apply the same technique to a cell range by selecting the range, then dragging the fill handle to the top (or left) of the range.

Step 6: The Function Wizard

➤ Click in cell **C6.** Pull down the **Insert menu** and click **Function** (or click the **Function Wizard button** on the Standard toolbar) to display step 1 of the Function Wizard.

➤ Click **Financial** in the Function Category list box. Click **PMT** in the Function Name list box. Click the **Next command button** to display the dialog box in Figure 3.6c.

➤ Click the text box for the rate. Type **A6/12.**

➤ Click the text box for the number of periods (nper). Type **15*12** (indicating 15 years and 12 months per year).

➤ Click the text box for the present value (pv). Type **−$C$1.** (Be sure to include the minus sign.)

➤ Check that the computed values on your monitor match those in Figure 3.6c. Make corrections as necessary.

➤ Click the **Finish command button** to insert the function into the worksheet. Cell C6 should display $927.01.

Step 7: Copy the 15-year payments

➤ Check that cell **C6** is still selected. Point to the **fill handle** in the lower-right corner of cell C6. The mouse pointer changes to a thin cross.

➤ Drag the **fill handle** to copy the PMT function to cells C7 through C11; if you have done the step correctly, cell C11 will display $1,232.52. Adjust the width of the cell if you see a series of pound signs.

➤ Save the workbook.

Step 8: Compute the monthly difference (pointing)

➤ Click in cell **D6.** Type = to begin the formula.

➤ Press the **left arrow key** (or click in cell **C6**), which produces the marquee (flashing box) around the entry in cell C6. The status bar indicates the point mode as shown in Figure 3.6d.

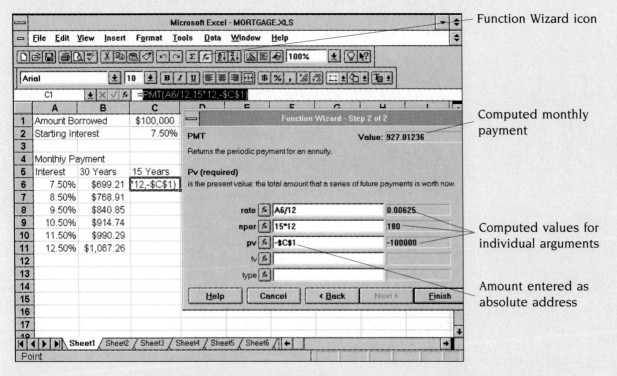

(c) The Function Wizard (step 6)

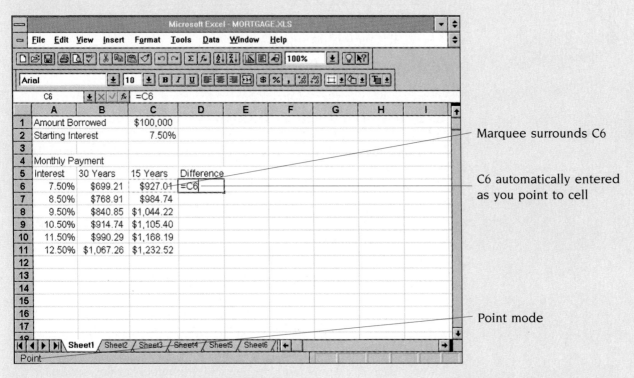

(d) Pointing (step 8)

FIGURE 3.6 Hands-on Exercise 1 (continued)

➤ Press the **minus sign,** then press the **left arrow key** twice (or click in cell B6).

➤ Press **enter** to complete the formula. Cell D6 should display $227.80.

➤ Use the fill handle to copy the contents of cell D6 to cells D7 through D11. If you have done the step correctly, cell D11 will display $165.26 as shown in Figure 3.6e.

➤ Save the workbook.

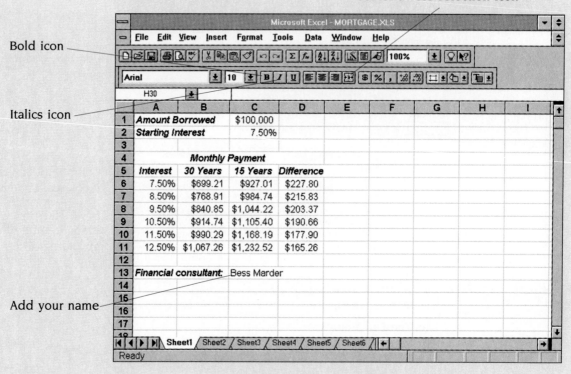

(e) The Completed Spreadsheet (step 9)

FIGURE 3.6   Hands-on Exercise I (continued)

THE OPTIMAL (BEST FIT) COLUMN WIDTH

The appearance of pound signs within a cell indicates that the cell width (column width) is insufficient to display the computed results in the selected format. Double click the right border of the column heading to change the column width to accommodate the widest entry in that column. For example, to increase the width of column B, double click the border between the column headings for columns B and C.

Step 9: The finishing touches

➤ Add formatting as necessary, using Figure 3.6e as a guide.

➤ Click cell **A4.** Drag the mouse over cells A4 through D4. Click the **Center Across Columns button** on the Formatting toolbar to center the entry over columns A through D.

➤ Add boldface and/or italics to the text and/or numbers as you see fit.

➤ Type **Financial Consultant** in cell A13. Enter **your name** in cell C13.

➤ Save the workbook.

Step 10: Print the worksheet

➤ Pull down the **File menu** and click **Print Preview** (or click the **Print Preview icon** on the Standard toolbar).

➤ Click the **Setup command button** to display the Page Setup dialog box.
  — Click the **Margins tab.** Check the box to center the worksheet horizontally.
  — Click the **Sheet tab.** Check the boxes to include Row and Column headings and Gridlines.
  — Click **OK** to exit the Page Setup dialog box.

➤ Click the **Print command button** to display the Print dialog box, then click **OK** to print the worksheet.

➤ Press **Ctrl+`** to display the cell formulas. (The left quotation mark is on the same key as the ~.) Widen the cells as necessary to see the complete cell formulas.

➤ Click the **Print icon** on the Standard toolbar to print the cell formulas.

➤ Exit Excel.

THE GRADE BOOK REVISITED

Figure 3.7 contains an expanded version of the professor's grade book that includes more students, an additional test, a potential homework bonus, and the automatic determination of a student's letter grade. The worksheet was built by using several additional capabilities, each of which is explained shortly. Consider:

Date entered with TODAY function   IF function   Table Lookup function

	A	B	C	D	E	F	G	H	I	J
1	6/13/94						Professor's Grade Book			
2										
3	Name	Soc Sec Num	Test 1	Test 2	Test 3	Test 4	Test Avg	Homework	Final Avg	Grade
4	Adams, John	111-22-3333	80	71	70	84	77.8	Poor	77.8	C
5	Barber, Maryann	444-55-6666	96	98	97	90	94.2	OK	97.2	A
6	Boone, Dan	777-88-9999	78	81	70	78	77.0	OK	80.0	B
7	Borow, Jeff	123-45-6789	65	65	65	60	63.0	OK	66.0	D
8	Brown, James	999-99-9999	92	95	79	80	85.2	OK	88.2	B
9	Carson, Kit	888-88-8888	90	90	90	70	82.0	OK	85.0	B
10	Coulter, Sara	100-00-0000	60	50	40	79	61.6	OK	64.6	D
11	Fegin, Richard	222-22-2222	75	70	65	95	80.0	OK	83.0	B
12	Ford, Judd	200-00-0000	90	90	80	90	88.0	Poor	88.0	B
13	Glassman, Kris	444-44-4444	82	78	62	77	75.2	OK	78.2	C
14	Goodman, Neil	555-55-5555	92	88	65	78	80.2	OK	83.2	B
15	Milgrom, Marion	666-66-6666	94	92	86	84	88.0	OK	91.0	A
16	Moldof, Adam	300-00-0000	92	78	65	84	80.6	OK	83.6	B
17	Smith, Adam	777-77-7777	60	50	65	80	67.0	Poor	67.0	D
18										
19	Average		82	78	71	81	HW Bonus	3	Grading Criteria	
20	High		96	98	97	95			(Minimum Req'd)	
21	Low		60	50	40	60				F
22	Range		36	48	57	35			60	D
23									70	C
24	Exam Weights		20%	20%	20%	40%			80	B
25									90	A

Statistical functions

FIGURE 3.7 Extended Grade Book

Statistical functions: The AVERAGE, MAX, and MIN functions are used to compute statistics for the class as a whole. The range of grades is computed by subtracting the minimum value from the maximum value.

IF function: The IF function is used to conditionally add a homework bonus to the student's test average and potentially raise the final average prior to determining the grade. The bonus is awarded to those students whose homework is "OK". Students whose homework grade is poor do not receive a bonus.

Table lookup function: The expanded grade book converts a student's final average to a letter grade, in accordance with the table shown in the lower-right portion of the worksheet. A student needs an average of 60 or higher to earn a D, 70 or higher for a C, and so on.

Date function: The current date appears in the upper-left corner of the worksheet. Date arithmetic (that is, the elapsed time between two dates) is also possible, although it is not illustrated explicitly in the figure.

Large worksheets: The expanded grade book is larger than the applications considered so far, and requires additional commands for viewing on the monitor and for printing.

Statistical Functions

The **MAX, MIN,** and **AVERAGE** functions return the highest, lowest, and average values, respectively, from an argument list. The list may include individual cell references, ranges, numeric values, functions, or mathematical expressions (formulas). The functions are illustrated in the worksheet of Figure 3.8.

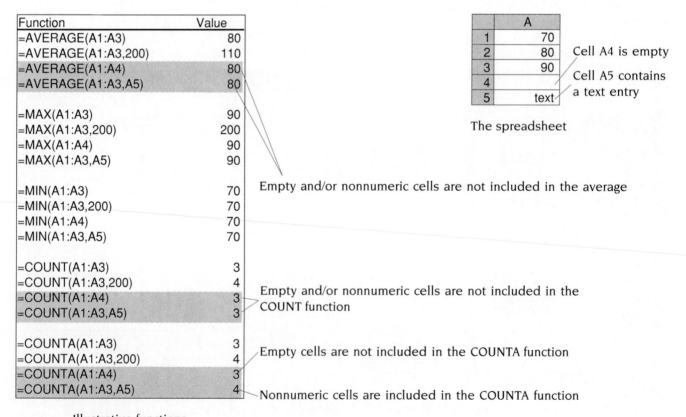

Illustrative functions

FIGURE 3.8 Statistical Functions with a Text Entry

The first example, =AVERAGE(A1:A3), computes the average for cells A1 through A3 by adding the values in the indicated range (70, 80, and 90), then dividing the result by three, to obtain an average of 80. Additional arguments in the form of values and/or cell addresses can be specified within the parentheses; for example, the function =AVERAGE(A1:A3,200) computes the average of cells A1, A2, and A3, and the number 200.

Empty and nonnumeric cells are *not* included in the computation. Thus, since cell A4 is empty, the function =AVERAGE(A1:A4) also returns an average of 80 (240/3), which is the same result as the function =AVERAGE(A1:A3). In similar fashion, the function =AVERAGE(A1:A3,A5) includes only three values in its computation (cells A1, A2, and A3), because the nonnumeric entry in cell A5 is excluded. The results of the MIN and MAX functions are obtained in a comparable way as indicated in Figure 3.8.

The COUNT and COUNTA functions each tally the number of entries in the argument list with a subtle difference. The **COUNT function** returns the number of nonempty cells with numeric entries, including formulas that evaluate to numeric results. The **COUNTA function** returns the number of nonempty cells, including both nonnumeric and numeric values. In Figure 3.8 the functions =COUNT(A1:A3) and =COUNTA(A1:A3) both return a value of 3. The functions =COUNT(A1:A4) and =COUNTA(A1:A4) also return a value of 3 because cell A4 is empty and thus is excluded from both functions. The function =COUNTA(A1:A3,A5) returns a value of 4 because it includes the nonnumeric entry in cell A5.

FIND AND REPLACE

Anyone familiar with a word processor knows the advantages of the Find and Replace commands. The identical capability is available in Excel. Pull down the Edit menu and click Replace, then supply the necessary information in the appropriate text boxes. You may not use the command often, but it is invaluable should the need arise.

Arithmetic Expressions versus Functions

Many worksheet calculations, such as an average or a sum, can be performed in two ways. You can enter a formula such as =(B1+B2+B3)/3, or you can use the equivalent function =AVERAGE(B1:B3). *The use of functions is generally preferable* as shown in Figure 3.9.

The two worksheets in Figure 3.9a may appear equivalent, but the SUM function in the worksheet on the left is superior to the arithmetic expression in the worksheet on the right. The entries in cell A5 of both worksheets return a value of 100.

Now consider what happens if a new row is inserted between existing rows 2 and 3, with the entry in the new cell equal to 25. The SUM function adjusts automatically to include the new value (returning a sum of 125 in the worksheet on the left) because the SUM function was defined originally for the cell range *A1 through A4*. The new row is inserted within these cells, moving the entry in cell A4 to cell A5, and changing the range to include cell A5.

No such accommodation is made in the worksheet on the right because the arithmetic expression was defined to include four *specific* cells, rather than a range of cells. The addition of the new row modifies the cell references (since the values in cells A3 and A4 have been moved to cells A4 and A5), but does not include the new row in the adjusted expression.

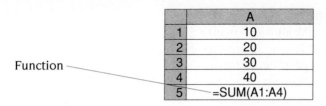

Function —————

	A
1	10
2	20
3	30
4	40
5	=SUM(A1:A4)

	A
1	10
2	20
3	30
4	40
5	=A1+A2+A3+A4

————— Formula

(a) Spreadsheets as Initially Entered

Range is adjusted
automatically, returning
a sum of 125

	A
1	10
2	20
3	25
4	30
5	40
6	=SUM(A1:A5)

	A
1	10
2	20
3	25
4	30
5	40
6	=A1+A2+A4+A5

Addresses for
old cells A3 and
A4 are changed;
the new entry in
cell A3 is not
included in the
sum

(b) Spreadsheets after the Addition of a New Row

Range is adjusted
automatically, returning
a sum of 80

	A
1	10
2	30
3	40
4	=SUM(A1:A3)

	A
1	10
2	30
3	40
4	=A1+#REF!+A2+A3

#REF! displayed
since entry in A2 has
been deleted;
addresses for cells A3
and A4 are changed
to A2 and A3

(c) Spreadsheets after the Deletion of a Row

FIGURE 3.9   Arithmetic Expressions versus Functions

Similar reasoning holds for deleting a row. Figure 3.9c deletes row 2 from the *original* worksheets, which moves the entry in cell A4 to cell A3. The SUM function in the worksheet on the left adjusts automatically to =SUM(A1:A3) and returns the value 80. The formula in the worksheet on the right, however, returns an error (to indicate an illegal cell reference) because it is still attempting to add the entries in four cells, one of which no longer exists. In summary, a function expands and contracts to adjust for insertions or deletions, and should be used wherever possible.

#REF!—ILLEGAL CELL REFERENCE

The #REF! error value is displayed if Excel is unable to evaluate a formula because of an illegal cell reference. The most common cause of the error is deleting the row or column that contained the original cell reference.

IF function

The *IF function* enables decision making to be implemented within a worksheet—for example, a conditional bonus for students whose homework is satisfactory. Students with inferior homework do not get this break.

The IF function has three arguments: a condition that is evaluated as true or false, a value if the condition is true, and a value if the condition is false. Consider:

=IF(condition,value-if-true,value-if-false)

        └── Displayed value for a false condition
      └── Displayed value for a true condition
└── Condition is either true or false

The IF function returns either the second or third argument, depending on the result of the *logical test* of the condition. If the condition is true, the function returns the second argument, whereas if the condition is false, the function returns the third argument.

The condition uses one of the six *relational operators* in Figure 3.10a. The IF function is illustrated in the worksheet in Figure 3.10b, which produced the examples in Figure 3.10c. In every instance the condition is evaluated, then the second or third argument is displayed, depending on whether the condition is true or false. The arguments may be numeric (1000 or 2000), a cell reference to display the contents of the specific cell (B1 or B2), a formula (B1+10 or B1-10), a function (MAX(B1:B2) or MIN(B1:B2)), or a text entry enclosed in quotation marks ("Go" or "Hold").

Operator	Description
=	Equal to
<>	Not equal to
<	Less than
>	Greater than
<=	Less than or equal to
>=	Greater than or equal to

(a) Relational Operators

	A	B	C
1	10	15	April
2	10	30	May

(b) The Spreadsheet

IF function	Evaluation
=IF(A1=A2,1000,2000)	1000
=IF(A1<>A2,1000,2000)	2000
=IF(A1<>A2,B1,B2)	30
=IF(A1<B1,MAX(B1:B2),MIN(B1:B2))	30
=IF(A1<A2,B1+10,B1−10)	5
=IF(A1=A2,C1,C2)	April
=IF(SUM(A1:A2)>20,"Go","Hold")	Hold

(c) Examples

FIGURE 3.10 The IF Function

The IF function is used in the grade book of Figure 3.7 to award a bonus for homework. Students whose homework is "OK" receive the bonus, whereas other students do not. The IF function to implement this logic for the first student is entered in cell H4 as follows:

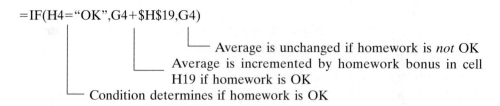

=IF(H4="OK",G4+$H$19,G4)

— Average is unchanged if homework is *not* OK
— Average is incremented by homework bonus in cell H19 if homework is OK
— Condition determines if homework is OK

The IF function compares the value in cell H4 (the homework grade) to the literal "OK." If the condition is true (the homework is OK), the bonus in cell H19 is added to the student's test average in cell G4. If, however, the condition is false (the homework is not OK), the average is unchanged.

The bonus is specified as a cell address rather than a specific value so that the number of bonus points can be easily changed; that is, the professor can make a single change to the worksheet by increasing (decreasing) the bonus in cell H19 and see immediately the effect on every student without having to edit or retype any other formula. An absolute (rather than a relative) reference is used to reference the homework bonus, so that when the IF function is copied to the other rows in the column, the address will remain constant. A relative reference, however, was used for the student's homework and semester averages in cells H4 and G4, because these addresses change from one student to the next.

Table Lookup Function

Consider for a moment how the professor assigns letter grades to students at the end of the semester. He or she computes a test average for each student and conditionally awards the bonus for homework. The professor then determines a letter grade according to a predetermined scale; for example, 90 or above is an A, 80 to 89 is a B, and so on.

The *table lookup function* duplicates this process within a worksheet, by assigning an entry to a cell based on a numeric value contained in another cell. In other words, just as the professor knows where on the grading scale a student's numerical average will fall, the table lookup function determines where within a specified table a numeric value (a student's average) is found, and retrieves the corresponding entry (the letter grade).

The table lookup function requires three arguments: the numeric value to look up, the range of cells containing the table, and the column number within the table that contains the result. These concepts are illustrated in Figure 3.11, which was taken from the expanded grade book in Figure 3.7. The table in Figure 3.11 extends over two columns (I and J) and five rows (21 through 25); that is, the table is located in the range I21:J25. The *break points,* or comparison values (the lowest numeric value for each grade), are contained in column I (the first column in the table) and are in ascending order. The corresponding letter grades are found in column J.

The table lookup function in cell J4 determines the letter grade (for John Adams) based on the computed average in cell I4. Consider:

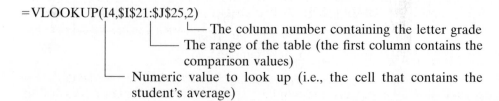

=VLOOKUP(I4,$I$21:$J$25,2)

— The column number containing the letter grade
— The range of the table (the first column contains the comparison values)
— Numeric value to look up (i.e., the cell that contains the student's average)

	A		G	H	I	J	
1							
2							
3	**Name**	...	**Test Avg**	**Homework**	**Final Avg**	**Grade**	Cell J4 contains =VLOOKUP(14,$I$21:$J$25,2)
4	Adams, John	...	77.8	Poor	77.8	C	
.	.	.	.	.	.	.	
.	.	.	.	.	.	.	
.	.	.	.	.	.	.	
18							
19	*Average*		*HW Bonus*	3	*Grading Criteria*		
20	*High*				*(Minimum Req'd)*		Grades are in column J
21	*Low*					F	
22	*Range*				60	D	Cells I22 through I25 contain the break points in ascending order
23					70	C	
24	*Exam Weights*				80	B	
25					90	A	

FIGURE 3.11   Table Lookup Function

The first argument is the value to look up, which in this example is Adams's computed average, found in cell I4. A relative reference is used so that the address will adjust when the formula is copied to the other rows in the worksheet.

The second argument is the range of the table, found in cells I21 through J25, as explained earlier. Absolute references are specified so that the addresses will not change when the function is copied to determine the letter grades for the other students. The first column in the table (column I in this example) contains the break points, which must be in ascending order.

The third argument indicates the column where the letter grades are found. To determine the letter grade for Adams (whose computed average is 77.8), the table lookup function searches cells I21 through I25 for the first value greater than 77.8 (the computed average in cell I4). The lookup function finds the number 80 in cell I24. It then backs up one row and retrieves the corresponding letter grade from the second column of the table in that row (cell J23). Adams, with an average of 77.8, is assigned a grade of C.

Date Functions and Date Arithmetic

Excel provides several functions that enable you to work with dates, two of which are illustrated in Figure 3.12. The **TODAY() function** returns the current date, which is the date a worksheet is created or retrieved. The **DATE(yy,mm,dd)** function displays a specific date, such as May 13, 1994. The TODAY() function will display May 13, 1994 only on that specific date. The DATE(94,5,13) function will display May 13, 1994 regardless of the current date.

In actuality, both functions store the date as a **serial date** corresponding to the number of days in this century. January 1, 1900 is stored as the number 1, January 2, 1900 as the number 2, etc. May 13, 1994 corresponds to the number 34467 as can be seen in Figure 3.12.

The fact that dates are stored as serial numbers enables you to compute the number of days between two dates by subtraction. Age, for example, can be computed by subtracting the date of birth from the current date, and dividing the result by 365. Realize, too, that while the subtraction provides the exact number of elapsed days, the subsequent division is only approximate, in that leap years (with 366 days) are not accounted for. Note, too, the IF function in Figure 3.12a, which examines the computed age, then displays an appropriate message indicating whether the individual is legal or still under the age of 21.

Another example of **date arithmetic** is shown in Figure 3.12b, in which a constant is added to the date of purchase in order to obtain the due date. In this example the formula in cell D4 adds the date in cell C4 to the number of days in cell

Displays current date (date spreadsheet is retrieved)

Always displays same date

Serial number stored by Excel

	A	B	C	D
		Cell Formulas	Date Format	Numeric Format
1				
2	Today's Date	=TODAY()	13-May-94	34467
3	Birthdate	=DATE(73,10,31)	31-Oct-73	26968
4				
5	Elapsed Time (days)	=B2–B3		7499
6	Age (years)	=B5/365		20.5
7				
8		=IF(D6>=21,"LEGAL","Minor")		Minor

(a) Date Functions and Date Arithmetic
(current date: May 13, 1994)

Formula entered: =C4+$C$10

	A	B	C	D
1			Accounts Receivable	
2				
3	Customer	Account Number	Date of Purchase	Date Due
4	Ruce, Doug	R23456	15-Dec-93	14-Jan-94
5	Dembrow, Harriet	D34987	22-Jan-94	21-Feb-94
6	Center, Sol	C12987	31-Jan-94	2-Mar-94
7	Morris, Gail	M87698	3-Feb-94	5-Mar-94
8	Black, Chuck	B09875	26-Feb-94	28-Mar-94
9				
10		Number of days until due:	30	

(b) Date Arithmetic

FIGURE 3.12 Date Functions and Date Arithmetic

C10. The formula is not displayed in the figure but is entered into the worksheet as =C4+$C$10. The combination of a relative and an absolute reference enables the entry in cell D4 to be copied to the remaining cells in that column. A relative reference is used for the purchase date because the cell address changes from row to row. An absolute reference is used for the number of days because that cell address remains constant.

All dates can be formatted to display the month, day, and year as shown in Figure 3.12. You can also enter a date directly (without having to use the DATE function) by typing 5/13/94 or May 13, 1994 in the appropriate cell.

DAYLIGHT SAVINGS TIME

The TODAY function uses the computer's internal clock and calendar to obtain the current time and date. But what if your computer has the wrong information? Open the Main group in Program Manager, double click the Control Panel icon, then double click the Date/Time icon to open a dialog box. Enter the correct time and date, click OK to accept the new settings, then close the Control Panel application.

Scrolling

A large worksheet, such as the extended grade book, can seldom be seen on the monitor in its entirety; that is, only a portion of the worksheet is in view at any given time. The specific rows and columns that are displayed are determined by an operation called *scrolling,* which shows different parts of a worksheet at different times. Scrolling enables you to see any portion of the worksheet at the expense of not seeing another portion. The worksheet in Figure 3.13a, for example, displays column J containing the students' grades, but not columns A and B, which contain the students' names. In similar fashion you can see rows 21 through 25 that display the grading criteria, but you cannot see the column headings.

Can't see columns A and B or rows 1–9

	C	D	E	F	G	H	I	J
10	60	50	40	79	61.6	OK	64.6	D
11	75	70	65	95	80.0	OK	83.0	B
12	90	90	80	90	88.0	Poor	88.0	B
13	82	78	62	77	75.2	OK	78.2	C
14	92	88	65	78	80.2	OK	83.2	B
15	94	92	86	84	88.0	OK	91.0	A
16	92	78	65	84	80.6	OK	83.6	B
17	60	50	65	80	67.0	Poor	67.0	D
18								
19	82	78	71	81	*HW Bonus*	3	*Grading Criteria*	
20	96	98	97	95			*(Minimum Req'd)*	
21	60	50	40	60				F
22	36	48	57	35			60	D
23							70	C
24	20%	20%	20%	40%			80	B
25							90	A
26								

(a) Scrolling

FIGURE 3.13   Large Spreadsheets

Scrolling comes about automatically as the active cell changes and may take place in both a horizontal and a vertical direction. Clicking the right arrow on the horizontal scroll bar (or pressing the right arrow key when the active cell is already in the rightmost column of the screen) causes the entire screen to move one column to the right. In similar fashion, clicking the down arrow in the vertical scroll bar (or pressing the down arrow key when the active cell is in the bottom row of the screen) causes the entire screen to move down one row.

SCROLLING: THE MOUSE VERSUS THE KEYBOARD

You can use either the mouse or the keyboard to scroll within the worksheet, but there is one critical difference. Scrolling with the keyboard also changes the active cell. Scrolling with the mouse does not.

Freezing Panes

Scrolling brings distant portions of a large worksheet into view, but moves the text headings for existing rows and/or columns off the screen. You can, however, retain the row and/or column headings by *freezing panes* as shown in Figure 3.13b. The grades and grading criteria are visible as in the previous figure, but so too are the students' names and column headings.

Look closely at this figure and you will see that columns B through D (social security number, test 1, and test 2) are missing as are rows 4, 5, and 6 (the first three students). You will also notice a horizontal line under row 3, and a vertical line after column A, to indicate that these rows and columns have been frozen. Scrolling still takes place as you move beyond the rightmost column or below the bottom row, but you will always see column A and rows 1, 2, and 3 displayed on the monitor.

The Freeze (Unfreeze) Panes command is found in the pull-down Window menu. It offers the advantage of providing permanent labels for the rows and columns displayed in the monitor regardless of the scrolling in effect. It is especially helpful when viewing or entering data in a large worksheet.

Column A remains on screen; columns B, C, and D are missing

Rows 4, 5, and 6 are missing

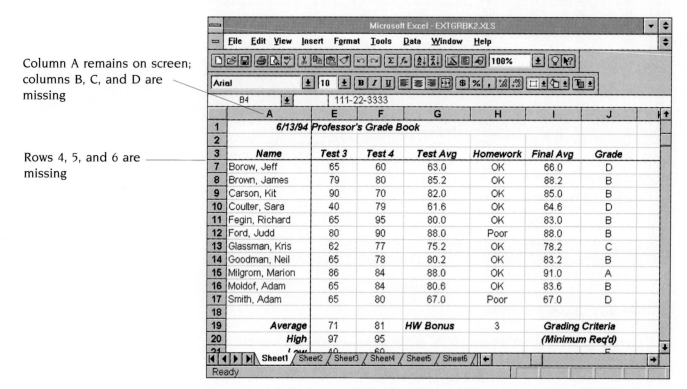

(b) Freezing Panes

FIGURE 3.13   Large Spreadsheets (continued)

THE AUTOFILL CAPABILITY

The last shortcut we will introduce is the *autofill capability,* which creates a series based on the initial value(s) you supply. It is a wonderful shortcut and the quickest way to enter certain types of data. If, for example, you needed the months of the year in 12 successive cells, you would enter January (or Jan) in the first cell, then drag the fill handle over the next 11 cells in the direction you want to fill. Excel will enter the remaining months of the year in those cells.

Excel guesses at the type of series you want and fills the cells accordingly. You can type Monday (rather than January) and Excel will return the days of the week. You can enter a text and numeric combination, such as Quarter 1 or 1st Quarter, and Excel will extend the series appropriately. You can also create a numeric series by entering the first two numbers in that series; for example, to enter the years 1990 through 1999, type 1990 and 1991 in the first two cells, select both of these cells, and drag the fill handle in the appropriate direction over the destination range.

HANDS-ON EXERCISE 2:

Extended Grade Book

Objective To develop the extended grade book; to use statistical (AVERAGE, MAX, and MIN), logical (IF and VLOOKUP), and date functions (TODAY); to demonstrate scrolling and the Freeze Panes command. Use Figure 3.14 as a guide.

Step 1: Open the extended grade book
➤ Pull down the **File menu** and click **Open** (or click the **Open icon** on the Standard toolbar). Double click the **EXTGRBK.XLS** workbook to open a partially completed version of the extended grade book discussed in the chapter.
➤ Pull down the **File menu.** Click **Save As.** Save the workbook as **EXTGRBK2** so that you can return to the original workbook if necessary.

MISSING SCROLL BARS

The horizontal and vertical scroll bars are essential, especially with larger worksheets that cannot be seen in their entirety. If either scroll bar is missing, it is because a previous user elected to hide it. Pull down the Tools menu, click Options, and click the View tab. Click the check boxes to display the Horizontal and Vertical scroll bars, then click the OK command button to exit the dialog box and return to the worksheet.

Step 2: Enter today's date
➤ Click in cell **A1,** the cell that is to contain today's date.
➤ Click the **Function Wizard icon** on the Standard toolbar. Click **Date & Time** in the Function Category list box in step 1 of the Function Wizard.
➤ Click the **down arrow** on the Function Name list box to see the additional Date and Time functions. Click **TODAY** as shown in Figure 3.14a. Click the **Next command button** to move to step 2 of the Function Wizard.
➤ The dialog box on your screen shows there are no arguments for the TODAY function. (The indication of a volatile value means that the date will change every time you open the workbook.) Click the **Finish command button** to insert the date into your worksheet.
➤ Save the workbook.

Step 3: The autofill feature
➤ Click in cell **C3,** the cell containing the label Test 1.
➤ Point to the **fill handle** in the lower-right corner. The mouse pointer changes to a thin cross.
➤ Drag the fill handle over cells **D3, E3,** and **F3.** A border appears to indicate the destination range.

➤ Release the mouse. Cells D3, E3, and F3 now contain the labels Test 2, Test 3, and Test 4, respectively.

CREATE A CUSTOM SERIES

A custom series is very helpful if you repeatedly enter the same lists of data. Pull down the Tools menu, click Options, then click the Custom Lists tab. Click New List in the Custom Lists box, click the Add command button, then enter the items in the series (e.g., Tom, Dick, and Harry) using the enter key to separate one item from the next. The next time you type Tom in a cell and drag the fill handle, you will see the series Tom, Dick, and Harry repeated through the entire range.

Function appears in formula bar

Select category

Select TODAY function

Click here to move to next step

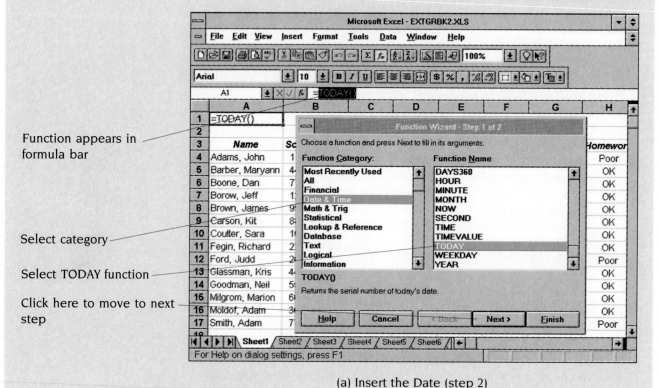

(a) Insert the Date (step 2)

FIGURE 3.14 Hands-on Exercise 2

NOW VERSUS TODAY

The NOW and TODAY functions both return a serial value for the current date. The difference is that the NOW function includes a decimal portion, which reflects the time of day, but the TODAY function does not. The distinction is important only with date arithmetic when the day is half over (after 12PM) because the serial value in the NOW function will be rounded up to the next day. The results of a calculation using the NOW function will differ by one day from the "identical" calculation using the TODAY function.

Step 4: Scrolling and freezing panes

➤ Press **Ctrl+Home** to move to cell A1. Click the **right arrow** on the horizontal scroll bar until column A scrolls off the screen. Cell A1 is still the active cell because scrolling with the mouse does not change the active cell.

➤ Press **Ctrl+Home.** Press the **right arrow key** until column A scrolls off the screen. The active cell changes as you scroll with the keyboard.

➤ Press **Ctrl+Home** to return to cell A1. Click the **down arrow** on the vertical scroll bar (or press the **down arrow key** until row 1 scrolls off the screen). Note whether the active cell changes or not.

➤ Press **Ctrl+Home** again, then click in cell **B4.** Pull down the **Window menu.** Click **Freeze Panes** as shown in Figure 3.14b. You will see a line to the right of column A and below row 3; that is, column A and rows 1 through 3 will always be visible regardless of scrolling.

➤ Click the **right arrow** on the horizontal scroll bar (or press the **right arrow key**) repeatedly until column J is visible. Note that column A is visible (frozen), but that one or more columns are not shown.

➤ Click the **down arrow** on the vertical scroll bar (or press the **down arrow key**) repeatedly until row 25 is visible. Note that rows 1 through 3 are visible (frozen), but that one or more rows are not shown.

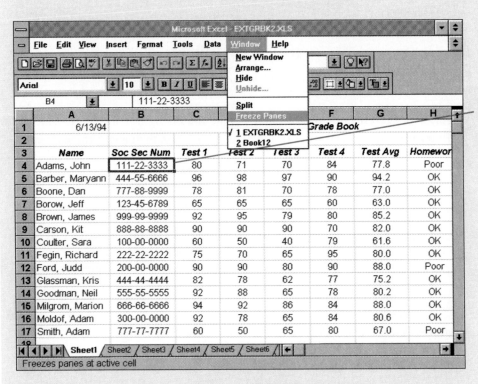

Select B4 to freeze rows above (1–3) and column to the left (A)

(b) Freeze Panes Command (step 4)

FIGURE 3.14   Hands-on Exercise 2 (continued)

Step 5: The IF function

➤ Pull down the **Window Menu.** Click **Unfreeze Panes.**

➤ Scroll to the top of the worksheet, then scroll until Column I is visible on the screen. Click in cell **I4.**

➤ Click the **Function Wizard icon** on the Standard toolbar. Click **Logical** in the Function Category list box in step 1 of the Function Wizard. Click **IF** in the Function Name list box, then click the **Next command button** to move to

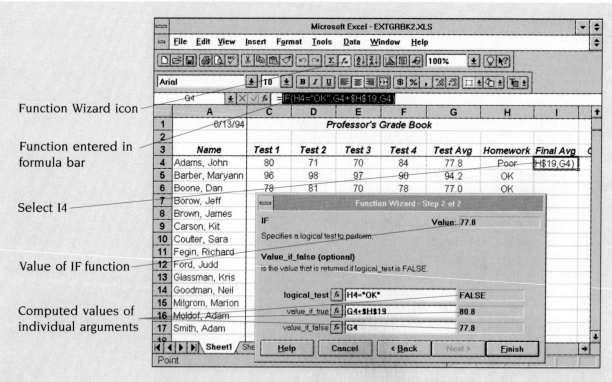

Function Wizard icon

Function entered in formula bar

Select I4

Value of IF function

Computed values of individual arguments

(c) The IF Function (step 5)

FIGURE 3.14   Hands-on Exercise 2 (continued)

step 2 of the Function Wizard and display the dialog box in Figure 3.14c.

➤ Enter the arguments for the IF function as shown in the figure. You can enter the arguments directly or you can use pointing as follows:

— Click the **logical_test** text box. Click cell **H4** in the worksheet. (You may need to move the dialog box to access cell H4. Click and drag the title bar to move the dialog box out of the way.) Type **="OK"** to complete the logical test.

— Click the **value_if_true** text box. Click cell **G4** in the worksheet, type a **plus sign,** click cell **H19** in the worksheet (scrolling if necessary), and finally press the **F4 key** (see tip below) to convert the reference to cell H19 to an absolute reference.

— Click the **value_if_false** text box. Click cell **G4** in the worksheet, scrolling if necessary.

➤ Check that the computed values on your worksheet match those in the figure and make corrections as necessary. Click the **Finish command button** to insert the function into your worksheet.

THE F4 KEY

The F4 key cycles through relative, absolute, and mixed addresses. Click on any reference within the formula bar; for example, click on A1 in the formula =A1+A2. Press the F4 key once and it changes to an absolute reference. Press the F4 key a second time and it becomes a mixed reference, A$1; press it again and it is a different mixed reference, $A1. Press the F4 key a fourth time and it returns to the original relative address, A1.

KEYBOARD SHORTCUTS: MOVING WITHIN A WORKSHEET

Press PgUp or PgDn to scroll an entire screen in the indicated direction. Press Ctrl+Home or Ctrl+End to move to the beginning or end of a worksheet—that is, to cell A1 and to the cell in the lower-right corner, respectively. If these keys do not work, it is because the transition navigation keys (i.e., Lotus conventions) are in effect. Pull down the Tools menu, click Options, and click the Transition tab. Clear the check in the Transition Navigation Keys check box, then click OK.

Step 6: The VLOOKUP function

➤ Click in cell **J4.**

➤ Click the **Function Wizard icon** on the Standard toolbar.

➤ Click **Lookup & Reference** in the Function Category list box in step 1 of the Function Wizard.

➤ Scroll in the Function Name list box until you can select **VLOOKUP.**

➤ Click the **Next command button** to move to step 2 of the Function Wizard and display the dialog box in Figure 3.14d.

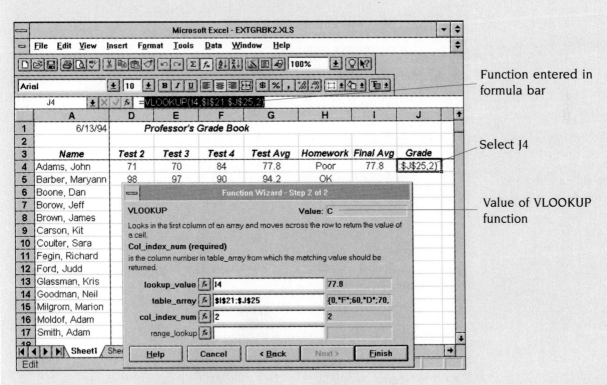

(d) The VLOOKUP Function (step 6)

FIGURE 3.14   Hands-on Exercise 2 (continued)

➤ Enter the arguments for the VLOOKUP function as shown in the figure. You can enter the arguments directly or you can use pointing as follows:
— Click the **lookup_value** text box. Click cell **I4** in the worksheet.

— Click the **table_array** text box. Click cell **I21** and **drag to cell J25** (scrolling if necessary). Press the **F4 key** (see tip on page 108) to convert to an absolute reference.

— Click the **col_index_num** text box. Type **2.**

➤ Check that the computed values on your worksheet match those in the figure and make corrections as necessary. Click the **Finish command button** to insert the function into your worksheet.

➤ Save the workbook.

Step 7: Copy the IF and VLOOKUP functions (the fill handle)

➤ Scroll to the top of the worksheet. Select cells **I4** and **J4** as in Figure 3.14e.

➤ Point to the **fill handle** in the lower-right corner of the selected range. The mouse pointer changes to a thin cross.

➤ Drag the fill handle over cells **I5 through J17.** A border appears to indicate the destination range as shown in Figure 3.14e. Release the mouse to complete the copy operation. If you have done everything correctly, Adam Smith should have a grade of D based on a final average of 67.0.

➤ Save the workbook.

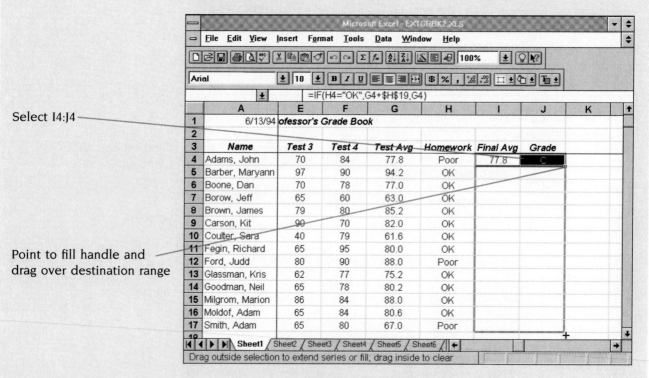

(e) The Fill Handle (step 7)

FIGURE 3.14 Hands-on Exercise 2 (continued)

Step 8: Statistical functions

➤ Click in cell **C19.** Type **=AVERAGE(C4:C17).** Press **enter.** Cell C19 should display 82.

➤ Click in cell **C20.** Type **=MAX(C4:C17).** Press **enter.** Cell C20 should display 96.

➤ Click in cell **C21.** Type **=MIN(C4:C17).** Press **enter.** Cell C21 should display 60.

➤ Click in cell **C22.** Type **=C20-C21.** Press **enter.** Cell C22 should display 36.

#NAME? AND OTHER ERRORS

Excel displays an error value when it is unable to calculate the formula in a cell. Misspelling a function name (e.g., using AVG instead of AVER-AGE) results in #NAME?, which is perplexing at first, but easily corrected once you know the meaning of the error. All error values begin with a number sign (#); pull down the Help menu, click Search, then enter # for a listing and explanation of the error values.

Step 9: Copy the statistical functions (shortcut menu)
➤ Select cells **C19 through C22** as shown in Figure 3.14f. Click the **right mouse button** to display the shortcut menu shown in the figure. Click **Copy.** A marquee appears around the selected cells.
➤ Drag the mouse over cells **D19 through F19.** Click the **Paste icon** on the Standard toolbar to complete the copy operation. If you have done everything correctly, cells F19, F20, F21, and F22 will display 81, 95, 60, and 35, respectively.
➤ Save the workbook.

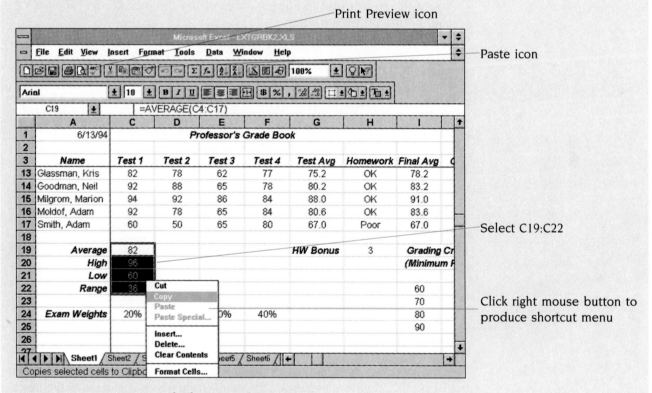

(f) Shortcut Menus (step 9)

FIGURE 3.14   Hands-on Exercise 2 (continued)

Step 10: Print the worksheet
➤ Click the **Print Preview** icon on the Standard toolbar. Click the **Setup command button** to display the Page Setup dialog box.
  — Click the **Page tab.** Click the **Landscape option button.** Click the option button to Fit to one page.

— Click the **Sheet tab.** Check the boxes for Row and Column Headings and for Gridlines.

— Click **OK** to exit the Page Setup dialog box.

— Click the **Print command button,** then click **OK** to print the worksheet.

➤ Press **Ctrl+`** to display the cell formulas. (The left quotation mark is on the same key as the ~.)

➤ Click the **Print Preview** icon. Adjust the margins and column widths as necessary, click the **Print command button,** then click **OK** to print the worksheet with cell formulas.

➤ Exit Excel.

SEE THE WHOLE WORKSHEET

Press Ctrl+Home to move to the beginning of the worksheet. Press the F8 key to enter the extended selection mode (EXT will appear on the status bar), then press Ctrl+End to move to the end of the worksheet and simultaneously select the entire worksheet. Pull down the View menu, click Zoom, then click the Fit Selection option button. Click OK to close the dialog box. The magnification shrinks to display the entire worksheet; how well you can read the display depends on the size of your monitor and the size of the worksheet.

MAKE IT FIT

The Page Setup command offers different ways to make a large worksheet fit on one page. Click the Print Preview icon on the Standard toolbar to view the worksheet prior to printing, click the Margins command button to display (hide) sizing handles for the page margins and column widths, then drag any handle to adjust the margin or column width. You can also click the Setup command button from the Print Preview screen to display the Page Setup dialog box. Use the Page tab to change to *landscape* printing and/or to select the scaling option to Fit to one page.

SUMMARY

The PMT function requires three arguments (the interest rate per period, the number of periods, and the amount of the loan), from which it computes the associated payment.

The fill handle is used to copy a cell or group of cells to a range of adjacent cells. Pointing is a more accurate way to enter a cell reference into a formula as it uses the mouse or cursor keys to reference the cell directly. The Function Wizard helps you choose the appropriate function, then enter the arguments in the proper sequence. The autofill capability creates a series based on the value(s) you supply.

The AVERAGE, MAX, and MIN functions return the average, highest, and lowest values for the designated entries. The COUNT function indicates the number of cells with numeric entries; the COUNTA function displays the number of cells with numeric and/or nonnumeric entries.

The IF function has three arguments: a logical test that is evaluated as true or false, a value if the test is true, and a value if the test is false. The VLOOKUP (table lookup) function also has three arguments: the numeric value to look up, the range of cells containing the table, and the column number within the table that contains the result.

The TODAY() function returns the current date, while the DATE(yy,mm,dd) function returns a specific date. Both functions store the date as a serial number corresponding to the number of days in this century, thus enabling date arithmetic.

Scrolling enables you to view any portion of a large worksheet but moves the headings for existing rows and/or columns off the screen. The Freeze Panes command keeps the row and/or column headings on the screen while scrolling in a large worksheet.

Key Words and Concepts

=AVERAGE	Arguments	Marquee
=COUNT	Assumptions	Point mode
=COUNTA	Autofill capability	Pointing
=DATE	Break point	Portrait
=IF	Custom series	Relational operator
=MAX	Date arithmetic	Relative reference
=MIN	Edit Clear command	Scaling
=NOW	Enter mode	Scrolling
=PMT	Fill handle	Serial date
=SUM	Freezing panes	Spell check
=TODAY	Function Wizard	Table lookup
=VLOOKUP	Landscape	Template
Absolute reference	Logical test	

Multiple Choice

1. Which of the following options may be used to print a large worksheet?
   (a) Landscape orientation
   (b) Scaling
   (c) Reduced margins
   (d) All of the above

2. If the results of a formula contain more characters than can be displayed according to the present format and cell width,
   (a) The extra characters will be truncated under all circumstances
   (b) All of the characters will be displayed if the cell to the right is empty
   (c) A series of asterisks will be displayed
   (d) A series of pound signs will be displayed

3. Which cell—A1, A2, or A3—will contain the amount of the loan, given the function =PMT(A1,A2,A3)?
   (a) A1
   (b) A2
   (c) A3
   (d) Impossible to determine

4. Which of the following will compute the average of the values in cells D2, D3, and D4?
   (a) The function =AVERAGE(D2:D4)
   (b) The function =AVERAGE(D2,D4)
   (c) Both (a) and (b)
   (d) Neither (a) nor (b)

5. The function =IF(A1>A2,A1+A2,A1*A2) returns
   (a) The product of cells A1 and A2 if cell A1 is greater than A2
   (b) The sum of cells A1 and A2 if cell A1 is less than A2
   (c) Both (a) and (b)
   (d) Neither (a) nor (b)

6. Which of the following is the preferred way to sum the values in cells A1 to A4?
   (a) =SUM(A1:A4)
   (b) =A1+A2+A3+A4
   (c) Either (a) or (b) is equally good
   (d) Neither (a) nor (b) is correct

7. Which of the following will return the highest and lowest arguments from a list?
   (a) HIGH/LOW
   (b) LARGEST/SMALLEST
   (c) MAX/MIN
   (d) All of the above

8. Which of the following is a *required* technique to develop the worksheet for the mortgage analysis?
   (a) Pointing
   (b) Copying with the fill handle
   (c) Both (a) and (b)
   (d) Neither (a) nor (b)

9. Given that cells B6, C6, and D6 contain the numbers 10, 20, and 30, respectively, what value will be returned by the function =IF(B6>10,C6*2,D6*3)?
   (a) 10
   (b) 40
   (c) 60
   (d) 90

10. Which formula will compute the age of a person born on March 16, 1977?
    (a) =TODAY() − DATE(77,3,16)
    (b) =TODAY() − DATE(77,3,16)/365
    (c) =(TODAY() − DATE(77,3,16))/365
    (d) =AGE(77,3,16)

11. What is the best way to enter January 21, 1994 into a worksheet, given that you create the worksheet on that date, and further, given that you always want to display that specific date?
   (a) =TODAY()
   (b) 1/21/94
   (c) Both (b) and (b) are equally acceptable
   (d) Neither (a) nor (b)

12. Which function returns the number of *numeric entries* in the range A2:A6?
   (a) =COUNT(A2:A6)
   (b) =COUNTA(A2:A6)
   (c) =COUNT(A2,A6)
   (d) =COUNTA(A2,A6)

13. What happens if you select a range, then press the right mouse button?
   (a) The range will be deselected
   (b) Nothing; that is, the button has no effect
   (c) The Edit and Format menus will be displayed in their entirety
   (d) A shortcut menu with commands from both the Edit and Format menus will be displayed

14. The worksheet displayed in the monitor shows columns A and B, skips columns D, E, and F, then displays columns G, H, I, J, and K. What is the most likely explanation for the missing columns?
   (a) The columns were previously deleted
   (b) The columns are empty and thus are automatically hidden from view
   (c) Either (a) or (b) is a satisfactory explanation
   (d) Neither (a) nor (b) is a likely reason

15. Given the function =VLOOKUP(C6,D12:F18,3)
   (a) The entries in cells D12 through D18 are in ascending order
   (b) The entries in cells D12 through D18 are in descending order
   (c) The entries in cells F12 through F18 are in ascending order
   (d) The entries in cells F12 through F18 are in descending order

ANSWERS

1. d	**4.** a	**7.** c	**10.** c	**13.** d
2. d	**5.** d	**8.** d	**11.** b	**14.** d
3. c	**6.** a	**9.** d	**12.** a	**15.** a

EXPLORING EXCEL

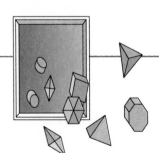

1. Use Figure 3.15 to match each action with its result; a given action may be used more than once, or not at all.

Action	Result
a. Click at 12, type =AVERAGE(, then click at 8, drag to 11, and press enter	___ Freeze column A and rows 1, 2, and 3 on the screen for scrolling

b. Click at 6, then click at 5

c. Click at 1

d. Click at 2

e. Click at 3

f. Click in the lower-right corner of 7, then drag to 10

g. Click at 17, then click at 4

h. Click at 12, drag to 13, then click at 9

i. Click the right mouse button at 17

j. Click at 14, type =, click at 16, type −, click at 15, then press enter

___ Use the autofill feature to enter the column titles for Test 2, Test 3, and Test 4

___ Increase the number of decimal places for the test averages

___ Use the Function Wizard to enter the current date in cell A1

___ Preview the worksheet prior to printing

___ Save the worksheet

___ Enter the formula to compute the range for the scores on Test 1

___ Display a shortcut menu in order to format the date that will be entered in cell A1

___ Enter the function to compute the test average for John Adams

___ Spell check the worksheet

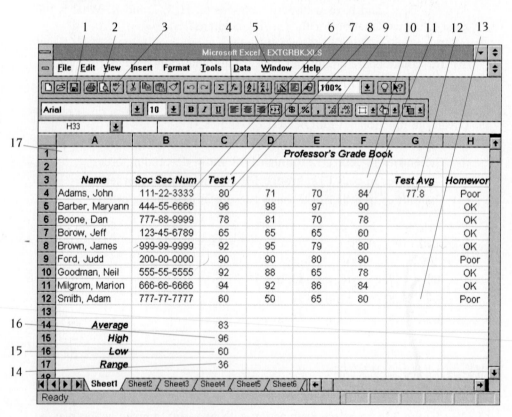

FIGURE 3.15   Screen for Problem 1

2. Consider the two worksheets shown in Figure 3.16 and the entries, =AVER-AGE(A1:A4) versus =(A1+A2+A3+A4)/4, both of which calculate the average of cells A1 through A4. Assume that a new row is inserted in the worksheet between existing rows 2 and 3, with the entry in the new cell equal to 100.

a. What value will be returned by the AVERAGE function in worksheet 1 after the new row has been inserted?

b. What value will be returned by the formula in worksheet 2 after the new row has been inserted?

c. In which cell will the AVERAGE function itself be located after the new row has been inserted?

Return to the original problem, but this time delete row 2.

d. What value will be returned by the AVERAGE function in worksheet 1 after the row has been deleted?

e. What will be returned by the formula in worksheet 2 after the row has been deleted?

	A
1	10
2	20
3	30
4	40
5	=AVERAGE(A1:A4)

(a) Worksheet 1

	A
1	10
2	20
3	30
4	40
5	=(A1+A2+A3+A4)/4

(b) Worksheet 2

FIGURE 3.16 Worksheet for Problem 2

3. Answer the following with respect to Figure 3.17. (Cell B5 is empty.) What value will be returned by the worksheet functions?

a. =IF(A1=0,A2,A3)

b. =SUM(A1:A5)

c. =MAX(A1:A5,B1:B5)

d. =MIN(A1:A3,5,A5)

e. =AVERAGE(B1:B4)

f. =AVERAGE(B1:B5)

g. =MIN(10,MAX(A2:A4))

h. =MAX(10,MIN(A2:A4))

i. =COUNTA(A1:A5)

j. =COUNTA(B1:B5)

k. =COUNT(A1:A5)

l. =COUNT(B1:B5)

m. =VLOOKUP(15,A1:B5,2)

n. =VLOOKUP(20,A1:B5,2)

	A	B
1	10	60
2	20	70
3	30	80
4	40	90
5	50	

FIGURE 3.17 Worksheet for Problem 3

4. Refer to the worksheet in Figure 3.3b, which used the PMT function to compute the amortization schedule for a loan.

a. What formula (function) should be entered into cell C6?

b. What formula (function) should be entered into cell D9?

c. What formula should be entered into cell B10? (The amount of each payment that goes toward interest is the interest rate per period times the unpaid balance of the loan.)

d. What formula should be entered into cell C10? (The amount of each payment that goes toward the principal is the payment amount minus the amount that goes toward interest.)

e. What formula should be entered into cell D10?

f. Implement the worksheet in Excel, but supply your own parameters for the principal, interest, and length of the loan. Add your name somewhere in the worksheet, then print the worksheet as well as the cell formulas. Prepare a cover page and submit both printouts to your instructor.

5. The Autofill command: Create the worksheet in Figure 3.18, then select the cells in the range A1 through G1. Point to the fill handle and drag it to row 12.

a. What are the contents of cells A2 through A12? of cells B2 through B12? What can you conclude about the fill handle and the months of the year?

b. What are the contents of cells C2 through C12? of cells D2 through D12? What can you conclude about a repeating series?

c. What are the contents of cells E2 through E12? of cells F2 through F12? Are these results consistent with those of part b?

d. What are the contents of cells G2 through G12? How would you use the autofill feature to enter the years 1993, 1994, and so on in cells G2 through G12?

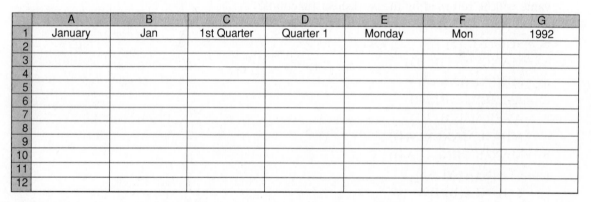

	A	B	C	D	E	F	G
1	January	Jan	1st Quarter	Quarter 1	Monday	Mon	1992
2							
3							
4							
5							
6							
7							
8							
9							
10							
11							
12							

FIGURE 3.18 The Autofill Command

6. Figure 3.19 contains a worksheet used to determine information about Certificates of Deposit purchased at First National Bank of Miami. Retrieve PROB0306.XLS from the data disk, then complete the worksheet following the steps below:

➤ Enter the function to display the current date in B1.

➤ Enter the formula to calculate the Maturity Date in cell E9. (To determine the Maturity Date, add the duration of the certificate to the date purchased.) Copy the formula to the remaining entries in the column.

➤ Move to cell F9 and enter the formula to calculate the number of days remaining until the certificate matures, or if the certificate has already matured, the text *Matured* should appear in the cell. The determination of whether or not the CD has matured can be made by comparing the Maturity Date to the current date; that is, if the Maturity Date is greater than the current date, the CD has not yet matured.

- Format all of the dates so that they are displayed in the dd-mm-yy format (e.g., 15-May-94 rather than 5/15/94).
- Format the Amount of CD with dollar signs and commas, but no decimal places.
- Center the entries in A3 and A4 over the width of the worksheet. Change the font to 14 point Arial bold italic.
- Boldface the column headings.
- Save and print the worksheet.

	A	B	C	D	E	F
1	Date:					
2						
3	Certificates of Deposit					
4	First National Bank of Miami					
5						
6						# of Days
7			Date		Maturity	Remaining
8	Customer	Amount of CD	Purchased	Duration	Date	Till Mature
9	Harris	500000	12/1/93	180		
10	Bodden	50000	1/30/94	180		
11	Dorsey	25000	2/3/94	180		
12	Rosell	10000	3/30/94	365		
13	Klinger	10000	4/1/94	365		

FIGURE 3.19   Spreadsheet for Problem 6

7. Figure 3.20 contains a worksheet used to determine information about software purchases for HOT SPOT Software Sales. Figure 3.20a shows the worksheet as it exists on disk, while Figure 3.20b shows the completed worksheet. Retrieve PROB0307.XLS from the data disk and complete it so that it is identical to the worksheet in Figure 3.20b. In doing so, you will need the following facts:

- The total sale is determined by multiplying the current price by the number of units sold.
- A discount is given if the total sale is equal to or greater than the discount threshold. (The amount of discount is determined by multiplying the total sale by the discount percentage. The exact percentage to be used is indicated in the assumption area at the bottom of the worksheet.) If the total sale is less than the discount threshold, no discount is given.
- The discounted total is determined by subtracting the amount of discount from the total sale.
- The sales tax is determined by multiplying the discounted total by the sales tax percentage (as indicated in the assumption area).
- The amount due is determined by adding the sales tax to the discounted total.
- The number of customers, highest current price, fewest units sold, average discount, and total amount due are determined by entering the appropriate functions in the indicated cells.

Would it be a good idea to lower the discount threshold to $500 and lower the discount percentage to 10%? Why or why not? Why should the discount threshold, discount percentage, and sales tax percentage be isolated from the main body of the worksheet? What advantages does this give you in working with the worksheet?

(a) Spreadsheet on Disk

	A	B	C	D	E	F	G	H	I
1	HOT SPOT Software Sales								
2	Miami, Florida								
3									
4	Customer		Current	Units	Total	Amount of	Discounted	Sales	Amount
5	Name	Program	Price	Sold	Sale	Discount	Total	Tax	Due
6	Macy's	Windows	59.99	2					
7	Kings Bay Athletics	Word for Windows	295	5					
8	Bloomingdale's	After Dark	29.95	10					
9	Service Merchandise	Excel	495	3					
10	Lord & Taylor	Lotus for Windows	595	3					
11	Burdine's	WordPerfect	245	2					
12	Sports Authority	Word for Windows	295	3					
13	The Gap	Excel	495	7					
14	Home Depot	Windows	59.99	12					
15	Brookstone	Lotus for Windows	595	8					
16	Coconuts	WordPerfect	245	10					
17	Express	Windows	59.99	3					
18									
19									
20	Discount Threshold:		1000				Number of Customers:		
21	Discount Percentage:		0.15				Highest Current Price:		
22	Sales Tax:		0.065				Fewest Units Sold:		
23							Average Discount:		
24							Total Amount Due:		

(a) Spreadsheet on Disk

(b) Completed Spreadsheet

	A	B	C	D	E	F	G	H	I
1				**HOT SPOT Software Sales**					
2									
3				**Miami, Florida**					
4	Customer		Current	Units	Total	Amount of	Discounted	Sales	Amount
5	Name	Program	Price	Sold	Sale	Discount	Total	Tax	Due
6	Macy's	Windows	$59.99	2	$119.98	$0.00	$119.98	$7.80	$127.78
7	Kings Bay Athletics	Word for Windows	$295.00	5	$1,475.00	$221.25	$1,253.75	$81.49	$1,335.24
8	Bloomingdale's	After Dark	$29.95	10	$299.50	$0.00	$299.50	$19.47	$318.97
9	Service Merchandise	Excel	$495.00	3	$1,485.00	$222.75	$1,262.25	$82.05	$1,344.30
10	Lord & Taylor	Lotus for Windows	$595.00	3	$1,785.00	$267.75	$1,517.25	$98.62	$1,615.87
11	Burdine's	WordPerfect	$245.00	2	$490.00	$0.00	$490.00	$31.85	$521.85
12	Sports Authority	Word for Windows	$295.00	3	$885.00	$0.00	$885.00	$57.53	$942.53
13	The Gap	Excel	$495.00	7	$3,465.00	$519.75	$2,945.25	$191.44	$3,136.69
14	Home Depot	Windows	$59.99	12	$719.88	$0.00	$719.88	$46.79	$766.67
15	Brookstone	Lotus for Windows	$595.00	8	$4,760.00	$714.00	$4,046.00	$262.99	$4,308.99
16	Coconuts	WordPerfect	$245.00	10	$2,450.00	$367.50	$2,082.50	$135.36	$2,217.86
17	Express	Windows	$59.99	3	$179.97	$0.00	$179.97	$11.70	$191.67
18									
19									
20	Discount Threshold:		$1,000				Number of Customers:		12
21	Discount Percentage:		15.0%				Highest Current Price:		$595.00
22	Sales Tax:		6.5%				Fewest Units Sold:		2
23							Average Discount:		$192.75
24							Total Amount Due:		$16,828.42

(b) Completed Spreadsheet

FIGURE 3.20 Spreadsheet for Problem 7

8. Figure 3.21 suggests how a worksheet can be extended to the preparation of sales invoices. The figure assumes the existence of a template that the user retrieves for each new order. All entries in the shaded area are made after the template is retrieved, depending on the particular order.

a. What formula should you enter in cell D9 to compute the amount due for the first item?

b. What entry should you use in cell D14 to compute the subtotal? Your answer should accommodate the potential insertion of additional rows (after row 12) should the customer order more than four items.

	A	B	C	D
1	*INVOICE*			16-Mar-94
2				
3	Customer:	Mr. John Doe		
4		10000 Sample Road		
5		Coral Springs, FL 33065		
6	Tax Status:	Exempt		
7				
8	Quantity	Item	Unit Price	Amount
9	15	Widgets (small)	$14.00	$210.00
10	6	Widgets (medium)	$20.00	$120.00
11	2	Widgets (large)	$25.00	$50.00
12	14	Widgets (extra large)	$30.00	$420.00
13				
14		Subtotal		$800.00
15		Discount	10%	$80.00
16		Sales Tax		$0.00
17			Total	$720.00
18				
19				
20				
21				
22				
23	Sales Tax		Discount	
24	6%		$200	2%
25			$400	5%
26			$750	10%

FIGURE 3.21 Spreadsheet for Problem 8

   c. What entry should you use in cell C15 to determine the discount percentage (based on the table shown in the lower-right portion of the worksheet)?

   d. What entry should you use in cell D15 to compute the discount?

   e. What formula should you use to compute the sales tax? (Customers with a tax status of "Exempt" pay no tax; all other customers pay the tax rate shown in cell A24 for the discounted order.)

   f. What formula should you use in cell D17 for the total due?

   g. Implement the worksheet in the figure, add your name as the customer, and submit the assignment to your instructor.

9. Use Figure 3.1 at the beginning of the chapter as the basis for this exercise.

   a. Open the PROB0309.XLS on the data disk.

   b. Enter the parameters for your specific car in cells B1, B2, and B3 as in Figure 3.1. Enter the terms of the loan in cells B5 and B6 to determine the projected monthly payment.

   c. The monthly payment is only one expense; that is, a realistic estimate requires insurance, gas, and maintenance. Enter these labels in cells A8, A9, and A10, then put the projected expenses in cells B8, B9, and B10.

   d. Add the label *Total* in cell A11, and the formula to compute this amount in cell B11.

   e. Insert two rows at the top of the worksheet to accommodate the title of the worksheet. Click in cell A1 and type the title of the worksheet, *Can I Afford It?*, followed by your name.

   f. Format the title in boldface, italics, and/or a larger typeface. Leave row 2 blank to offset the title from the remainder of the worksheet.

   g. The worksheet can make the decision for you. Click in cell A13 and enter the label, *The Decision. . :* Enter an IF function in cell B13 that will display Yes if the total expenses are $500 or less, and No otherwise.

h. Save the updated workbook.

i. Print the entire worksheet two ways, once with computed values and once with cell formulas. Submit both worksheets to your instructor.

10. Inserting an object: This exercises requires the availability of the ClipArt subdirectory in Word for Windows (or any other clip art collection). Use Figure 3.22 as a guide in the exercise.

a. Open the MORTGAGE.XLS workbook from the first hands-on exercise.

b. Click anywhere in column E, the place where you want the picture to go.

c. Pull down the Insert menu. Click Picture.

d. Click on drive C (or whichever drive contains the WINWORD subdirectory).

e. Double click on the WINWORD subdirectory. Double click the CLIPART subdirectory within the WINWORD directory.

f. If necessary, check the Preview Picture box so that you can see the picture prior to inserting it into the worksheet. Click the picture you want—for example, HOUSES.WMF—then click OK.

g. The picture is now in the worksheet where you can use the normal Windows commands to size and/or move the object.

h Pull down the File menu to save the workbook with the embedded graphic.

i. Print the completed worksheet, graphic and all.

	A	B	C	D	E	F	G	H
1	Amount Borrowed		$100,000					
2	Starting Interest		7.50%					
3								
4		Monthly Payment						
5	Interest	30 Years	15 Years	Difference				
6	7.50%	$699.21	$927.01	$227.80				
7	8.50%	$768.91	$984.74	$215.83				
8	9.50%	$840.85	$1,044.22	$203.37				
9	10.50%	$914.74	$1,105.40	$190.66				
10	11.50%	$990.29	$1,168.19	$177.90				
11	12.50%	$1,067.26	$1,232.52	$165.26				
12								
13	Financial consultant:		Bess Marder					

FIGURE 3.22 Inserting an Object (problem 10)

Case Studies

Startup Airlines

You have been hired as the spreadsheet expert for a small start-up airline that needs to calculate the fuel requirements and associated cost for its available flights. The airline currently has two types of aircraft, a Boeing-727 and a DC-9, which consume 10,000 and 8,000 gallons of fuel, respectively, for each hour in the air. The fuel needed for any given flight depends on the aircraft and number of flying hours; for example, a five-hour flight in a DC-9 can be expected to use 40,000 gallons. In addition, the plane must carry an additional 10% of the required fuel to maintain a holding pattern (4,000 gallons in this example) and an additional 20% as reserve (8,000 gallons in this example). Use the data in AIRLINES.XLS to compute the fuel necessary for the listed flights as well as the estimated cost based on a fuel price of $1.00 per gallon. Your worksheet should be completely flexible and amenable to change; that is, the hourly fuel requirements, price per gallon, and holding and reserve percentages are all subject to change at a moment's notice.

The Financial Consultant

A friend of yours is in the process of buying a home and has asked you to compare the payments and total interest on a 15- and a 30-year loan. You want to do as professional a job as possible and have decided to analyze the loans in Excel, then incorporate the results into a memo written in Word for Windows. As of now the principal is $150,000, but it is very likely that your friend will change his mind several times, and so you want to use the OLE capability within Windows to dynamically link the worksheet to the word processing document. Your memo should include a letterhead that takes advantage of the formatting capabilities within Word; a graphic logo would be a nice touch.

Compensation Analysis

A corporation typically uses several different measures of compensation in an effort to pay its employees fairly. Most organizations closely monitor an employee's salary history, keeping both the present and previous salary in order to compute various statistics, including:

➤ The percent salary increase, which is computed by taking the difference between the present and previous salary, and dividing by the previous salary.

➤ The months between increase, which is the elapsed time between the date the present salary took effect and the date of the previous salary. (Assume 30 days per month for ease of calculation.)

➤ The annualized rate of increase, which is the percent salary increase divided by the months between increase (expressed as a fraction of a year); for example, a 5% raise after 6 months is equivalent to an annualized increase of 10%; a 5% raise after two years is equivalent to an annual increase of 2.5%.

Use the data in SALARIES.XLS to compute salary statistics for the employees who have had a salary increase; employees who have not received an increase should have a suitable indication in the cell. Compute the average, minimum, and maximum value for each measure of compensation for those employees who have received an increase.

The Automobile Dealership

The purchase of a car usually entails extensive bargaining between the dealer and the consumer. The dealer has an asking price but typically settles for less. The commission paid to a salesperson depends on how close the selling price is to the asking price. Exotic Motors has the following compensation policy for its sales staff:

➤ A 3% commission on the actual selling price for cars sold at 95% or more of the asking price.

➤ A 2% commission on the actual selling price for cars sold at 90% or more (but less than 95%) of the asking price.

➤ A 1% commission on the actual selling price for cars sold at less than 90% of the asking price. The dealer will not go below 85% of his asking price.

The dealer's asking price is based on the dealer's cost plus a 20% markup; for example, the asking price on a car that cost the dealer $20,000 would be $24,000.

Develop a worksheet to be used by the dealer, which shows his profit (the selling price minus the salesperson's commission) on every sale. The worksheet should be completely flexible and allow the dealer to vary the markup or commission percentages without having to edit or recopy any of the formulas. Use the data in EXOTIC.XLS to test your worksheet.

The Birthday Problem

How much would you bet *against* two people in your class having the same birthday? Don't be too hasty, for the odds of two classmates sharing the same birthday (month and day) are much higher than you would expect; for example, there is a 50% chance in a class of 23 students that two people will have been born on the same day. The probability jumps to 70% in a class of 30, and to 90% in a class of 41.

You need a basic knowledge of probability to prove these statements, but the solution is readily amenable to a spreadsheet. In essence, you calculate the probability of individuals *not* having the same birthday, then subtract this number from 1, to obtain the probability of the event coming true. In a group of two people, for example, the probability of *not* being born on the same day is 365/366; that is, the second person can be born on any of 365 days and still have a different birthday. The probability of two people having the same birthday becomes 1 − 365/366.

The probability for *different* birthdays in a group of three people is (365/366)*(364/366); the probability of *not* having different birthdays; that is, of two people having the same birthday, is 1 minus this number. In similar fashion the probability for different birthdays in a group of four people is (365/366)*(364/366)*(363/366), and so on. Can you develop a worksheet that shows the probability of two people being born on the same day in classes of up to 50 students?

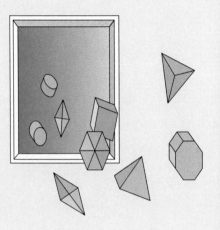

Graphs and Charts: Delivering a Message

CHAPTER OBJECTIVES

After reading this chapter you will be able to:

1. Distinguish between different types of charts, stating the advantages and disadvantages of each.
2. Distinguish between a chart embedded in a worksheet versus one in a separate chart sheet; explain how many charts can be associated with the same worksheet.
3. Use the ChartWizard to create and/or modify a chart.
4. Enhance a chart by using arrows and text.
5. Differentiate between data series specified in rows versus data series specified in columns.
6. Describe how a chart can be statistically accurate, yet totally misleading.
7. Create a compound document consisting of a word processing memo, a worksheet, and a chart.

OVERVIEW

Business has always known that the graphic representation of data is an attractive, easy-to-understand way to convey information. Indeed, business graphics has become one of the most exciting Windows applications, enabling charts (graphs) to be easily created from a worksheet, with just a few simple keystrokes or mouse clicks.

The chapter begins by emphasizing the importance of determining the message to be conveyed by a chart. It describes the different types of charts available within Excel and how to choose among them. It explains how to create a chart by using the ChartWizard, how to embed a chart within a worksheet, and how to create a chart in a separate chart sheet. It also describes how to enhance a chart with arrows and additional text.

The second half of the chapter explains how one chart can plot multiple sets of data, and how several charts can be based on the same worksheet. It describes how to create a compound document, in which a chart and its associated worksheet are dynamically linked to a memo created by a word processor. All told, we think you will find this to be one of the most enjoyable chapters in the text.

CHART TYPES

A **chart** is a graphic representation of data in a worksheet. The chart is created from values in the worksheet known as **data points.** The data points are grouped into one or more **data series.** Each data series appears as a row or column in the worksheet.

The worksheet in Figure 4.1 will be used throughout the chapter as the basis for the charts we will create. Your manager believes that the sales data can be understood more easily from charts than from the strict numerical presentation of a worksheet. You have been given the assignment of analyzing the data in the worksheet and are developing a series of charts to convey that information.

	A	B	C	D	E	F
1	Superior Software Monthly Sales					
2						
3		*Miami*	*Denver*	*New York*	*Boston*	*Total*
4	Word Processing	$50,000	$67,500	$9,500	$141,000	$268,000
5	Spreadsheets	$44,000	$18,000	$11,500	$105,000	$178,500
6	Database	$12,000	$7,500	$6,000	$30,000	$55,500
7	Total	$106,000	$93,000	$27,000	$276,000	$502,000

FIGURE 4.1   Superior Software

The sales data in the worksheet can be presented several ways—for example, by city, by product, or by a combination of the two. Ask yourself which type of chart is best suited to answer the following questions:

➤ What percentage of total revenue comes from each city? from each product?
➤ What is the dollar revenue produced by each city? by each product?
➤ What is the rank of each city with respect to sales?
➤ How much revenue does each product contribute in each city?

In every instance realize that a chart exists only to deliver a message, and that you cannot create an effective chart unless you are sure of what that message is. The next several pages discuss the different types of business charts, each of which is best suited to a particular type of message.

KEEP IT SIMPLE

Keep it simple. This rule applies to both your message and the means of conveying that message. Excel makes it almost too easy to change fonts, styles, type sizes, and colors, and such changes often detract from a chart rather than enhance it. More is not necessarily better, and just because the features are there, does not mean you have to use them. Remember that a chart must ultimately succeed on the basis of content and content alone.

Pie Charts

A *pie chart* is the most effective way to display proportional relationships. It is the type of chart to select whenever words like *percentage* or *market share* appear in the message to be delivered. The pie, or complete circle, denotes the total amount. Each slice of the pie corresponds to the appropriate percentage of the total.

The pie chart in Figure 4.2a divides the pie representing total sales into four slices, one for each city. The size of each slice is proportional to the percentage of total sales in that city. The chart depicts a single data series, which appears in cells B7 through E7 on the associated worksheet. The data series has four data points corresponding to the total sales in each city.

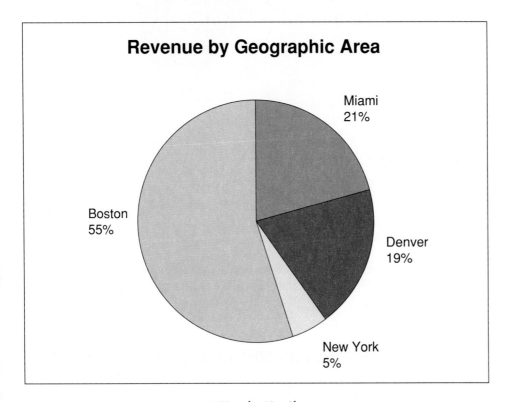

(a) Simple Pie Chart

FIGURE 4.2   Pie Charts

To create the pie chart, Excel computes the total sales ($502,000 in our example), calculates the percentage contributed by each city, and draws each slice of the pie in proportion to its computed percentage. Boston's sales of $276,000 account for 55 percent of the total, and so this slice of the pie is allotted 55 percent of the area of the circle.

An *exploded pie chart,* as shown in Figure 4.2b, separates one or more slices of the pie for emphasis. Another way to achieve emphasis in a chart is to choose a title that reflects the message you are trying to deliver. The title in Figure 4.2a, for example, *Revenue by Geographic Area,* is neutral and leaves the reader to develop his or her own conclusion about the relative contribution of each area. By contrast, the title in Figure 4.2b, *New York Accounts for only 5% of Revenue,* is more suggestive and emphasizes the problems in this office. Alternatively, the chart could be retitled to *Boston Exceeds 50% of Total Revenue* if the intent were to emphasize the contribution of Boston.

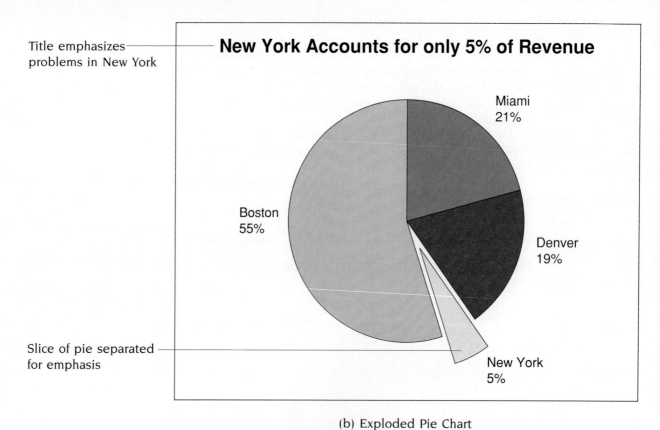

Title emphasizes problems in New York

Slice of pie separated for emphasis

(b) Exploded Pie Chart

FIGURE 4.2   Pie Charts (continued)

Three-dimensional pie charts may be created in exploded or nonexploded format as shown in Figures 4.2c and 4.2d. Excel also enables you to add arrows and text for emphasis.

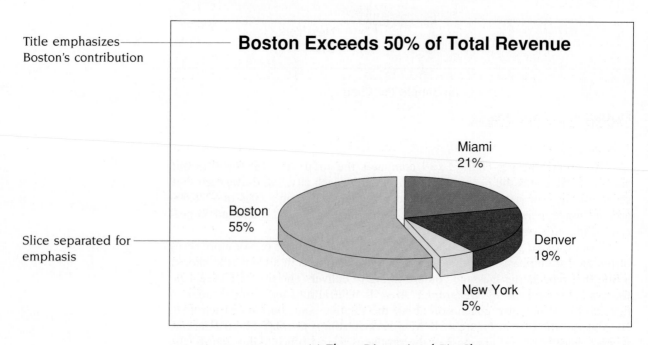

Title emphasizes Boston's contribution

Slice separated for emphasis

(c) Three-Dimensional Pie Chart

FIGURE 4.2   Pie Charts (continued)

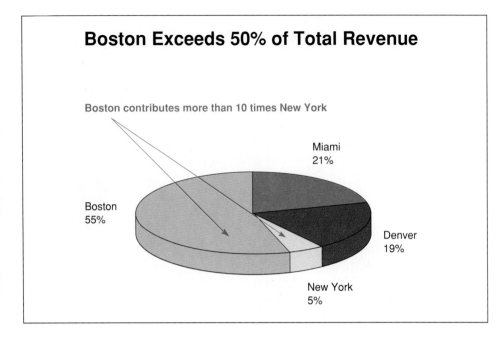

(d) Enhanced Pie Chart

FIGURE 4.2   Pie Charts (continued)

A pie chart is easiest to read when the number of slices is limited (not more than six or seven), and when small categories (percentages less than five) are not plotted individually. The latter may be avoided by grouping small categories into a single class labeled *Other*.

EXPLODED PIE CHARTS

Click and drag wedges in and out of a pie chart to convert an ordinary pie chart to an exploded pie chart. For best results, pull the wedge out only slightly from the main body of the pie.

Column and Bar Charts

A **column chart** is used when there is a need to show actual numbers rather than percentages. The column chart in Figure 4.3a plots the same data series as the earlier pie chart, but displays it differently. The values for the descriptive category (Miami, Denver, New York, and Boston) are shown along the *X* (horizontal) **axis.** The values of the quantitative variable (monthly sales) are plotted along the *Y* (vertical) **axis.** The height of each column reflects the value of the quantitative variable.

A column chart can be given a horizontal orientation and converted to a **bar chart** as in Figure 4.3b. Some individuals prefer the bar chart over the corresponding column chart because the longer horizontal bars accentuate the difference between the cities. Bar charts are also preferable when the descriptive labels are long and you want to eliminate the crowding that can occur along the horizontal axis of a column chart. As with the pie chart, a title can be developed to lead the reader and further emphasize the message—for example, *Boston Leads All Cities,* in Figure 4.3b.

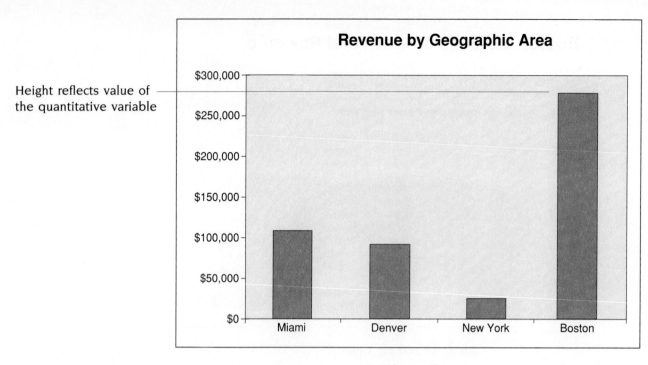

Height reflects value of
the quantitative variable

Revenue by Geographic Area

(a) Column Chart

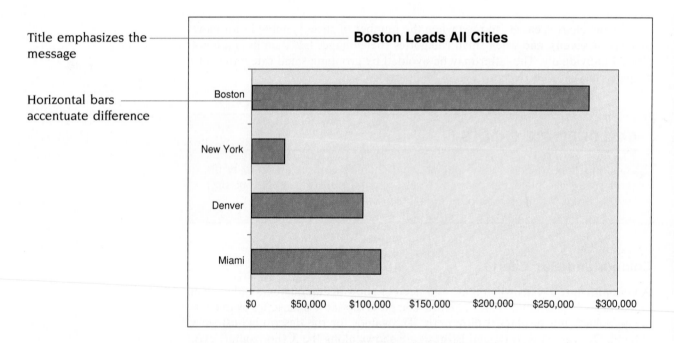

Title emphasizes the
message

Horizontal bars
accentuate difference

Boston Leads All Cities

(b) Horizontal Bar Chart

FIGURE 4.3   Column/Bar Charts

A three-dimensional column chart can produce added interest as shown in Figures 4.3c and 4.3d. Figure 4.3d plots a different set of numbers than we have seen so far (the sales for each application, rather than the sales for each city). And again, arrows and text can be added to any chart to enhance the message.

As with a pie chart, column and bar charts are easiest to read when the number of categories is relatively small (seven or less). Otherwise the columns (bars) are plotted so close together that labeling becomes impossible.

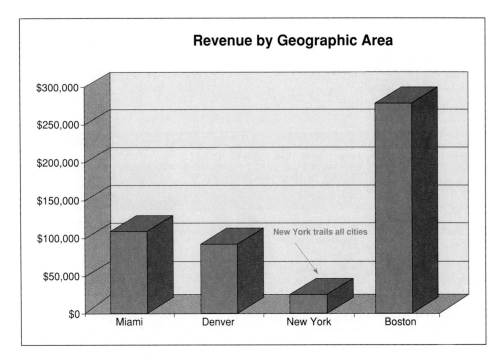

(c) Three-dimensional Column Chart

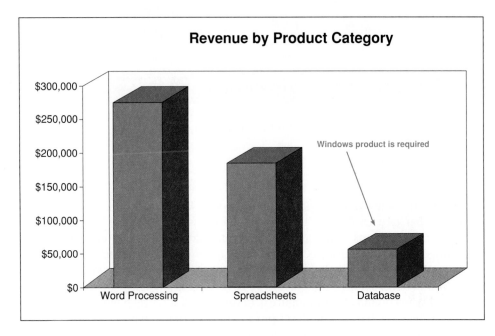

(d) Alternate Column Chart

FIGURE 4.3 Column/Bar Charts (continued)

CREATING A CHART

There are two ways to create a chart in Excel. You can *embed* the chart in a worksheet, or you can create the chart in a separate *chart sheet.* Figure 4.4a displays an embedded column chart. Figure 4.4b shows a pie chart in its own chart sheet. Both techniques are equally valid. The choice between the two depends on personal preference.

Regardless of where it is kept (embedded in a worksheet or in its own chart sheet), a chart is linked to the worksheet on which it is based. The charts in Figure 4.4 plot the same data series (the total sales for each city). Change any of these data points on the worksheet, and both charts will be updated automatically to reflect the new data.

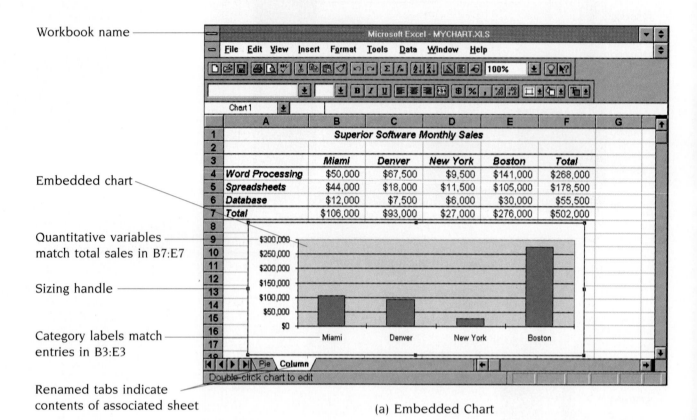

FIGURE 4.4   Creating a Chart

(a) Embedded Chart

Both charts are part of the same workbook (MYCHART.XLS as indicated in the title bar of each figure). The tabs within the workbook have been renamed to indicate the contents of the associated sheet. Additional charts may be created and embedded in the worksheet and/or created in additional chart sheets. And, as previously stated, if you change the worksheet, the chart (or charts) based upon it will also change.

Study the column chart in Figure 4.4a to see how it corresponds to the worksheet on which it is based. The descriptive names on the X axis are known as *cat-egory labels* and match the entries in cells B3 through E3. The quantitative values (data points) plotted on the Y axis match the total sales in cells B7 through E7. Even the numeric format matches; that is, the currency format used in the worksheet appears automatically on the scale of the Y axis.

The *sizing handles* on the embedded chart indicate it is currently selected and can be sized, moved, or deleted the same way as any Windows object:

➤ To size the selected chart, point to a sizing handle (the mouse pointer changes to a double arrow), then drag the handle in the desired direction.

➤ To move the selected chart, point to its border (the mouse pointer is a single arrow), then drag the chart to its new location.

➤ To delete the selected chart, press the Del key.

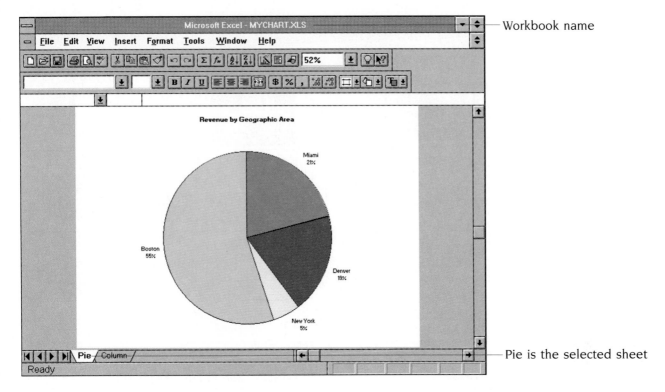

(b) Chart Sheet

FIGURE 4.4 Creating a Chart (continued)

The same operations apply to any of the objects within the chart (e.g., its title) as will be discussed in the section on enhancing a chart.

The ChartWizard

The *ChartWizard* is the easiest way to create a chart. Just select the cells that contain the data, click the ChartWizard icon on the Standard toolbar, and let the Wizard do the rest. The process is illustrated in Figure 4.5, which shows how the Wizard creates a column chart to plot total sales by geographic area.

The steps in Figure 4.5 appear automatically, one after the other, as you click the Next command button to move from one step to the next. You can retrace

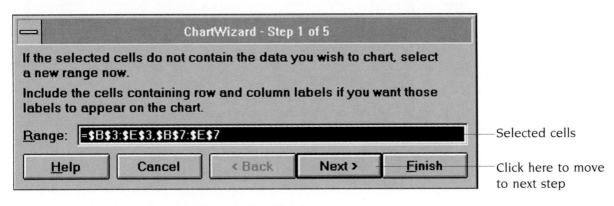

(a) Step 1—Define the Range

FIGURE 4.5 The ChartWizard

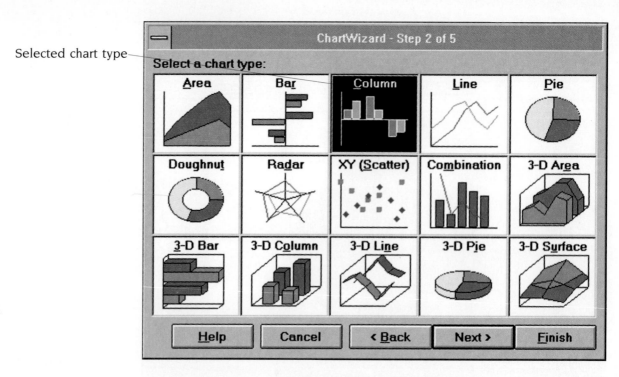

Selected chart type

(b) Step 2—Select the Chart Type

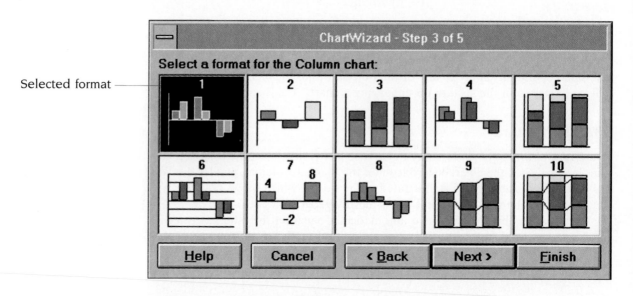

Selected format

(c) Step 3—Select the Format for the Column Chart

FIGURE 4.5   The ChartWizard (continued)

your steps at any time by pressing the Back command button, access the on-line help facility with the Help command button, or negate the process with the Cancel command button.

Step 1, shown in Figure 4.5a, confirms the range of selected cells, $B$3:$E$3 (containing the city names) and $B$7:$E$7 (containing the total sales for each city). Step 2 asks you to choose one of the available chart types, and step 3 has you choose the specific format for the type of chart you selected. Step 4 shows you a preview of the completed chart. (The distinction between data series in rows

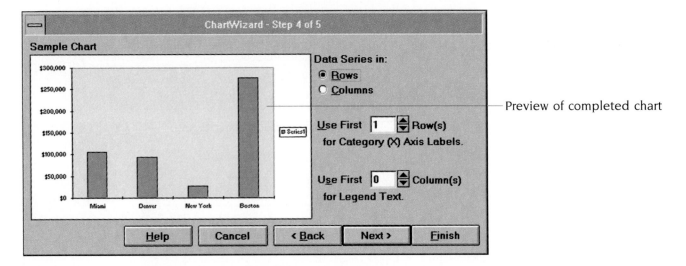

(d) Step 4—Preview the Chart

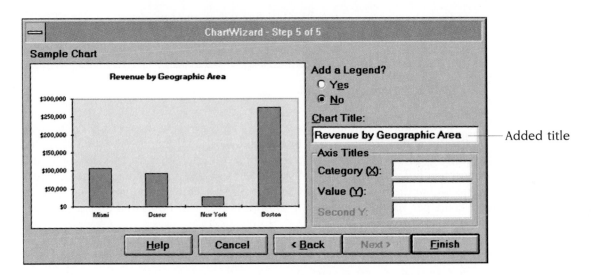

(e) Step 5—Add Legends and Titles

FIGURE 4.5 The ChartWizard (continued)

versus columns is explained after the hands-on exercise.) Step 5 enables you to add a title and a legend. It's that simple and the entire process takes but a few minutes.

Enhancing a Chart

After you create a chart, you can enhance it in several ways. You can change the chart type, add (remove) a legend, and/or add (remove) gridlines. You can select any part of the chart (e.g., the title) and change its formatting. You can also add arrows and text.

Figure 4.6 displays an enhanced version of the column chart that was created by using the ChartWizard in Figure 4.5. The chart type has been changed to a three-dimensional column chart, and gridlines have been added. Both changes were accomplished by using icons on the *Chart toolbar.*

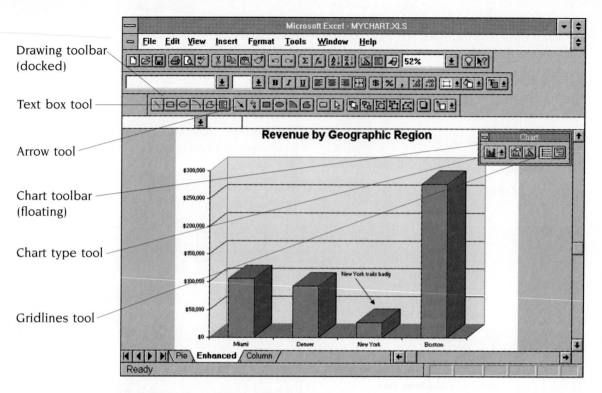

Drawing toolbar (docked)

Text box tool

Arrow tool

Chart toolbar (floating)

Chart type tool

Gridlines tool

FIGURE 4.6   Enhancing a Chart

A text box and an arrow have been added by using the corresponding tools on the ***Drawing toolbar.*** A ***text box*** is a block of text that is added to a chart (or worksheet) for emphasis. You can format all or part of the text by selecting it and choosing a different font or point size. You can also apply boldface or italics. Text wraps within the box as it is entered. The text box and ***arrow tool*** are not part of the chart per se, but are inserted as objects that can be moved and sized independently of the chart.

FLOATING TOOLBARS

Any toolbar can be docked along the edge of the application window, or it can be displayed as a floating toolbar within the application window. To move a ***docked toolbar,*** drag the toolbar background. To move a ***floating toolbar*** drag its title bar. To size a floating toolbar, drag any border in the direction you want to go. Double click the background of any toolbar to toggle between a floating toolbar and a docked (fixed) toolbar.

HANDS-ON EXERCISE 1:

The ChartWizard

Objective To create and modify a chart by using ChartWizard; to embed a chart within a worksheet; to create a chart in its own sheet; to enhance a chart to include arrows and text.

Step 1: Open the Superior Software workbook

➤ Load Excel. Pull down the **File menu** and click **Open** (or click the **Open icon** on the toolbar). Open the **SOFTWARE.XLS** workbook.

➤ Pull down the **File menu.** Save the workbook as **MYCHART** so that you can return to the original workbook if necessary.

➤ Pull down the **Tools menu,** click **Options,** click the **General tab,** check the box to **Reset TipWizard,** and click **OK.**

Step 2: Start the ChartWizard

➤ Drag the mouse over cells **B3 through E3** to select the category labels (the names of the cities) as shown in Figure 4.7a.

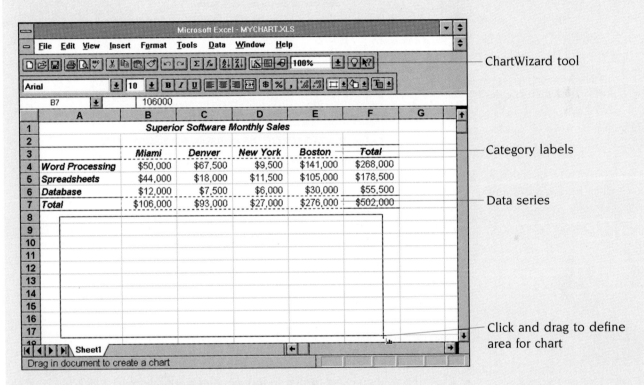

(a) Define the Data Range (step 2)

FIGURE 4.7 Hands-on Exercise 1

➤ Press and hold the **Ctrl key** as you drag the mouse over cells **B7 through E7** to select the data series (the cells containing the total sales for the individual cities).

➤ Check that both ranges **B3:E3** and **B7:E7** are selected.

➤ Click the icon for the **ChartWizard.** A marquee will appear around the selected ranges, and the mouse pointer changes to a tiny cross with a tiny bar chart.

➤ Click below cell A7, then drag the mouse to define the area to hold the chart as shown in Figure 4.7a. Release the mouse.

Step 3: The ChartWizard (continued)

➤ You should see the dialog box for step 1 of ChartWizard as shown in Figure 4.7b. If the range is correct (i.e., the ChartWizard displays $B$3:$E$3 and $B$7:$E$7), click the **Next command button.** If the range is incorrect, click **Cancel** and begin again, or correct the entry.

Reflects selected cells

Click here to continue

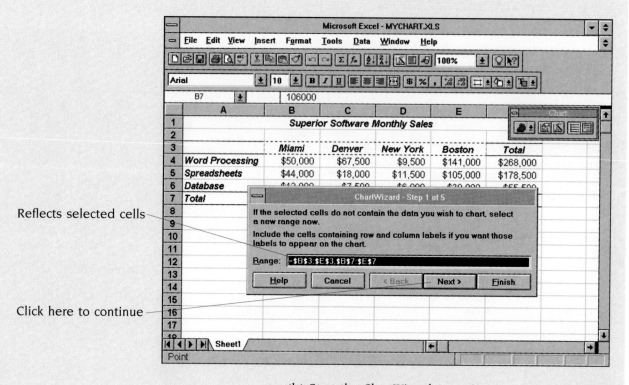

(b) Start the ChartWizard (step 3)

FIGURE 4.7   Hands-on Exercise 1 (continued)

➤ Click the icon for a **column chart** (the default). Click the **Next command button.**
➤ Click the column chart format in **box number 6** (the default). Click the **Next command button.**
➤ View the sample chart shown in step 4 of the ChartWizard:
  — If you are satisfied with your chart, click the **Next command button** to move to step 5 of the ChartWizard.
  — If you are not satisfied, click the **Back command button** to return to the previous step, where you can change the chart format.
➤ Complete the chart in step 5 of the ChartWizard as shown in Figure 4.7c:
  — Click the **No option button** to suppress the legend.
  — Click in the text box to add the title. Type **Revenue by Geographic Area.**
  — Click the **Finish command button** to exit the ChartWizard.
➤ You should see the chart in Figure 4.7d. The sizing handles indicate that the chart is selected and will be affected by subsequent commands.
➤ Save the workbook.

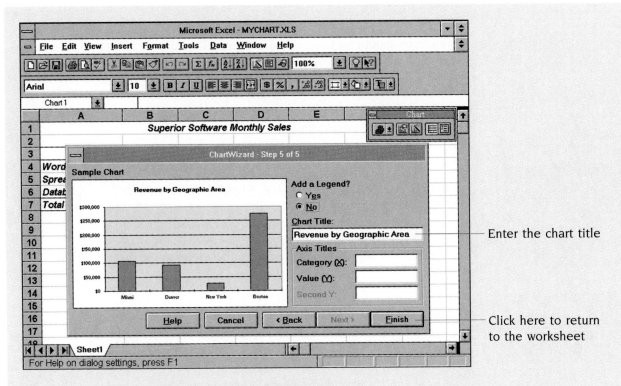

Enter the chart title

Click here to return to the worksheet

(c) The ChartWizard (step 3)

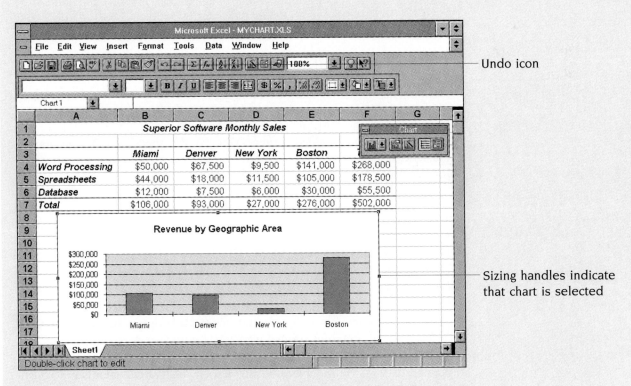

Undo icon

Sizing handles indicate that chart is selected

(d) The Embedded Chart (step 4)

FIGURE 4.7 Hands-on Exercise 1 (continued)

Step 4: Delete the chart

➤ The chart should be selected from the previous step; if not, click just above the top gridline to select it.

➤ Press the **Del key.** The chart disappears from the worksheet. Click the **Undo icon** on the Standard toolbar to cancel the last command. The chart is back in the worksheet.

➤ Click anywhere outside the chart to deselect it.

MOVING AND SIZING THE EMBEDDED CHART

To move the embedded chart within a worksheet, click anywhere in the chart to select the chart, then drag it to a new location. To size the chart, select it, then drag any of the eight sizing handles in the desired direction.

Step 5: Change the worksheet

➤ Click in cell **B4.** Change the entry to **$300,000.** Press the **enter key.** The totals in cells F4, B7, and F7 change automatically to reflect the increased sales for word processing in the Miami office.

➤ The column for Miami also changes in the chart and is now larger than the column for Boston.

➤ Click the **Undo** button on the Standard toolbar to return to the initial value of $50,000.

➤ The worksheet and chart are restored to their values as shown in Figure 4.7d.

THE FORMAT OBJECT COMMAND

Dress up an embedded chart by changing its border. Select the chart, pull down Format menu, then click Object to produce the Format Object dialog box. Click the Patterns tab, which displays check boxes to choose a shadow effect and rounded corners. You can also specify a different border style, thickness, or color as well as a background color and/or pattern for the entire chart. Click OK to exit the dialog box.

Step 6: Modify the chart

➤ Double click anywhere in the chart to select it for editing. The chart is enclosed in a hashed line as shown in Figure 4.7e.

➤ Pull down the **Format menu.** Click **Chart Type** to display the dialog box in Figure 4.7e.

➤ Click the box containing a **Pie chart.** Click the **3-D option button.** Click **OK.** You will see a three-dimensional pie chart, but the slices are not yet labeled.

➤ Pull down the **Format menu** a second time. Click **AutoFormat** to display a dialog box with various types of pie charts. Click format **number 7,** which will label the slices of the pie with percentages and the city names. Click **OK.** The completed pie chart is shown in Figure 4.7f.

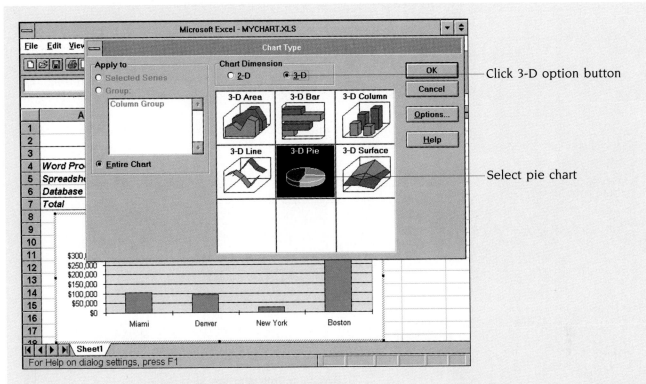

Click 3-D option button

Select pie chart

(e) Change the Chart Type (step 6)

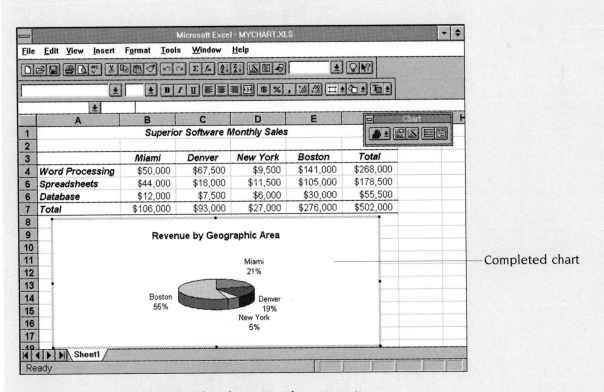

Completed chart

(f) The Completed 3-D Pie Chart (step 6)

FIGURE 4.7   Hands-on Exercise 1 (continued)

Step 7: Create a second chart

➤ Drag the mouse over cells **A4 through A6** to select the category labels (the software categories) as shown in Figure 4.7g.

➤ Press and hold the **Ctrl key** as you drag the mouse over cells **F4 through F6** to select the data series (the cells containing the total sales for the product categories).

➤ Pull down the **Insert menu.** Click **Chart.** Click **As New Sheet** as shown in Figure 4.7g.

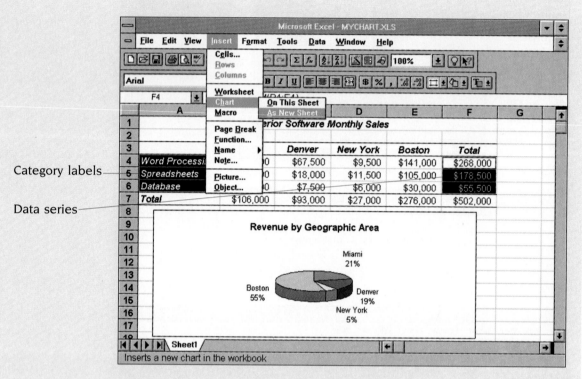

Category labels

Data series

(g) Insert Chart Command (step 7)

FIGURE 4.7 Hands-on Exercise 1 (continued)

Step 8: The ChartWizard

➤ You should see step 1 of the ChartWizard with cells A4:A6 and F4:F6 selected. Click the **Next command button** if the range is correct; click the **Cancel command button** if the range is incorrect and begin again.

➤ Click the icon for a **3-D Column chart.** Click the **Next command button.**

➤ Click the column chart format in **box number 1** (the default). Click the **Next command button.**

➤ View the sample chart shown in step 4 of the ChartWizard:
— If you are satisfied, click the **Next command button.**
— If you are not satisfied, click the **Back command button** to return to the previous step, where you can change the chart format.

➤ Complete the chart in step 5 of the ChartWizard:
— Click the **No option button** to suppress the legend.
— Click in the text box. Type **Revenue by Product Category.**
— Click the **Finish command button.**

➤ You should see the chart in Figure 4.7h, but without the text box and arrow.

➤ Save the workbook.

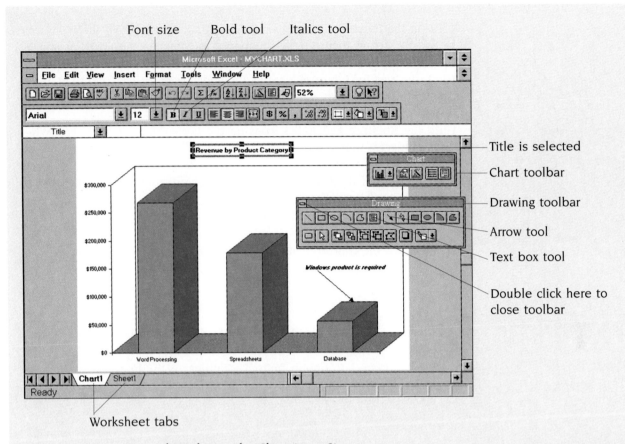

Font size   Bold tool   Italics tool

Title is selected

Chart toolbar

Drawing toolbar

Arrow tool

Text box tool

Double click here to close toolbar

Worksheet tabs

(h) Enhance the Chart (step 9)

FIGURE 4.7   Hands-on Exercise I (continued)

Step 9: Workbook tabs

➤ The 3-D column chart has been created in the chart sheet labeled Chart1. Click the **Sheet1 tab** to return to the worksheet and embedded chart from the first part of the exercise.

➤ Click the **Chart1 tab** to return to the chart sheet containing the 3-D column chart.

THE SHORTCUT MENU

Point to a cell (or group of selected cells), a worksheet tab, a toolbar, or chart (or a selected part of the chart), then click the **right mouse button** to display a shortcut menu. All shortcut menus are context sensitive and display commands appropriate for the selected item.

Step 10: Enhance the chart

➤ Point to any visible toolbar. Click the **right mouse button** to display the Toolbar shortcut menu. Click **Drawing** to display the Drawing toolbar, which will be used to enhance the chart.

➤ Click the **black arrow button** on the Drawing toolbar. The mouse pointer changes to a thin cross.

GRAPHS AND CHARTS   **143**

- ➤ Click in the chart where you want the arrow to begin, drag the mouse to extend the arrow, then release the mouse to complete the arrow as shown in Figure 4.7h.
- ➤ Click the **text box button** on the Drawing toolbar. The mouse pointer changes to a thin cross. Click in the chart where you want the text box to begin, drag the mouse to extend the box, then release the mouse.
- ➤ Click the **Boldface** and **Italics icons** on the Formatting toolbar. Type **Windows product is required** as shown in Figure 4.7h. Click outside the text box to complete the entry.
- ➤ Click the title of the Chart. You will see sizing handles around the title to indicate it has been selected.
- ➤ Click the arrow on the Font Size box on the Formatting toolbar. Click **18** to increase the size of the title.
- ➤ Double click the control-menu box on the Drawing toolbar to close it.
- ➤ Save the workbook.

Step 11: Print the worksheet
- ➤ Pull down the **File menu** and click **Print** to display the dialog box in Figure 4.7i.
- ➤ Click the appropriate option button according to the item(s) you wish to print; for example, click **Selected Sheet(s)** to print just the column chart. Click **OK** to print the selection.

(i) Print the Chart (step 10)

FIGURE 4.7 Hands-on Exercise 1 (continued)

➤ Click the **TipWizard icon** to open the TipWizard box. Click the **up arrow** on the tip box to review the suggestions made by the TipWizard during the exercise.

➤ Pull down the **File menu.** Click **Exit** to quit Excel.

MULTIPLE DATA SERIES

The charts presented so far displayed only a single data series—for example, the total sales by location or the total sales by product category. Although such charts are useful, it is often necessary to view *multiple data series* on the same chart.

Figure 4.8a displays the sales in each location according to product category. We see the rankings within each city, and further, that word processing is the leading application in three of the four cities. Figure 4.8b plots the identical data but in stacked columns rather than side-by-side.

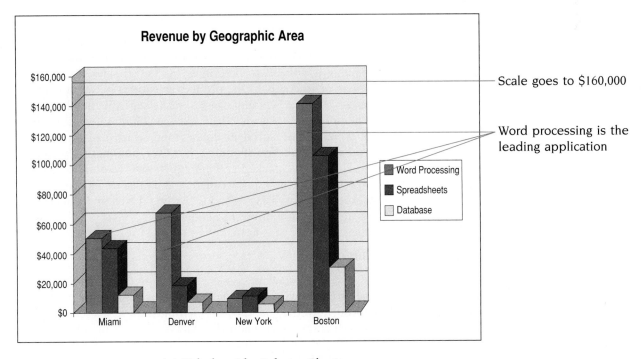

(a) Side-by-side Column Chart

FIGURE 4.8   Column Charts

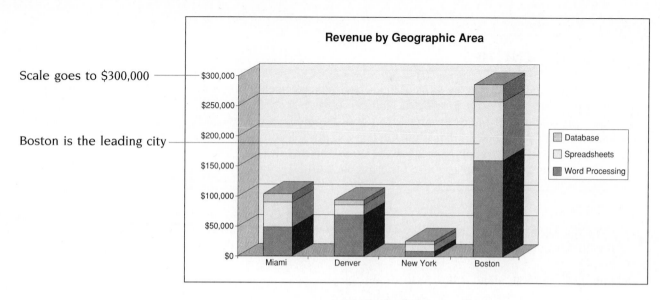

Scale goes to $300,000

Boston is the leading city

(b) Stacked Column Chart

FIGURE 4.8   Column Charts (continued)

The choice between the two types of charts depends on your message. If, for example, you want your audience to see the individual sales in each product category, the ***side-by-side columns*** are more appropriate. If, on the other hand, you want to emphasize the total sales for each city, the ***stacked columns*** are preferable. Note, too, the different scale on the Y axis in the two charts. The side-by-side columns in Figure 4.8a show the sales of each product category and so the Y axis goes only to $160,000. The stacked columns in Figure 4.8b, however, reflect the total sales for each city and thus the scale goes to $300,000.

The biggest difference is that the stacked column explicitly totals the sales for each city while the side-by-side column does not. The advantage of the stacked column is that the city totals are clearly shown and can be easily compared, and further, the relative contributions of each product category within each city are apparent. The disadvantage is that the segments within each column do not start at the same point, making it difficult to determine the actual sales for the individual product categories or to compare the product categories between cities.

Realize too, that for a stacked column chart to make sense, its numbers must be additive. This is true in Figure 4.8b, where the stacked columns consist of three components, each of which is measured in dollars, and which can be logically added together to produce a total. You shouldn't, however, automatically convert a side-by-side column chart to its stacked column equivalent. It would not make sense, for example, to convert a column chart that plots unit sales and dollar sales side by side, to a stacked column chart that adds the two. Units and dollars represent different physical concepts, and are not additive.

Rows versus Columns

Figure 4.9 illustrates a critical concept associated with multiple data series—whether the data series are in rows or columns. Figure 4.9a displays the worksheet we have been using throughout the chapter with multiple data series selected. Figure 4.9b contains the resultant chart when the data series are in rows (B4:E4, B5:E5, and B6:E6). Figure 4.9c displays the chart based on data series in columns (B4:B6, C4:C6, D4:D6, and E4:E6).

Both charts plot a total of twelve data points (three product categories for each of four locations) but group the data differently. Figure 4.9b displays the data

	A	B	C	D	E	F
1	Superior Software Monthly Sales					
2						
3		*Miami*	*Denver*	*New York*	*Boston*	*Total*
4	Word Processing	$50,000	$67,500	$9,500	$141,000	$268,000
5	Spreadsheets	$44,000	$18,000	$11,500	$105,000	$178,500
6	Database	$12,000	$7,500	$6,000	$30,000	$55,500
7	Total	$106,000	$93,000	$27,000	$276,000	$502,000

(a) The Worksheet

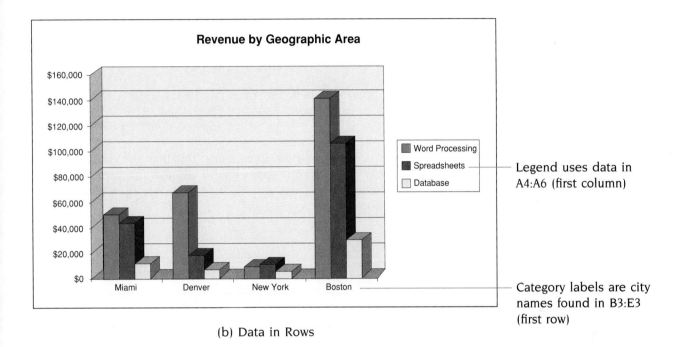

Revenue by Geographic Area

Legend uses data in A4:A6 (first column)

Category labels are city names found in B3:E3 (first row)

(b) Data in Rows

Revenue by Product Category

Legend uses data in B3:E3 (first row)

Category labels are product categories found in A4:A6 (first column)

(c) Data in Columns

FIGURE 4.9   Multiple Data Series

by city; that is, the sales of three product categories are shown for each of four cities. Figure 4.9c is the reverse and groups the data by product category; this time the sales of the four cities are shown for each of three product categories. The choice between the two depends on your message and whether you want to emphasize revenue by city or by product category. It sounds complicated, but it's not and Excel will create either chart for you according to your specifications.

➤ If you specify that the data are in rows (Figure 4.9b), the Wizard will
  — Use the first row (cells B3 through E3) in the selected range for the category labels on the X axis
  — Use the first column (cells A4 through A6) for the legend text
➤ If you specify that the data are in columns (Figure 4.9c), the Wizard will
  — Use the first column (cells A4 through A6) in the selected range for the category labels on the X axis
  — Use the first row (cells B3 through E3) for the legend text

Stated another way, the data series in Figure 4.9b are in rows. Thus there are three data series, one for each product category. The first data series plots the word processing sales in Miami, Denver, New York, and Boston; the second series plots the spreadsheet sales for each city, and so on.

The data series in Figure 4.9c are in columns. This time there are four data series, one for each city. The first series plots the Miami sales for word processing, spreadsheets, and database; the second series plots the Denver sales for each software category, and so on.

DEFAULT SELECTIONS

Excel makes a default determination as to whether the data are in rows or columns by assuming that you want fewer data series than categories. Thus, if the selected cells contain more rows than columns, it will assume that the data series are in columns. If, on the other hand, there are more columns than rows, it will assume the data series are in rows. You can override the default selection by editing the chart with the ChartWizard.

HANDS-ON EXERCISE 2:

Multiple Data Series

Objective To plot multiple data series in the same chart; to differentiate between data series in rows and columns; to create and save multiple charts associated with the same worksheet.

Step 1: Open the Software workbook
➤ Load Excel. Pull down the **File menu** and click **Open** (or click the **Open icon** on the Standard toolbar).
➤ Open the **SOFTWARE.XLS** workbook from the first exercise. Save this workbook as **MYCHART2.XLS** so that you can return to the original workbook if necessary.

- ➤ Reset the TipWizard as you have been doing throughout the text.
- ➤ Drag the mouse over cells **A3 through E6** as shown in Figure 4.10a.

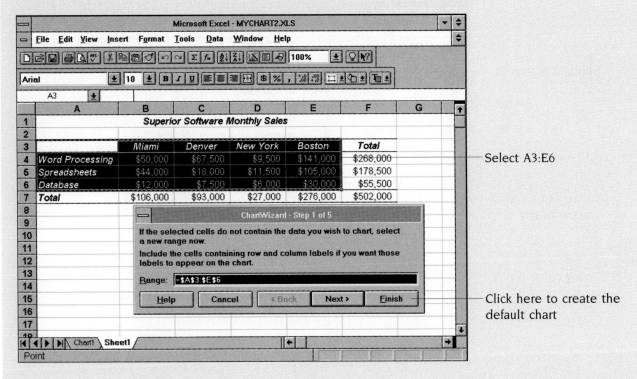

(a) Multiple Data Ranges (step 2)

FIGURE 4.10 Hands-on Exercise 2

THE F11 KEY

The F11 key is the fastest way to create a chart in its own worksheet. Select the data, including the legends and category labels, then press the F11 key to create the chart according to the default format built into Excel. After the *default chart* has been created, you can use the chart toolbar or shortcut menus to choose a different chart type and/or customize the formatting.

Step 2: Create the default chart
- ➤ Be sure that cells A3 through E6 are still selected. Pull down the **Insert menu.** Click **Chart.** Click **As New Sheet** to bring up step 1 of the ChartWizard as shown in Figure 4.10a.
- ➤ Click the **Finish command button** to skip the remaining steps in the ChartWizard and create the default chart in Figure 4.10b.
- ➤ The workbook now has two worksheets. The newly created chart is in the chart sheet labeled Chart1. The data on which the chart is based is in the worksheet labeled Sheet1.
- ➤ Save the workbook.

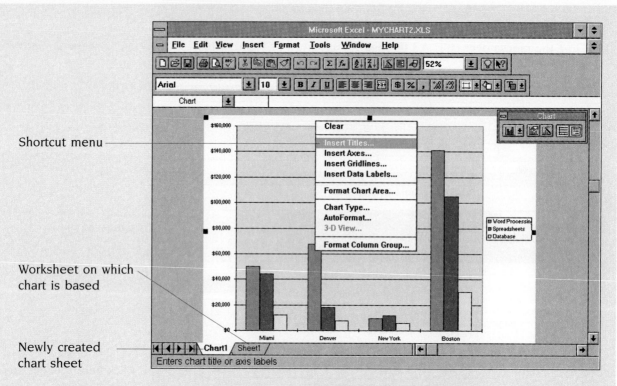

Shortcut menu

Worksheet on which chart is based

Newly created chart sheet

(b) The Default Chart (step 3)

FIGURE 4.10 Hands-on Exercise 2 (continued)

MOVING BETWEEN WORKSHEETS

Press Ctrl+PgDn to move to the next sheet (worksheet or chart sheet) in a workbook. Press Ctrl+PgUp to return to the previous sheet.

Step 3: Add the title

➤ Point just above the top gridline and click the **right mouse button** to produce the shortcut menu in Figure 4.10b. (If you see a different shortcut menu, press Esc, point elsewhere in the chart, and click the right mouse button a second time.)

➤ Click **Insert Titles** on the shortcut menu to bring up the Titles dialog box. Click the **check box** next to Chart Title. Click **OK.**

➤ Type the title of the chart, **Revenue by Geographic Area.** Press the **enter key.** The title should still be selected.

➤ Click the arrow on the Font Size box on the Formatting toolbar as shown in Figure 4.10c. Click **18** to increase the size of the title. Click outside the title to deselect it.

Step 4: Change the chart type

➤ Pull down the **Format menu** and click **AutoFormat.** (You can also point to the chart and click the **right mouse button,** then select **AutoFormat** from the shortcut menu.)

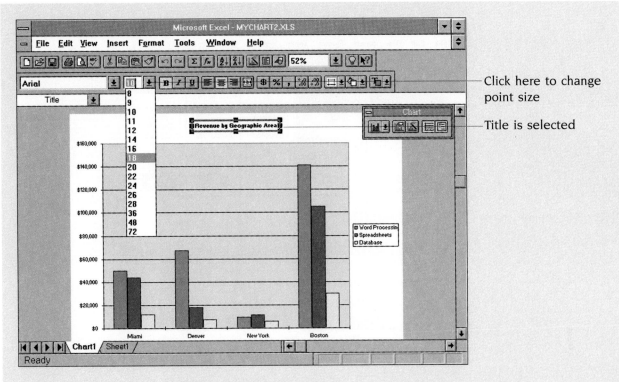

Click here to change point size

Title is selected

(c) Add the Title (step 3)

FIGURE 4.10 Hands-on Exercise 2 (continued)

➤ Click the **down arrow** on the Galleries list box to scroll through the chart types. Click **3-D Column** to produce the dialog box in Figure 4.10d.

➤ Click format number **1.** Click **OK.** The chart changes to a 3-D column chart.

Step 5: Renaming and copying sheets

➤ Point to the workbook tab labeled **Chart1.** Click the **right mouse button** to produce a shortcut menu pertaining to worksheet tabs. Click **Rename** to display the Rename Sheet dialog box. Type **Area.** Click **OK.**

➤ Point to the workbook tab labeled **Sheet1.** Click the **right mouse button** to produce a shortcut menu. Click **Rename** to display the Rename Sheet dialog box. Type **Sales Data.** Click **OK.**

➤ Point to the workbook tab named **Area** (that was previously Chart1). Click the **right mouse button.** Click **Move or Copy** to display the dialog box in Figure 4.10e.

➤ Click **Sales Data** in the Before Sheet list box. Click the check box to **Create a Copy.** Click **OK.**

➤ Excel pauses, then creates a duplicate chart sheet called Area (2).

COPYING A WORKSHEET

The fastest way to copy a worksheet (chart sheet) is to press and hold the Ctrl key as you drag the workbook tab to a second location in the workbook. Rename the copied tab (or any tab for that matter) by pointing to the tab and clicking the right mouse button to produce a shortcut menu. Click Rename, then enter the new name in the resulting dialog box.

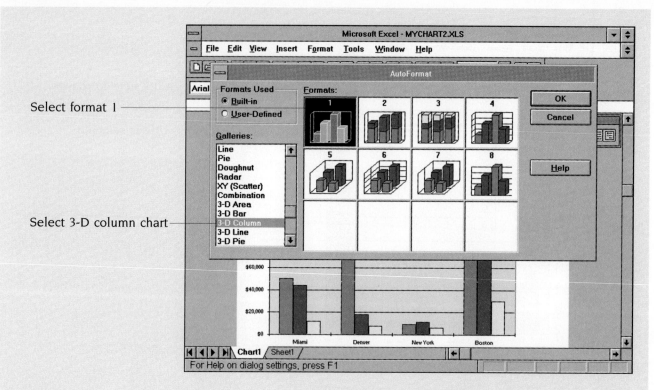

Select format 1

Select 3-D column chart

(d) The AutoFormat Command (step 4)

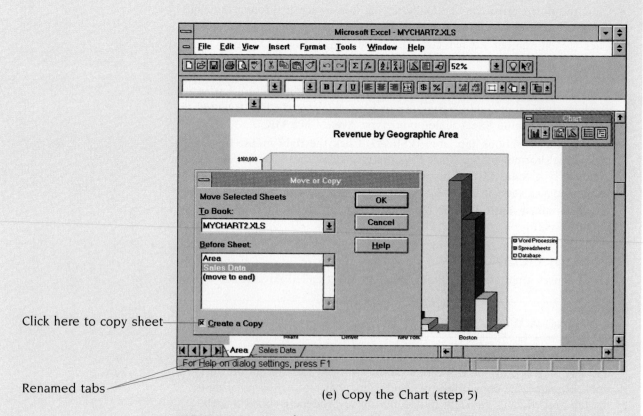

Click here to copy sheet

Renamed tabs

(e) Copy the Chart (step 5)

FIGURE 4.10 Hands-on Exercise 2 (continued)

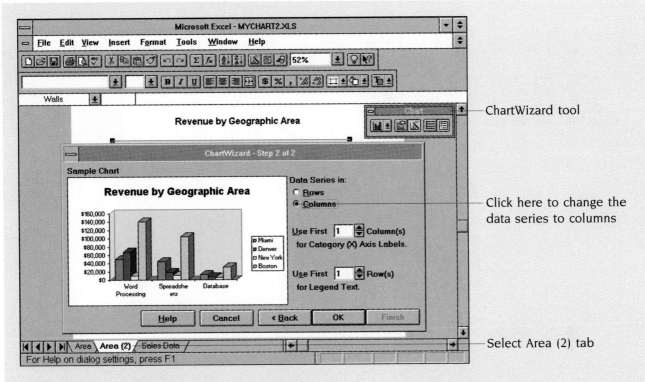

ChartWizard tool

Click here to change the data series to columns

Select Area (2) tab

(f) Change the Data Series (Step 6)

FIGURE 4.10   Hands-on Exercise 2 (continued)

Step 6: Change the data series
➤ Click the **Area (2) tab** to make it the active sheet. Click anywhere in the chart to select the chart.
➤ Click the **ChartWizard icon** on the Chart toolbar. You will see a dialog box indicating step 1 of 2 in ChartWizard. Click the **Next command button** to produce the dialog box in Figure 4.10f.
➤ Click the **Columns option button** to change the data series to columns, which will display the data by product category rather than location. Click **OK** to produce the chart in Figure 4.10g.
➤ Click anywhere in the title of the chart to select the title. Drag the mouse over **Geographic Area** to select this text. Type **Product Category.**
➤ Point to the workbook tab labeled **Area (2).** Click the **right mouse button** to produce a shortcut menu. Click **Rename** to produce the Rename Sheet dialog box. Type **Product.** Click **OK.** The workbook tabs are labeled Area, Product, and Sales Data, respectively.

Step 7: The stacked column chart
➤ Pull down the **Format menu** and click **AutoFormat.** (You can also point to the chart and click the **right mouse button,** then select **AutoFormat** from the shortcut menu.)
➤ Click format **2** in the Formats area. Click **OK.** The chart changes to a stacked bar chart as shown in Figure 4.10h.
➤ Double click the **control-menu box** or pull down the **File menu** and click **Exit** to quit Excel. Save the workbook if you are prompted to do so.

Chart title was changed

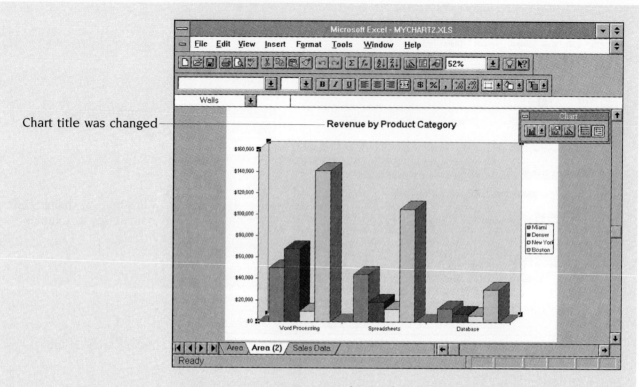

(g) Revenue by Product Category (step 6)

Stacked columns

Renamed tab

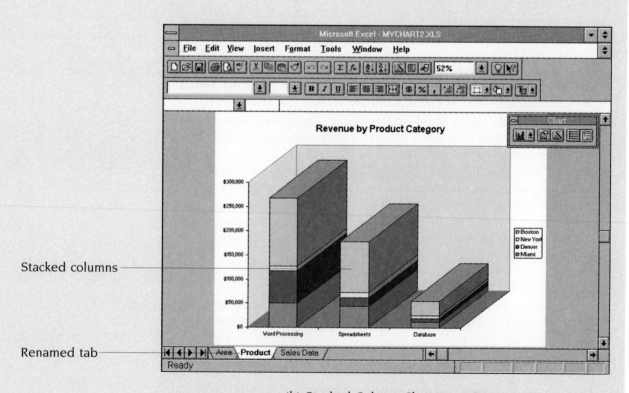

(h) Stacked Column Chart (step 7)

FIGURE 4.10   Hands-on Exercise 2 (continued)

OBJECT LINKING AND EMBEDDING

One of the primary advantages of Windows is the ability to produce a **compound document**—that is, a document with data from multiple applications. The memo in Figure 4.11 was created in Word for Windows and contains a worksheet and a chart that were created in Excel.

Pasting is the simplest way to develop a compound document and is done with the cut, copy, and paste commands present in all Windows applications. You cut or copy data onto the clipboard, then paste it into a different application to produce a compound document. There are, however, two disadvantages to the simple paste operation. First, it is *static,* meaning that if the data is subsequently changed in the original document, the change is not reflected in the compound document. Second, once data has been pasted into a compound document, it can no longer be edited using the original application.

Object Linking and Embedding *(OLE)* offers a superior way to share data. In actuality, there are two distinct techniques, linking and embedding. Our discussion focuses on linking. (See Appendix A in Grauer and Barber, *Exploring Word for Windows 6.0,* Prentice Hall, 1994, for an example of embedding.) The following terminology is essential:

➤ An **object** is any piece of data created by a Windows application—for example, a worksheet or a chart created in Excel.

➤ The **source document** is the place where the object originates. The source document—for example, an Excel worksheet—is created by the **server application,** Excel 5.0.

➤ The **destination document** is the file into which the object is placed. The destination document—for example, a Word document—is created by the **client application,** Word for Windows.

Linking provides a *dynamic* connection between the source and destination documents; that is, change the object in the source document and the object automatically changes in the destination document. The destination document does not contain the object per se, but a representation of the object, as well as a pointer (that is, a link) to the file containing the object. Linking requires that the object be saved prior to establishing the link.

The exercise that follows links two objects, a worksheet and a chart, to a Word document. As you do the exercise, both applications (Word and Excel) will be open, and it will be necessary to switch back and forth between the two. Thus the exercise also demonstrates the **multitasking** capability within Windows and the use of the **task list** to display the open applications. (See pages 53–77 in Grauer and Barber, *Exploring Windows,* Prentice Hall, 1994, for additional information on object linking and embedding, multitasking, and the common user interface.)

IN-PLACE EDITING

The in-place editing capability in Object Linking and Embedding 2.0 enables you to edit an embedded object by double clicking the object. The title bar continues to reflect the client application (e.g., Word for Windows), but the toolbar and pulldown menus will reflect the server application (e.g., Excel). There are two exceptions. The File and Window menus are those of the client application (Word) so that you can save the compound document and/or arrange multiple documents within the client application.

The May sales data clearly indicate that Boston is outperforming our other geographic areas. It is my feeling that Ms. Bost, the office supervisor, is directly responsible for its success and that she should be rewarded accordingly. In addition, we may want to think about transferring her to New York, as they are in desperate need of new ideas and direction. I will be awaiting your response after you have time to digest the information presented.

Superior Software Monthly Sales

	Miami	Denver	New York	Boston	Total
Word Processing	$50,000	$67,500	$9,500	$141,000	$268,000
Spreadsheets	$44,000	$18,000	$11,500	$105,000	$178,500
Database	$12,000	$7,500	$6,000	$30,000	$55,500
Total	$106,000	$93,000	$27,000	$276,000	$502,000

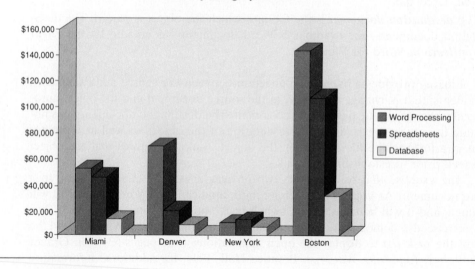

Revenue by Geographic Area

FIGURE 4.11   A Compound Document

HANDS-ON EXERCISE 3:

Object Linking and Embedding

Objective To create a compound document consisting of a memo, worksheet, and chart. The exercise is written for Word for Windows but will work with any Windows word processor that supports Object Linking and Embedding.

Step 1: Copy the worksheet to the clipboard
➤ Load Excel. Open the **MYCHART2.XLS** workbook that was used in the second exercise.
➤ Click the tab for **Sales Data.** Click cell **A1.** Drag the mouse over cells **A1 through F7** so that the entire worksheet is selected as shown in Figure 4.12a.

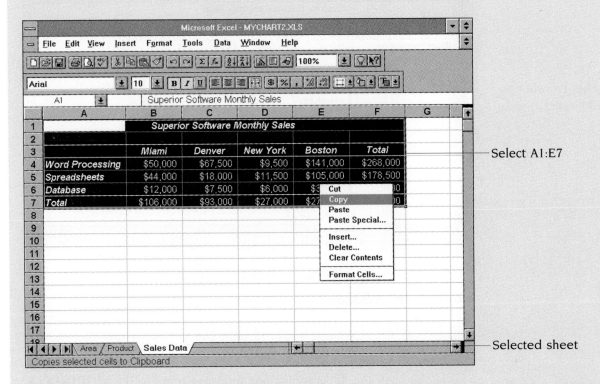

(a) Copy the Worksheet (step 1)

FIGURE 4.12 Hands-on Exercise 3 (continued)

➤ Press the **right mouse button** to display the shortcut menu. Click **Copy.** A flashing dashed line (the marquee) appears around the entire worksheet, indicating that it has been copied to the clipboard.

Step 2: Load Word
➤ Press **Ctrl+Esc** to display the task list as in Figure 4.12b. The contents of the task list depend on the applications open on your system. You should see Microsoft Excel - MYCHART2.XLS and Program Manager. You may also see other open applications.
➤ Double click **Program Manager** to switch to Program Manager.
➤ If necessary, open the group window that contains Word 6.0 (for example, Microsoft Office), then double click the **Microsoft Word 6.0 program icon** to load the word processor.

Step 3: Open the Word document
➤ Pull down the **File menu** and click **Open** (or click the **Open icon** on the standard toolbar).

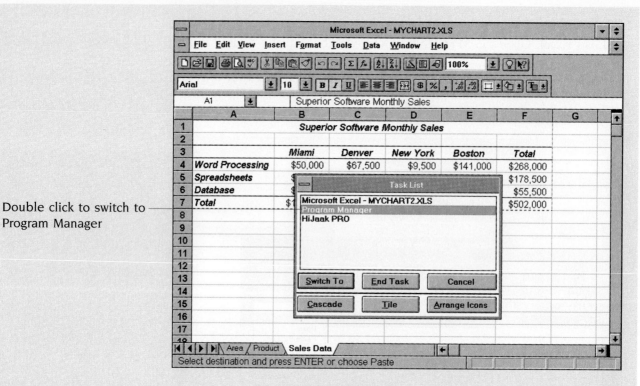

Double click to switch to Program Manager

(b) The Task List (step 2)

FIGURE 4.12   Hands-on Exercise 3 (continued)

➤ Click the **drop-down list box** to specify the appropriate drive (which is the same drive you have been using throughout the text).

➤ Scroll through the directory list box until you come to the **WORDDATA** directory. Double click this directory to make it the active directory.

➤ Double click **MEMO.DOC** to open this document. Type your name in the memo in place of Mr. White.

➤ Pull down the **View menu.** Click **Page Layout.** Pull down the **View menu** a second time. Click **Zoom.** Click the **Page Width** option button. Click **OK.** You should see the document in Figure 4.12c.

THE COMMON USER INTERFACE

The common user interface provides a sense of familiarity from one Windows application to the next. Even if you have never used Word for Windows, you will recognize many of the elements present in Excel. Both applications share a common menu structure with consistent ways to execute commands from those menus. The Standard and Formatting toolbars are present in both applications. Many keyboard shortcuts are also common—for example, Ctrl+Home and Ctrl+End to move to the beginning and end of a document or worksheet.

Step 4: Create the Link

➤ Press **Ctrl+End** to move to the end of the memo.

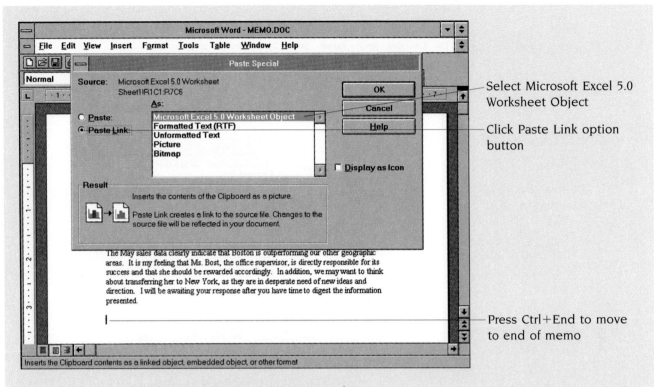

Select Microsoft Excel 5.0 Worksheet Object

Click Paste Link option button

Press Ctrl+End to move to end of memo

(c) The Word Document (steps 3 and 4)

FIGURE 4.12   Hands-on Exercise 3 (continued)

➤ Pull down the **Edit menu.** Click **Paste Special** to produce the dialog box in Figure 4.12c.

➤ Click **Microsoft Excel 5.0 Worksheet Object.** Click the **Paste Link** option button. Click **OK** to insert the worksheet into the document.

➤ Press the **enter key** twice (to allow for space between the worksheet and the chart that will be added in step 6).

➤ Pull down the **File menu** and click **Save** (or click the **Save button** on the Standard toolbar) to save the document.

Step 5: Return to Excel

➤ Press **Ctrl+Esc** to display the task list as in Figure 4.12d. Microsoft Excel and Word 6.0 are both on the task list because both applications are currently open. Microsoft Word - MEMO.DOC is currently highlighted because that is the active application and document.

➤ Double click **Microsoft Excel - MYCHART2.XLS** to return to the worksheet.

USE ALT+TAB TO SWITCH BETWEEN APPLICATIONS

Press and hold the Alt key while you press and release the Tab key repeatedly to cycle through the open applications. Release the Alt key when you see the title bar of the application you want.

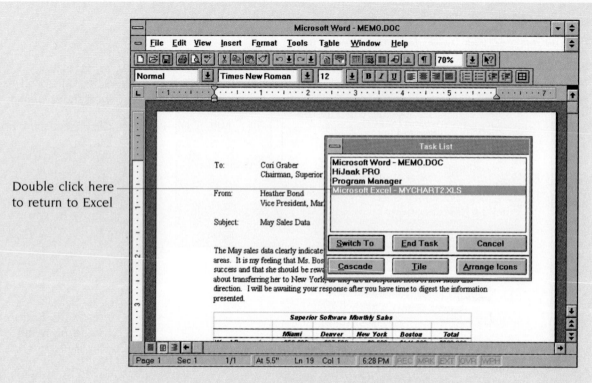

Double click here
to return to Excel

(d) Return to Excel (step 5)

FIGURE 4.12 Hands-on Exercise 3 (continued)

Step 6: Copy the chart to the clipboard
➤ Click outside the selected area to deselect the cells from step 1.
➤ Click the **Area tab** at the bottom of the worksheet window to activate the chart sheet.
➤ Point just inside the border of the chart. Click the left mouse button to select the chart. Be sure you have selected the entire chart and that you see the same sizing handles as in Figure 4.12e.
➤ Pull down the **Edit menu** and click **Copy** (or click the **Copy button** on the Standard toolbar). The marquee will appear around the chart to indicate it has been copied to the clipboard.
➤ Press and hold the **Alt key** while you press and release the **Tab key** repeatedly to cycle through the open applications. Release the Alt key when you see **Microsoft Word - MEMO.DOC** in a box in the middle of the screen as in Figure 4.12e.

Step 7: Add the chart to the document
➤ Press **Ctrl+End** to move to the end of the Word document.
➤ Pull down the **Edit menu.** Click **Paste Special.** Click the **Paste Link** option button. If necessary, click **Microsoft Excel 5.0 Chart Object.** Click **OK** to insert the chart into the document.
➤ Click the **up** or **down arrow** on the vertical scroll bar so that you will be able to see the worksheet and the chart as shown in Figure 4.12f. (Do not be concerned if you do not see all of the chart.)

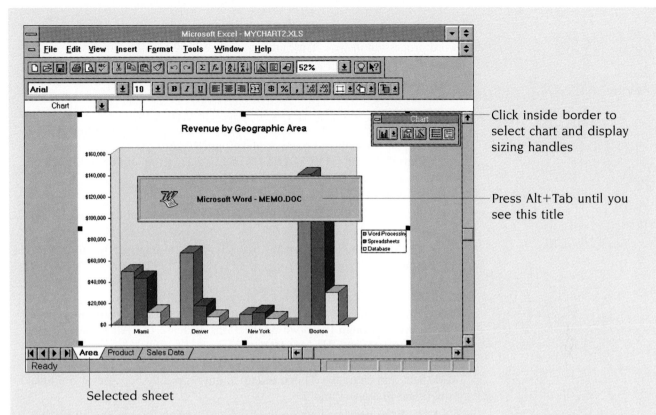

Click inside border to select chart and display sizing handles

Press Alt+Tab until you see this title

Selected sheet

(e) Copy the Chart (step 6)

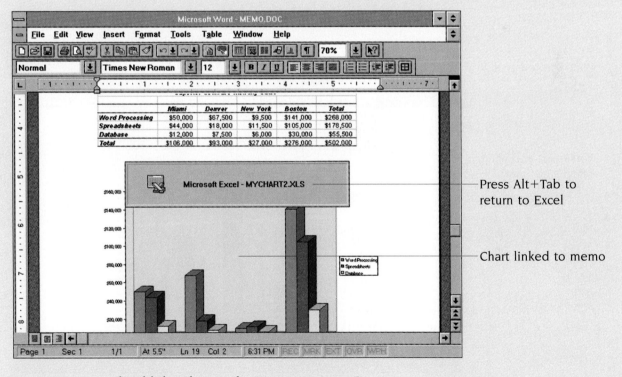

Press Alt+Tab to return to Excel

Chart linked to memo

(f) Add the Chart to the Document (step 7)

FIGURE 4.12 Hands-on Exercise 3 (continued)

➤ Look carefully at the worksheet and chart in the document. The sales for word processing in New York are currently $9,500 and the chart reflects this amount.

➤ Save the document.

Step 8: Modify the worksheet

➤ Press and hold the **Alt key** while you press and release the **Tab key** repeatedly to cycle through the open applications. Release the Alt key when you see **Microsoft Excel - MYCHART2.XLS** in a box in the middle of the screen as shown in Figure 4.12f.

➤ Click the **Sales Data tab** to return to the worksheet.

➤ Click in cell **D4.** Type **$200,000.** Press **enter.** You may need to widen the column to see the change.

➤ Click the **Area tab.** The chart has been modified automatically and reflects the increased sales for New York.

Step 9: The modified document.

➤ Press and hold the **Alt key** while you press and release the **Tab key** repeatedly to cycle through the open applications. Release the Alt key when you see **Microsoft Word - MEMO.DOC.**

➤ The active application changes back to Word as shown in Figure 4.12g. The worksheet and chart have been modified automatically because of the links established in steps 4 and 7.

➤ Click the **Print preview icon** on the Standard toolbar to view the entire document as shown in Figure 4.12h.

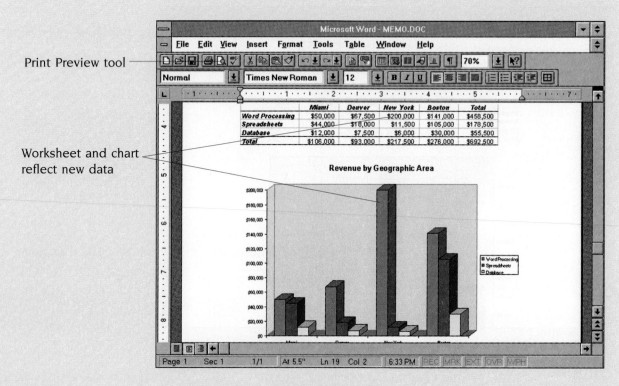

(g) The Modified Document (step 9)

FIGURE 4.12   Hands-on Exercise 3 (continued)

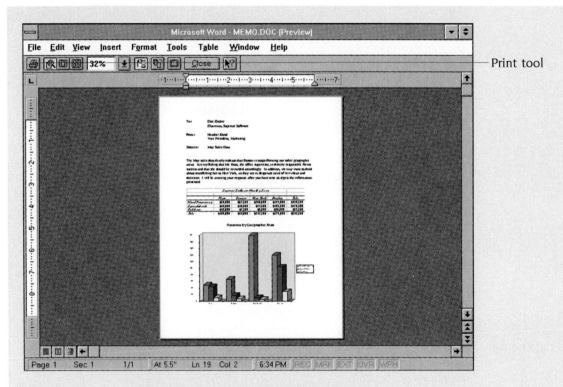

Print tool

(h) The Print Preview Command (step 9)

FIGURE 4.12 Hands-on Exercise 3 (continued)

➤ Click the **Print icon** to print the document. Click the **Close command button** to return to the document.
➤ Exit Word. Exit Excel. Exit Windows.

ADDITIONAL CHART TYPES

Excel offers a total of 15 chart types, each with several formats. The chart types are displayed in the ChartWizard (see Figure 4.5b) and are listed here for convenience. The chart types are: Area, Bar, Column, Line, Pie, Doughnut, Radar, XY (scatter), Combination, 3-D Area, 3-D Bar, 3-D Column, 3-D Line, 3-D Pie, and 3-D Surface.

It is not possible to cover every type of chart and so we concentrate on the most common. We have already presented the bar, column, and pie charts and continue with the line and combination charts. We use a different example, the worksheet in Figure 4.13a, which plots financial data for the National Widgets Corporation.

Line Chart

A *line chart* is appropriate for any message associated with time-related information—for example, the five-year trend of revenue and income in Figure 4.13b. A line chart plots one or more data series (e.g., revenue and income) against a descriptive category (e.g, year). As with a column chart, the quantitative values are plotted along the vertical scale (Y axis) and the descriptive category along the horizontal scale (X axis). The individual data points are connected by a straight line, and a legend is used to distinguish one data series from another.

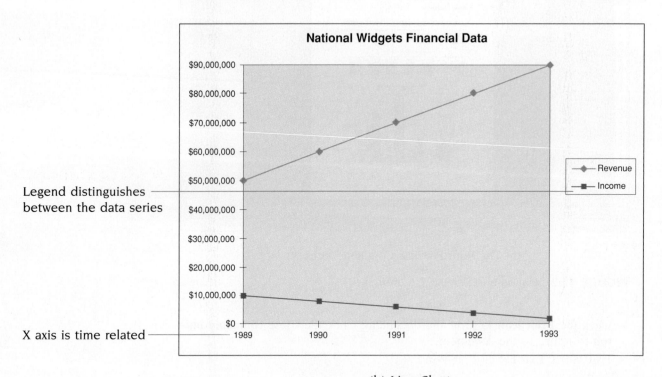

	A	B	C	D	E	F
1		*National Widgets Financial Data*				
2		*1989*	*1990*	*1991*	*1992*	*1993*
3	Revenue	$50,000,000	$60,000,000	$70,000,000	$80,000,000	$90,000,000
4	Income	$10,000,000	$8,000,000	$6,000,000	$4,000,000	$2,000,000
5	Stock Price	$40	$35	$36	$31	$24

(a) The Worksheet

Legend distinguishes between the data series

X axis is time related

(b) Line Chart

FIGURE 4.13   National Widgets Financial Data

Combination Chart

A *combination chart* is used when different scales are required for multiple data series that are plotted against the same descriptive variable. The chart in Figure 4.13c plots revenue, income, and stock price over the five-year period. The same scale can be used for revenue and income (both are in millions of dollars), but an entirely different scale is needed for the stock price. Note, too, how a line graph showing the declining price of the stock is imposed on the column chart showing the increased revenue. A picture is indeed worth a thousand words, and investors in National Widgets can see at a glance the true status of their company.

USE AND ABUSE OF CHARTS

The hands-on exercises in the chapter demonstrate how easily numbers in a worksheet can be converted to their graphic equivalent. *The numbers can, however, just as easily be converted into erroneous or misleading charts, a fact that is often overlooked.* Indeed, some individuals are so delighted just to obtain the charts, that they accept the data without question. Accordingly, we present two examples of

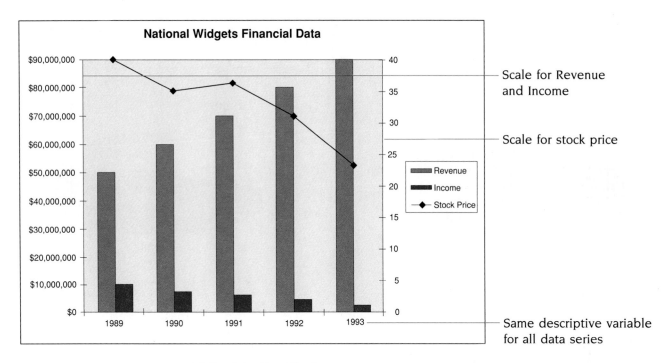

(c) Combination Chart

FIGURE 4.13   National Widgets Financial Data (continued)

statistically accurate, yet entirely misleading, graphical data, drawn from charts submitted by our students in response to homework assignments.

> Lying graphics cheapen the graphical art everywhere . . . When a chart on television lies, it lies millions of times over; when a *New York Times* chart lies, it lies 900,000 times over to a great many important and influential readers. The lies are told about the major issues of public policy—the government budget, medical care, prices, and fuel economy standards, for example. The lies are systematic and quite predictable, nearly always exaggerating the rate of recent change.
>
> **Edward Tufte**

Improper (omitted) Labels

The difference between *unit sales* and *dollar sales* is a concept of great importance, yet one that is often missed. Consider, for example, the two pie charts in Figures 4.14a and 4.14b, both of which are intended to identify the leading salesperson based on the underlying worksheet in Figure 4.14c. The charts yield two different answers, Jones and Smith, respectively, depending on which chart you use.

As you can see, the two charts reflect different percentages and would appear therefore to contradict each other. Both charts, however, are technically correct as the percentages depend on whether they express unit sales or dollar sales. *Jones is the leader in terms of units, whereas Smith is the leader in terms of dollars.* The latter is generally more significant, and hence the measure that is probably most important to the reader. Neither chart, however, was properly labeled (there is no

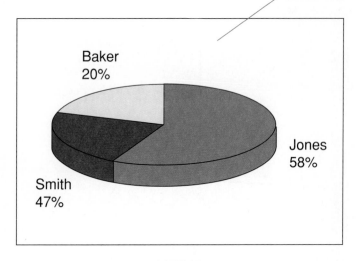

(a) Units

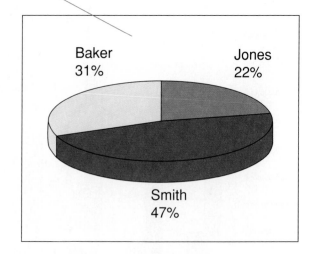

(b) Dollars

Sales Data - First Quarter								
		Jones		Smith		Baker		
		Units	Dollars	Units	Dollars	Units	Dollars	
Product 1	$1	200	$200	20	$20	30	$30	
Product 2	$5	50	$250	30	$150	30	$150	
Product 3	$20	5	$100	50	$1,000	30	$600	
	Totals:	255	$550	100	$1,170	90	$780	

(c) Underlying Spreadsheet

FIGURE 4.14   Omitted Labels

indication of whether units or dollars are plotted), which in turn may lead to erroneous conclusions on the part of the reader.

Adding Dissimilar Quantities

The conversion of a side-by-side column chart to a stacked column chart is a simple matter, requiring only a few mouse clicks. Because the procedure is so easy, however, it can be done without thought, and in situations where the stacked column chart is inappropriate.

Figures 4.15a and 4.15b display a side-by-side and a stacked column chart, respectively. One chart is appropriate and one chart is not. The side-by-side columns in Figure 4.15a indicate increasing sales in conjunction with decreasing profits. This is a realistic portrayal of the company, which is becoming less efficient because profits are decreasing as sales are increasing.

The stacked column chart in Figure 4.15b plots the identical numbers. It is deceptive, however, as it implies an optimistic trend whose stacked columns reflect a nonsensical addition. The problem is that although sales and profits are both measured in dollars, they should not be added together because the sum does not represent a meaningful concept.

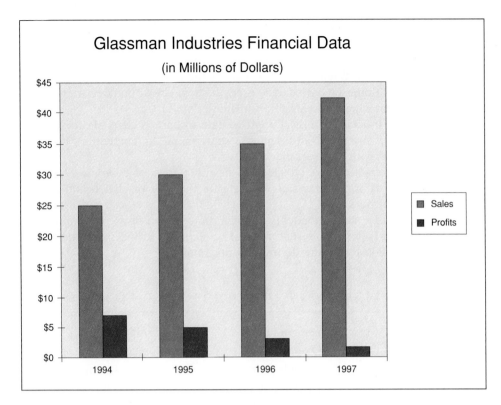

(a) Multiple Bar Chart

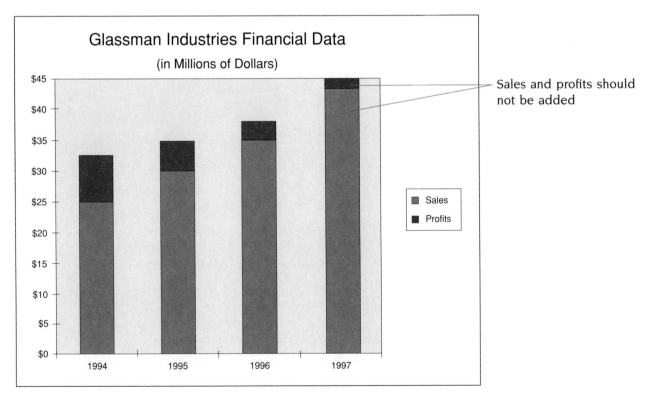

(b) Stacked Bar Chart

FIGURE 4.15 Adding Dissimilar Quantities

SUMMARY

A chart is a graphic representation of data in a worksheet. The type of chart chosen depends on the message to be conveyed. A pie chart is best for proportional relationships. A column or bar chart is used to show actual numbers rather than percentages. A line chart is preferable for time-related data.

The ChartWizard is the easiest way to create a chart. A chart may be embedded in a worksheet or created in a separate chart sheet. An embedded chart may be moved or sized within a worksheet.

Multiple data series may be specified in either rows or columns. Excel will choose the first row or column as appropriate for the category labels and legends to differentiate the series.

Object Linking and Embedding enables the creation of a compound document. The linking is dynamic in nature; that is, a change in the source document is automatically reflected in the destination document.

 ## Key Words and Concepts

3-D column chart	Data point	Multitasking
3-D pie chart	Data series	Object
Arrow tool	Default chart	Object Linking and
Bar chart	Destination document	Embedding (OLE)
Category label	Docked toolbar	Pie chart
Chart	Drawing toolbar	Server application
Chart sheet	Embedded chart	Side-by-side columns
Chart toolbar	Exploded pie chart	Sizing handles
ChartWizard	Floating toolbar	Source document
Client application	Legend	Stacked columns
Column chart	Line chart	Task list
Combination chart	Linking	Text box
Compound document	Multiple data series	

 ## Multiple Choice

1. Which type of chart is best to portray proportion or market share?
   (a) Pie chart
   (b) Line
   (c) Column chart
   (d) Combination chart

2. Which type of chart is typically used to display time-related data?
   (a) Pie chart
   (b) Line chart
   (c) Column chart
   (d) Combination chart

3. Which chart type is *not* suitable to display multiple data series?
   (a) Pie chart
   (b) Column chart
   (c) Both (a) and (b)
   (d) Neither (a) nor (b)

4. Which of the following is best to display *additive information* from multiple data series?
   (a) A column chart with the series stacked one on top of another
   (b) A column chart with the data series side by side
   (c) Both (a) and (b) are equally appropriate
   (d) Neither (a) nor (b) is appropriate

5. A workbook must contain:
   (a) A separate chart sheet for every worksheet
   (b) A separate worksheet for every chart sheet
   (c) Both (a) and (b)
   (d) Neither (a) nor (b)

6. Which of the following is true regarding an embedded chart?
   (a) It can be moved elsewhere within the worksheet
   (b) It can be made larger or smaller
   (c) Both (a) and (b)
   (d) Neither (a) nor (b)

7. Which of the following will produce a shortcut menu?
   (a) Pointing to a workbook tab and clicking the right mouse button
   (b) Pointing to an embedded chart and clicking the right mouse button
   (c) Pointing to a selected cell range and clicking the right mouse button
   (d) All of the above

8. Which of the following is done *prior* to invoking the ChartWizard?
   (a) The data series are selected
   (b) The location of the embedded chart within the worksheet is specified
   (c) Both (a) and (b)
   (d) Neither (a) nor (b)

9. Which of the following will display sizing handles when selected?
   (a) An embedded chart
   (b) The title of a chart
   (c) A text box or arrow
   (d) All of the above

10. Which of the following is true?
    (a) Ctrl+Esc displays the task list
    (b) Alt+Tab switches between open applications
    (c) Both a and b
    (d) Neither a nor b

11. Which of the following is true regarding the compound document (the memo containing the worksheet and chart) that was created in the chapter?
    (a) The worksheet is the source document and the memo is the destination document
    (b) Excel is the server application and Word for Windows is the client application
    (c) Both (a) and (b) above
    (d) Neither (a) nor (b)

12. In order to represent multiple data series on the same chart:
  (a) The data series must be in rows and the rows must be adjacent to one another on the worksheet
  (b) The data series must be in columns and the columns must be adjacent to one another on the worksheet
  (c) The data series may be in rows or columns so long as they are adjacent to one another
  (d) The data series may be in rows or columns with no requirement to be next to one another

13. If multiple data series are selected and rows are specified,
  (a) The first row will be used for the category (X axis) labels
  (b) The first column will be used for the legend
  (c) Both (a) and (b)
  (d) Neither (a) nor (b)

14. If multiple data series are selected and columns are specified,
  (a) The first column will be used for the category (X axis) labels
  (b) The first row will be used for the legend
  (c) Both (a) and (b)
  (d) Neither (a) nor (b)

15. Which of the following is true about the scale on the Y axis in a column chart that plots multiple data series side by side, versus one that stacks the values one on top of another?
  (a) The scale for the stacked columns will contain larger values than if the columns are plotted side by side
  (b) The scale for the side-by-side columns will contain larger values than if the columns are stacked
  (c) The values on the scale will be the same regardless of whether the columns are stacked or side by side
  (d) The values on the scale will be different, but it is not possible to tell which chart will contain the higher values

ANSWERS

1. a	**6.** c	**11.** c
2. b	**7.** d	**12.** d
3. a	**8.** a	**13.** c
4. a	**9.** d	**14.** c
5. d	**10.** c	**15.** a

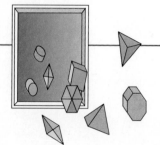

EXPLORING EXCEL

1. Use Figure 4.16a to match each action with its result; a given action may be used more than once or not at all.

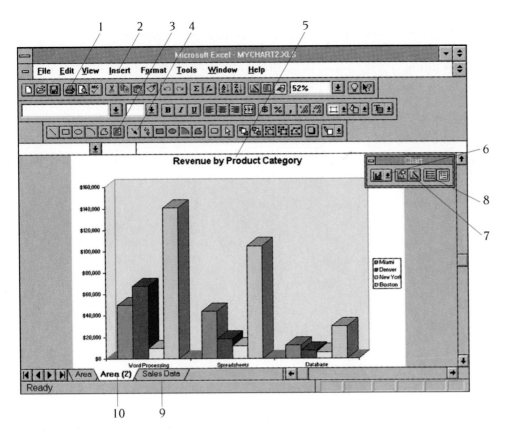

FIGURE 4.16 Screen for Problem 1

Action	Result
a. Click at 1	___ Activate the Sales Data sheet
b. Click at 2	___ Create gridlines on the chart
c. Click at 3	___ Change the font used for the chart title
d. Click at 4	
e. Double click at 5	___ Rename the current sheet
f. Click at 6	___ Place an arrow on the chart
g. Click at 7	___ Change the chart type
h. Click at 8	___ Create a new chart on its own sheet
i. Click at 9	___ Print the chart
j. Click the right mouse button at 10	___ Place a text box on the chart
	___ Change the data series from columns to rows

2. The value of a chart is aptly demonstrated by writing a verbal equivalent to a graphic analysis. Accordingly, write the corresponding written description of the information contained in Figure 4.8a. Can you better appreciate the effectiveness of the graphic presentation?

3. The worksheet of Figure 4.17c is the basis for the two charts of Figures 4.17a and 4.17b. Although the charts may at first glance appear to be satisfactory, each reflects a fundamental error. Discuss the problems associated with each.

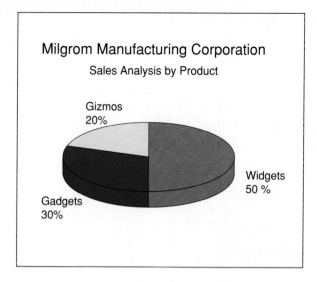

(a) Error 1

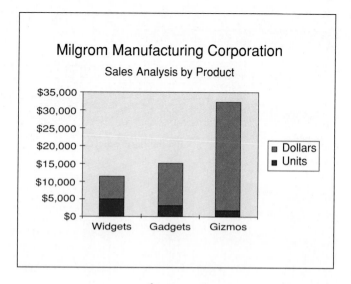

(b) Error 2

	Milgrom Manufacturing Corporation Sales Analysis by Product		
	Unit Price	Units Sold	Revenue
Widgets	$1.25	5,000	$6,250
Gadgets	$4.00	3,000	$12,000
Gizmos	$14.99	2,000	$29,980

(c) The Worksheet

FIGURE 4.17 Worksheet for Problem 3

4. Using the data disk: Answer the following with respect to the worksheet and embedded chart in Figure 4.18, which are found on the data disk in the file PROB0404.XLS.

   a. Retrieve the worksheet from the data disk.

   b. Change the number in cell B8 to 6,000,000. What corresponding changes take place in the chart?

   c. Change the format for cells B5 to F9 to comma with no decimals. What corresponding changes take place in the chart?

   d. Change the entry in cell A5 to Madrid. What corresponding changes take place in the chart?

   e. Change the chart to a three-dimensional pie chart.

   f. Use the text box and arrow tools to add an appropriate callout.

   g. Type your name in cell A11 of the worksheet.

   h. Print the worksheet and embedded chart and submit it to your instructor.

   i. What would happen if you press the Del key when the chart is selected? Is there anyway to retrieve the chart after it has been deleted?

	A	B	C	D	E	F
1			Unique Boutiques			
2			Sales 1990-1993			
3						
4	Store	1990	1991	1992	1993	Totals
5	Miami	$2,500,000	$2,750,000	$2,900,000	$2,700,000	$10,850,000
6	London	$4,300,000	$4,500,000	$3,800,000	$4,200,000	$16,800,000
7	Paris	$1,800,000	$2,200,000	$2,700,000	$2,900,000	$9,600,000
8	Rome	$1,750,000	$1,500,000	$1,900,000	$1,750,000	$6,900,000
9	Totals	$10,350,000	$10,950,000	$11,300,000	$11,550,000	$44,150,000
10						
11						
12						
13						
14						
15				Unique Boutiques		
16						
17			$18,000,000			
18						
19			$16,000,000			
20			$14,000,000			
21						
22			$12,000,000			
23			$10,000,000			
24						
25			$8,000,000			
26			$6,000,000			
27						
28			$4,000,000			
29			$2,000,000			
30						
31			$0			
32			Miami London Paris Rome			

FIGURE 4.18 Spreadsheet and Graph for Problem 4

5. Answer the following with respect to the worksheet and embedded chart of Figure 4.19.

   a. Are the data series in rows or columns?

   b. How many data series are there?

   c. Which cells contain the category labels?

   d. Which cells contain the legends?

   e. Create the worksheet and embedded chart as shown in Figure 4.19.

   f. Create a second chart in its own chart sheet, which reverses the data series by switching rows and columns.

   g. Add your name to the worksheet, then print the entire workbook and submit it to your instructor.

6. The worksheet in Figure 4.20 is to be used as the basis for several charts depicting information on hotel capacities.

   a. What type of chart is best to show the proportion of total capacity for each hotel?

   b. Which data range(s) should be selected prior to invoking the ChartWizard in order to produce the chart of part a?

   c. What type of chart is best to compare the capacities of the individual hotels to one another?

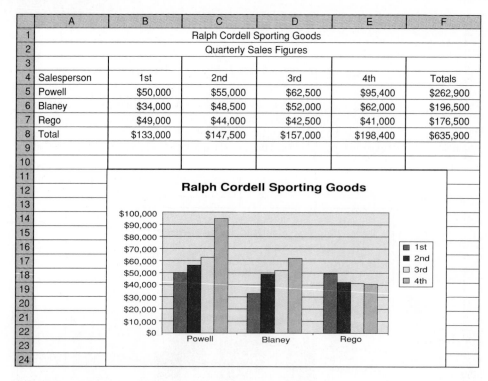

	A	B	C	D	E	F
1			Ralph Cordell Sporting Goods			
2			Quarterly Sales Figures			
3						
4	Salesperson	1st	2nd	3rd	4th	Totals
5	Powell	$50,000	$55,000	$62,500	$95,400	$262,900
6	Blaney	$34,000	$48,500	$52,000	$62,000	$196,500
7	Rego	$49,000	$44,000	$42,500	$41,000	$176,500
8	Total	$133,000	$147,500	$157,000	$198,400	$635,900

FIGURE 4.19 Spreadsheet and Graph for Problem 5

	A	B	C	D
1		*Hotel Capacities and Room Rates*		
2				
3		*Total*	*Standard*	*Deluxe*
4	*Hotel*	*Rooms*	*Rate*	*Rate*
5	Holiday Inn	250	$100	$150
6	Hyatt	450	$120	$175
7	Ramada Inn	300	$115	$190
8	Sheraton	750	$95	$150
9	Marriott	575	$100	$175
10	Hilton	600	$80	$120
11	Best Western	350	$75	$125
12	Days Inn	750	$50	$100

FIGURE 4.20 Spreadsheet for Problem 6

d. Which data range(s) should be selected prior to invoking the ChartWizard in order to produce the chart of part c?

e. What type of chart is best to show the comparison of the standard and deluxe room rates for all of the hotels, with the two different rates side-by-side for each hotel?

f. Which data range(s) should be selected prior to invoking the ChartWizard in order to produce the chart of part e?

g. Could the information in part f be conveyed in a stacked column chart?

h. The worksheet in Figure 4.20 exists on the data disk as PROB0406.XLS. Create the three charts in parts a, c, and e in separate sheets, then print each chart sheet and submit all three pages to your instructor.

7. Figure 4.21 contains a worksheet with sales data for the chain of four Michael Moldof clothing boutiques. Use the worksheet to develop the following charts:

a. A pie chart showing the percentage of total sales attributed to each store.

b. Redo part a as a column chart.

c. A stacked column chart showing total dollars for each store, broken down by clothing category.

d. A stacked column chart showing total dollars for each clothing category, broken down by store.

e. The worksheet in Figure 4.21 exists on the data disk as PROB0407.XLS. Create the charts in parts a, b, c, and d in separate sheets, then print each chart and submit all four pages to your instructor.

	A	B	C	D	E	F
1		Michael Moldof Men's Boutique - January Sales				
2						
3		Store 1	Store 2	Store 3	Store 4	Total
4	Slacks	$25,000	$28,750	$21,500	$9,400	$84,650
5	Shirts	$43,000	$49,450	$36,900	$46,000	$175,350
6	Underwear	$18,000	$20,700	$15,500	$21,000	$75,200
7	Accessories	$7,000	$8,050	$8,000	$4,000	$27,050
8						
9	Total	$93,000	$106,950	$81,900	$80,400	$362,250

FIGURE 4.21 Spreadsheet for Problem 7

8. The compound document in Figure 4.22 contains a memo and combination chart and is an excellent way to review the entire chapter.

a. Create the combination chart:
   ➤ Retrieve the PROB0408.XLS workbook from the data disk.
   ➤ Select cells A2 through F5.
   ➤ Click the ChartWizard icon and create the combination chart of Figure 4.13c, which appeared earlier in the chapter. (Select combination chart in step 2 and format 2 in step 3.)

b. Create the memo:
   ➤ Use Alt+Tab to switch to Program Manager. Open the program group that contains Word for Windows. Double click on the program icon to open the word processor.
   ➤ Enter the text of the memo as shown in Figure 4.22. Add your name as the financial consultant.
   ➤ Save the word processing document as PROB0408.DOC.

c. Create the compound document:
   ➤ Use Alt+Tab to return to Excel.
   ➤ Click the chart to select it. The sizing handles should appear to indicate that the chart has been selected. Pull down the Edit menu. Click Copy.
   ➤ Use Alt+Tab to return to Word for Windows.
   ➤ Pull down the Edit menu. Click Paste Special. Select Microsoft Excel 5.0 Chart Object as the data type from the list box. Click Paste Link to bring the chart into the memo.
   ➤ Save the memo. Print the memo and submit it to your instructor.

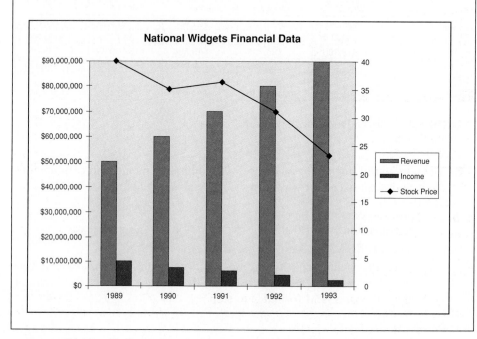

Steven Stocks
Financial Investments
100 Century Towers
New York, New York 10020

To: Carlos Rosell

From: Steven Stocks

Subject: Status Report on National Widgets Corporation

I have uncovered some information that I feel is important to the overall health of your investment portfolio. The graph below clearly shows that while revenues for National Widgets have steadily increased since 1989, income (profits) have steadily decreased. In addition, the stock price is continuing to decline. Although at one time I felt that a turnaround was imminent, I am no longer so optimistic and am advising you to cut your losses and sell your National Widgets stock as soon as possible.

FIGURE 4.22 Compound Document for Problem 8

Case Studies

University Enrollments

Your assistantship next semester has placed you in the Provost's office, where you are to help create a presentation for the Board of Trustees. The Provost is expected to make recommendations to the Board regarding the expansion of some programs and the reduction of others. You are expected to help the Provost by developing a series of charts to illustrate enrollment trends. The Provost has provided you with an Excel workbook (ENROLMNT.XLS, which is found on the data disk) with summary data over the last several years.

The Budget

Deficit reduction or not, the Federal government spends billions more than it takes in; for example, in fiscal year 1992, government expenditures totaled $1,380 billion versus income of only $1,090, leaving a deficit of $290 billion. Thirty percent of the income came from social security and Medicare taxes, 35% from personal income taxes, 7% from corporate income taxes, and 7% from excise, estate, and other miscellaneous taxes. The remaining 21% was borrowed.

Social security and Medicare accounted for 33% of the expenditures, and the defense budget another 24%. Social programs, including Medicare and Aid to Families with Dependent Children, totalled 17%. Community development (consisting of agricultural, educational, environmental, economic, and space programs) totalled 10% of the budget. Interest on the national debt amounted to 14%. The cost of law enforcement and government itself accounted for the final 2%.

Use the information contained within this problem to create the appropriate charts to reflect the distribution of income and expenditures. Do some independent research and obtain data on the budget, the deficit, and the national debt for the years 1945, 1967, and 1980. The numbers may surprise you; for example, how does the interest expense for the current year compare to the total budget in 1967 (at the height of the Viet Nam war) to the total budget in 1945 (at the end of World War II)? Create charts to reflect your findings, then write your representative in Congress. We are in trouble!

The Annual Report

Corporate America spends a small fortune to produce its annual reports, which are readily available to the public at large. Choose any company and obtain a copy of its most recent annual report. Consolidate the information in the company's report to produce a two-page document of your own. Your report should include a description of the company's progress in the last year, a worksheet with any data you deem relevant, and at least two charts in support of the worksheet or written material. Formatting is important, and you are expected to use a word processor in addition to the worksheet to present the information in an attractive manner.

One Step Beyond

What exactly is a macro? More important, how can macros help you be more productive in using Excel? How do you create a macro? What is the difference between playing and recording a macro? How can you assign a macro to a button that appears on the worksheet? Use the on-line help facility and/or the reference manual to teach yourself the basics of macros, then create three macros in conjunction with creating, displaying, and/or modifying a chart.

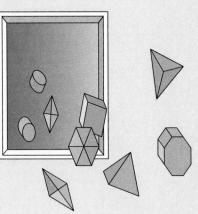

5

List and Data Management: Converting Data to Information

After reading this chapter you will be able to:

1. Create a list within Excel; explain the importance of proper planning and design prior to creating the list.

2. Add records to, edit records in, and delete records from an existing list; explain the significance of data validation.

3. Distinguish between data and information; describe how one is converted to the other.

4. Use the Sort command; distinguish between an ascending and a descending sort, and between a primary, secondary, and tertiary key.

5. Use the DSUM, DAVERAGE, DMAX, DMIN, and DCOUNT functions.

6. Use the AutoFilter and Advanced Filter commands to display a subset of a list.

7. Use the Subtotals command to summarize data in a list.

8. Create a pivot table.

OVERVIEW

All businesses maintain data in the form of lists. Companies have lists of their employees; magazines and newspapers keep lists of their subscribers; political candidates monitor voter lists; and so on. This chapter presents the fundamentals of list management as it is implemented in Excel.

We begin with the definition of basic terms such as field and record, then cover the commands to create a list, to add a new record, and to modify or delete an existing record. We distinguish between data and information and describe how one is converted to the other. We introduce the AutoFilter command to display selected records in a list and the Sort command to rearrange the list. We discuss the database functions and the associated criteria range. We also cover the use of subtotals and pivot tables, two powerful capabilities associated with lists.

All of this is accomplished using Excel, and although it may eventually be necessary for you to use a dedicated database program (e.g., Microsoft Access), you will be pleased at what you can do. The chapter contains three hands-on exercises, each of which focuses on a different aspect of data management.

LIST AND DATA MANAGEMENT

Imagine, if you will, that you are the personnel director of a medium-sized company with offices in several cities, and that you manually maintain employee data for the company. Accordingly, you have recorded the specifics of every individual's employment (the name, salary, location, title, and so on) in a manila folder, and you have stored the entire set of folders in a file cabinet. You have written the name of each employee on the label of his or her folder and have arranged the folders alphabetically in the filing cabinet.

File Terminology

The manual system just described illustrates the basics of data management terminology. The set of manila folders corresponds to a *file.* Each individual folder is known as a *record.* Each data item within a folder is called a *field.* The folders are arranged alphabetically in the file cabinet (according to the employee name on the label of each folder) to simplify the retrieval of any given folder. The records in a computer-based system can also be in sequence according to a specific field known as a *key.*

Excel maintains data in the form of a list. A *list* is an area in the worksheet that contains rows of similar data. A list is also a simple database, where the rows correspond to records and the columns correspond to fields. The first row contains the column headings or *field names.* Each additional row in the list contains a record. Each column represents a field. Each cell in the worksheet contains a value for a specific field in a specific record. Every record (row) contains the same fields (columns) in the same order.

Figure 5.1 contains an employee list with 13 records. There are four fields in every record—name, location, title, and salary. The field names should be meaningful and must be unique. (A field name may contain up to 255 characters, but you should keep them as short as possible so that a column does not become too wide and thus difficult to work with.) The arrangement of the fields within a record is consistent from record to record. The employee name was chosen as the key, and the records are shown in alphabetical order.

Normal business operations will require you to make repeated trips to the filing cabinet to maintain the accuracy of the data. You will have to add a folder whenever a new employee is hired. In similar fashion, you will have to remove the folder of any employee who leaves the company, or modify the data in the folder of any employee who receives a raise, changes location, and so on.

File Maintenance

Changes of this nature (additions, deletions, and modifications) are known as *file maintenance* and constitute a critical activity within any system. Indeed, without adequate file maintenance, the data in a system quickly becomes obsolete and the information useless. Imagine, if you will, the consequences of producing a payroll based on data that is six months old.

Nor is it sufficient simply to add, edit, or delete a record without adequate checks on the validity of the data. Look carefully at the entries in Figure 5.1 and ask yourself if a computer-generated report listing employees in the Chicago office

	A	B	C	D
1	Name	Location	Title	Salary
2	Adams	Atlanta	Trainee	$19,500
3	Adamson	Chicago	Manager	$52,000
4	Brown	Atlanta	Trainee	$18,500
5	Charles	Boston	Account Rep	$40,000
6	Coulter	Atlanta	Manager	$100,000
7	Frank	Miami	Manager	$75,000
8	James	Chicago	Account Rep	$42,500
9	Johnson	Chicag	Account Rep	$47,500
10	Manin	Boston	Accout Rep	$49,500
11	Marder	Chicago	Account Rep	$38,500
12	Milgrom	Boston	Manager	$57,500
13	Rubin	Boston	Account Rep	$45,000
14	Smith	Atlanta	Account Rep	$65,000

FIGURE 5.1 The Employee List

will include Johnson? Will a report listing account reps include Manin? The answer to both questions is *no* because the data for these employees was entered incorrectly. Chicago is misspelled in Johnson's record (the "o" was omitted). Account Rep is misspelled in Manin's title. You know that Johnson works in Chicago, but the computer does not, because it is searching for the correct spelling. It also will omit Manin from a listing of account reps because of the misspelled title.

GARBAGE IN, GARBAGE OUT (GIGO)

A computer does exactly what you tell it to do, which is not necessarily what you want it to do. It is absolutely critical, therefore, that you validate the data that goes into a system or else the associated information will not be correct. No system, no matter how sophisticated, can produce valid output from invalid input. In other words, garbage in—garbage out.

IMPLEMENTATION IN EXCEL

Creating a list is easy because there is nothing to do other than enter the data. You choose the area in the worksheet that will contain the list, then you enter the field names in the first row of the designated area. Each field name should be a unique text entry. The data for the individual records are entered in the rows immediately below the row of field names.

Once a list has been created, you can edit any field in any record just as you can change the entries in an ordinary worksheet. The **Insert Rows command** lets you add new rows (records) to the list. The **Insert Columns** (fields) **command** lets you add a new field. The **Delete command** in the Edit menu enables you to delete a row or column. You can also use shortcut menus to execute commands more quickly. And finally, you can also format the entries within a list just as you format the entries in a worksheet.

Data Form Command

A **data form** provides an easy way to add, edit, and delete records. The **Form command** in the Data menu displays a dialog box based on the fields in the list and containing the command buttons shown in Figure 5.2. Every record in the list contains the same fields in the same order—for example, Name, Location, Title, and Salary in Figure 5.2. (You do not have to enter a value for every field; that is, you may leave a field blank if the data is unknown.)

LIST SIZE AND LOCATION

A list can appear anywhere within a worksheet and can theoretically be as large as an entire worksheet (16,384 rows by 256 columns). Practically the list will be much smaller, giving rise to the following guideline for its placement within a worksheet: leave at least one blank column and one blank row between the list and the other entries in the worksheet. Excel can then select the list automatically in conjunction with commands for list management such as sorting or filtering.

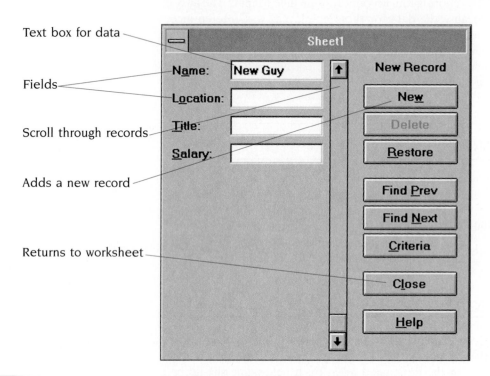

FIGURE 5.2 The Data Form Command

Next to each field name is a text box into which data can be entered for a new record, or edited for an existing record. The scroll bar to the right of the data is used to scroll through the records in the list. The functions of the various command buttons are explained briefly:

New   Adds a record to the end of a list, then lets you enter data in that record. The formulas for computed fields, if any, are automatically copied to the new record.

Delete   Removes the currently displayed record. The remaining records move up one row.

Restore   Cancels any changes made to the current record. (You must press the Restore button before pressing Enter or scrolling to a new record.)

	Displays the previous record that matches the existing criteria.
Find Prev	Displays the previous record that matches the existing criteria.
Find Next	Displays the next record that matches the existing criteria.
Criteria	Displays a dialog box to specify the criteria for the Find Prev or Find Next command buttons.
Close	Closes the data form and returns to the worksheet.
Help	Accesses on-line Help.

PRESS TAB, NOT ENTER

Press the Tab key to move to the next field within a data form. Press Shift+Tab to move to the previous field. Press the enter key only after the last field has been entered to move to the first field in the next record.

SORT COMMAND

The **Sort command** arranges the records in a list according to the value of one or more fields within the list. You can sort the list in **ascending** (low to high) or **descending** (high to low) **sequence.** (Putting a list in alphabetical order is considered an ascending sort.) You can also sort on more than one field at a time—for example, by location and then alphabetically within each location. The field(s) on which you sort the list is (are) known as the key(s).

The records in Figure 5.3a are listed alphabetically (in ascending sequence according to employee name). Adams comes before Adamson, who comes before Brown, and so on. Figure 5.3b displays the identical records but in descending sequence by employee salary. The employee with the highest salary is listed first and the employee with the lowest salary is last.

Figure 5.3c sorts the employees on two keys, by location and by descending salary within location. Location is the more important or **primary key.** Salary is the less important or **secondary key.** The Sort command groups employees according to like values of the primary key (location), then within the like values of the

	A	B	C	D	
1	**Name**	**Location**	**Title**	**Salary**	
2	Adams	Atlanta	Trainee	$19,500	
3	Adamson	Chicago	Manager	$52,000	Ascending order by name
4	Brown	Atlanta	Trainee	$18,500	
5	Charles	Boston	Account Rep	$40,000	
6	Coulter	Atlanta	Manager	$100,000	
7	Frank	Miami	Manager	$75,000	
8	James	Chicago	Account Rep	$42,500	
9	Johnson	Chicago	Account Rep	$47,500	
10	Manin	Boston	Account Rep	$49,500	
11	Marder	Chicago	Account Rep	$38,500	
12	Milgrom	Boston	Manager	$57,500	
13	Rubin	Boston	Account Rep	$45,000	
14	Smith	Atlanta	Account Rep	$65,000	

(a) Ascending Sequence (by name)

FIGURE 5.3 The Sort Command

Descending sequence
by salary

	A	B	C	D
1	**Name**	**Location**	**Title**	**Salary**
2	Coulter	Atlanta	Manager	$100,000
3	Frank	Miami	Manager	$75,000
4	Smith	Atlanta	Account Rep	$65,000
5	Milgrom	Boston	Manager	$57,500
6	Adamson	Chicago	Manager	$52,000
7	Manin	Boston	Account Rep	$49,500
8	Johnson	Chicago	Account Rep	$47,500
9	Rubin	Boston	Account Rep	$45,000
10	James	Chicago	Account Rep	$42,500
11	Charles	Boston	Account Rep	$40,000
12	Marder	Chicago	Account Rep	$38,500
13	Adams	Atlanta	Trainee	$19,500
14	Brown	Atlanta	Trainee	$18,500

(b) Descending Sequence (by salary)

Primary key (ascending)

Secondary key (descending)

	A	B	C	D
1	**Name**	**Location**	**Title**	**Salary**
2	Coulter	Atlanta	Manager	$100,000
3	Smith	Atlanta	Account Rep	$65,000
4	Adams	Atlanta	Trainee	$19,500
5	Brown	Atlanta	Trainee	$18,500
6	Milgrom	Boston	Manager	$57,500
7	Manin	Boston	Account Rep	$49,500
8	Rubin	Boston	Account Rep	$45,000
9	Charles	Boston	Account Rep	$40,000
10	Adamson	Chicago	Manager	$52,000
11	Johnson	Chicago	Account Rep	$47,500
12	James	Chicago	Account Rep	$42,500
13	Marder	Chicago	Account Rep	$38,500
14	Frank	Miami	Manager	$75,000

(c) Primary and Secondary Keys

FIGURE 5.3 The Sort Command (continued)

primary key arranges them in descending sequence (ascending could have been chosen just as easily) according to the secondary key (salary). Excel provides a maximum of three keys—primary, secondary, and tertiary.

CHOOSE A CUSTOM SORT SEQUENCE

Alphabetic fields are normally arranged in strict alphabetical order. You can, however, choose a custom sort sequence such as the days of the week or the months of the year. Pull down the Data menu, click Sort, click the Options command button, then click the arrow on the drop-down list box to choose a sequence other than the alphabet. You can also create your own sequence. Pull down the Tools menu, click Options, click the Custom Lists tab, then enter the items in ascending sequence in the List Entries Box.

HANDS-ON EXERCISE 1:

Creating and Maintaining a List

Objective To modify an employee list by adding, editing, and deleting records; to introduce the Data Form and Data Sort commands; to use the spell check.

Step 1: Open the employee workbook
➤ Load Excel. Pull down the **File menu** and click **Open** (or click the **Open icon** on the standard toolbar). Open the **EMPLOYEE.XLS** workbook.
➤ Pull down the **File menu.** Click the **Save As** command. Save the workbook as **EMPLOYE2.XLS.**

Step 2: Add a record (the Data Form command)
➤ Click a single cell anywhere within the employee list (cells A1 through D14).
➤ Pull down the **Data menu.** Click **Form** to produce a dialog box with data for the first record in the file (Adams). Click the **New command button** to clear the dialog boxes and begin entering a new record.
➤ Enter the data for **Elofson** as shown in Figure 5.4a, using the Tab key to move from field to field within the data form. Click the **Close command button** after entering the salary.
➤ Elofson has been added to the worksheet and appears in row 15.
➤ Save the workbook.

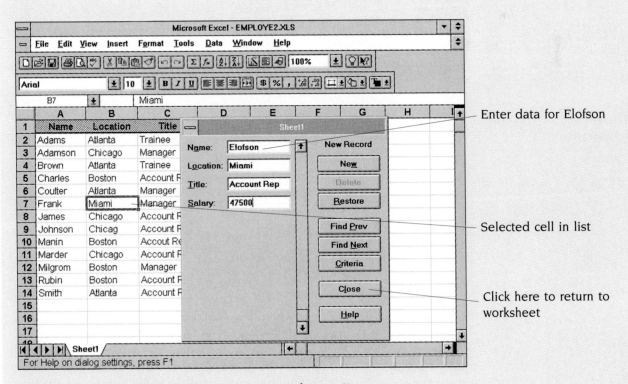

(a) The Data Form Command (step 2)

FIGURE 5.4 Hands-on Exercise 1

EMPHASIZE THE COLUMN HEADINGS (FIELD NAMES)

Use a different font, alignment, style (boldface and/or italics), pattern, or border to distinguish the first row containing the field names from the remaining rows (records) in a list. Do not use blank rows to separate the column headings as such entries will be interpreted as records within the list.

Step 3: Add a record (the Insert Rows command)

➤ Click the **row heading** for **row 8.**

➤ Pull down the **Insert menu.** Click **Rows** as shown in Figure 5.4b.

➤ Add the data for **Gillenson,** who works in **Miami** as an **Account Rep** with a salary of **$55,000.**

➤ Save the workbook.

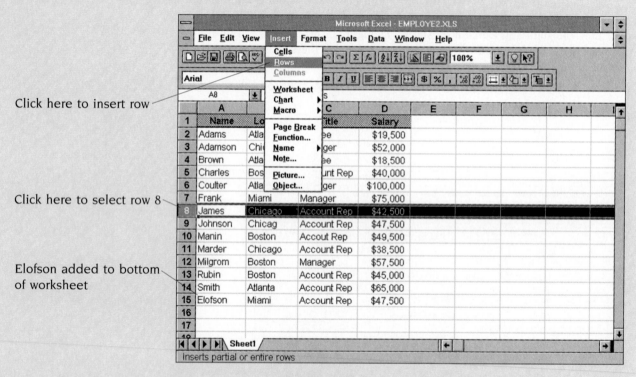

(b) The Insert Rows Command (step 3)

FIGURE 5.4   Hands-on Exercise I (continued)

Step 4: Sort the list

➤ Click a single cell anywhere within the employee list (cells A1 through D16).

➤ Pull down the **Data menu.** Click **Sort** to produce the dialog box in Figure 5.4c.

— Click the arrow in the **Sort By text box.** Select **Name** as the key.

— The Ascending option button is selected as the default sequence. Do not change this.

— The Header Row option button is selected, which indicates that the field names appear in the first row of the list. Do not change this.

➤ Click **OK** to sort the list and return to the worksheet.

➤ The employee names should be in alphabetical order. If you made a mistake, click the **Undo icon** on the Standard toolbar to cancel the sort and begin again.

➤ Save the workbook.

ONE KEY—ONE CLICK

Use the Ascending or Descending Sort button on the Standard toolbar if you are sorting on a single key. Click any cell in the column containing the desired key, then click the Ascending or Descending button to perform the sort. Click the Undo button immediately after executing the Sort command if the results are different from what you expect.

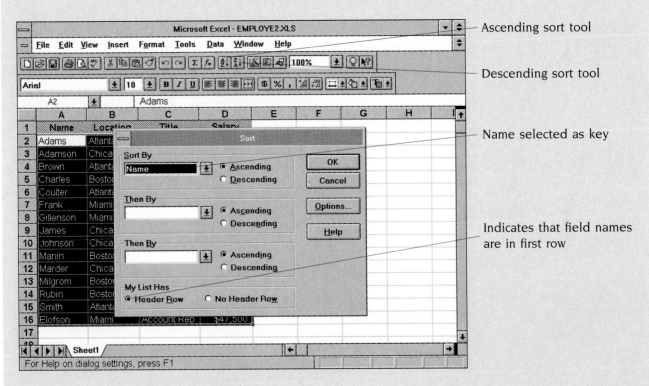

(c) Sort the Employee List (step 4)

FIGURE 5.4 Hands-on Exercise 1 (continued)

THE FREEZE PANES COMMAND

The Freeze Panes command is useful with large lists as it prevents the column headings (field names) from scrolling off the screen. Click in the first column in the row below the field names (the row containing the first record). Pull down the Window menu, then click the Freeze Panes command. A horizontal line will appear under the field names to indicate that the command is in effect.

Step 5: Delete a record

➤ A record may be deleted by using the Edit Delete command or the Data Form command; both methods will be illustrated to delete the record for Frank, which is currently in row 8.

➤ To delete a record by using the Edit Delete command:
  — Click the **row heading** in **row 8** (containing the record for Frank, which is slated for deletion).
  — Pull down the **Edit menu.** Click **Delete.** The record for Frank has been deleted.

➤ Click the **Undo icon** on the Standard toolbar. The record for Frank has been restored.

➤ To delete a record by using the Data Form command:
  — Click a single cell within the employee list.
  — Pull down the **Data menu.** Click **Form** to produce the data form.
  — Click the **down arrow** in the scroll bar until you come to the record for Frank.
  — Click the **Delete command button.**
  — Click **OK** in response to the warning message shown in Figure 5.4d. (The record cannot be undeleted as it could with the Edit Delete command.)
  — Click **Close** to close the Data Form.

➤ Save the workbook.

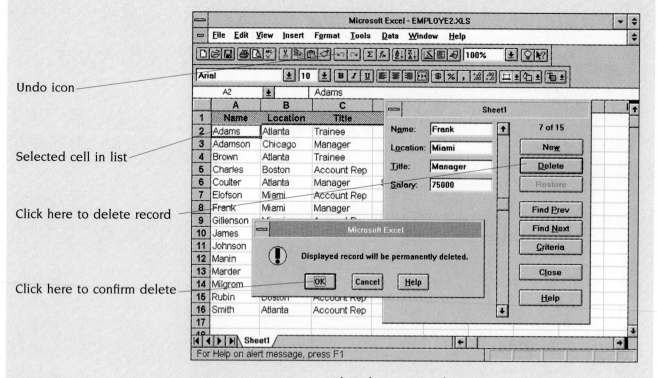

(d) Delete a Record (step 5)

FIGURE 5.4 Hands-on Exercise 1 (continued)

Step 6: Insert a field

➤ Click the **column heading** in column D.

➤ Click the **right mouse button** to produce a shortcut menu. Click **Insert.** The employee salaries have been moved to column E.

➤ Click cell **D1.** Type **Hire Date** and press **enter.** Adjust the column width if necessary.

HIRE DATE VERSUS LENGTH OF SERVICE

An individual's date of hire and length of service provide equivalent information as one is calculated from the other. It might seem easier, therefore, to store the length of service in the list and avoid the calculation, but this would be a mistake. The length of service changes continually, whereas the hire date remains constant. Thus the date, not the length of service, should be stored. Similar reasoning applies to a person's birth date and age.

Step 7: Enter the hire dates

➤ Dates may be entered in several different formats. Do not be concerned if Excel displays the date in a different format from the way you entered it.
— Type **11/24/93** in cell D2. Press the **down arrow key.**
— Type **Nov 24, 1993** in cell D3. Type a **comma** after the day but do not type a period after the month. Press the **down arrow key** to move to cell D4.
— Type **=Date(93,11,24)** in cell D4. Press the **down arrow key.**
— Type **11-24-93** in cell D5.
➤ For ease of data entry, assume that the next several employees were hired on the same day, 3/16/92.
— Click in cell **D6.** Type **3/16/92.** Press **enter.**
— Click in cell **D6.** Click the **Copy button** on the Standard toolbar, which produces a marquee around cell D6.
— Drag the mouse over cells **D7 through D10.** Click the **Paste** button on the Standard toolbar to complete the copy operation.
— Press **Esc** to remove the marquee around cell D6.
➤ The last five employees were hired one year apart, beginning October 31, 1989.
— Click in cell **D11** and type **10/31/89.**
— Click in cell **D12** and type **10/31/90.**
— Select cells **D11 and D12.**
— Drag the **fill handle** at the bottom of cell D12 over cells **D13, D14, and D15.** Release the mouse to complete the autofill operation.
➤ Save the workbook.

DATES AND THE FILL HANDLE

The AutoFill facility is the fastest way to create a series of dates. Enter the first two dates in the series, then select both cells and drag the fill handle over the destination range. Excel will create a series based on the increment between the first two cells; for example, if the first two dates are one month apart, the remaining dates will also be one month apart.

Step 8: Format the date

➤ Click in the column heading for **column D** to select the column of dates as in Figure 5.4e.
➤ Click the **right mouse button** to produce a shortcut menu. Click **Format Cells.**

➤ Click the **Number tab** in the Format Cells dialog box. Click **Date** in the Category list box. Click the first date format (m/d/yy). Click **OK.**

➤ Save the workbook.

Click here to select column D

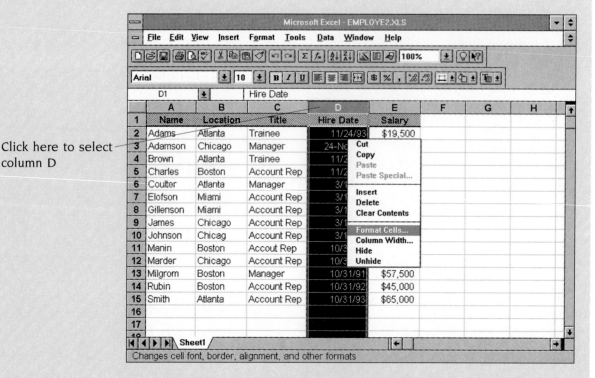

(e) Insert a Field (steps 6, 7, and 8)

Cells B2:C15 are selected

Misspelled word found

Click here to accept correct spelling

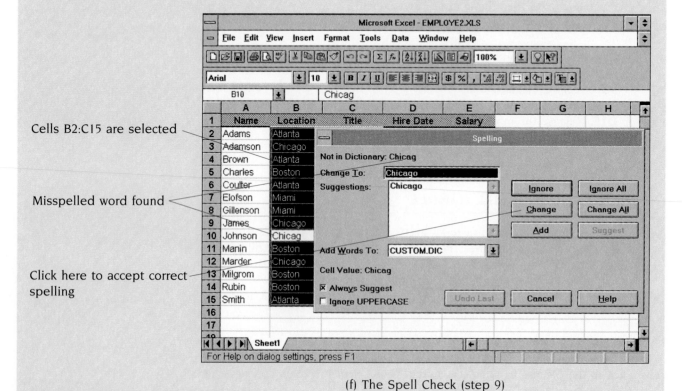

(f) The Spell Check (step 9)

FIGURE 5.4   Hands-on Exercise 1 (continued)

Step 9: The spell check
- ➤ Select cells **B2:C15** as in Figure 5.4f. Pull down the **Tools menu** and click **Spelling** (or click the **Spell Check icon**).
- ➤ Chicago is misspelled in cell B10 and flagged accordingly. Click the **Change command button** to accept the suggested correction and continue checking the document.
- ➤ Account is misspelled in cell C11 and flagged accordingly. Click **Account** in the Suggestions list box, then click the **Change command button** to correct the misspelling.
- ➤ Excel will indicate that it has finished checking the selected cells. Click **OK** to return to the worksheet.
- ➤ Save the workbook.
- ➤ Click the **TipWizard icon** to open the TipWizard box. Click the **up (down) arrow** to review the suggestions made by the TipWizard during the exercise.
- ➤ Exit Excel.

DATA VERSUS INFORMATION

Data and information are not synonymous. *Data* refers to a fact or facts about a specific record such as an employee's name, title, or salary. *Information,* on the other hand, is data that has been rearranged into a form perceived as useful by the recipient. A list of employees earning more than $35,000 or a total of all employee salaries are examples of information produced from data about individual employees. Put another way, data is the raw material and information is the finished product.

Decisions in an organization are based on information rather than raw data; for example, in assessing the effects of a proposed across-the-board salary increase, management needs to know the total payroll rather than individual salary amounts. In similar fashion, decisions about next year's hiring will be influenced, at least in part, by knowing how many individuals are currently employed in each job category.

Data is converted to information through a combination of database commands and functions whose capabilities are illustrated by the reports in Figure 5.5. The reports are based on the employee list as it existed at the end of the hands-on exercise. Each report presents the data in a different way, according to the information requirements of the end-user. As you view each report, ask yourself how it was produced; that is, what was done to the data to produce the information in the report?

Figure 5.5a contains a master list of all employees, listing employees by location and alphabetically within location. The report was created by sorting the list on two keys, location and name. Location is the more important or primary key. Name is the less important or secondary key. The sorted report groups employees according to like values of the primary key (location), then, within the primary key, groups the records according to the secondary key (name).

The report in Figure 5.5b displays a subset of records in the list by including only the employees that meet specific criteria. The criteria can be based on any field or combination of fields—in this case employees whose salaries are between $40,000 and $60,000. The employees are shown in descending order of salary. The employee with the highest salary is listed first.

The report in Figure 5.5c displays summary statistics for the selected employees—in this example, the salaries for the account reps within the company. Reports of this nature omit the salaries of individual employees (known as detail lines), in order to present an aggregate view of the organization.

Location Report

Name	Location	Title	Hire Date	Salary
Adams	Atlanta	Trainee	11/24/93	$19,500
Brown	Atlanta	Trainee	11/24/93	$18,500
Coulter	Atlanta	Manager	3/16/92	$100,000
Smith	Atlanta	Account Rep	10/31/93	$65,000
Charles	Boston	Account Rep	11/24/93	$40,000
Manin	Boston	Account Rep	10/31/89	$49,500
Milgrom	Boston	Manager	10/31/91	$57,500
Rubin	Boston	Account Rep	10/31/92	$45,000
Adamson	Chicago	Manager	11/24/93	$52,000
James	Chicago	Account Rep	3/16/92	$42,500
Johnson	Chicago	Account Rep	3/16/92	$47,500
Marder	Chicago	Account Rep	10/31/90	$38,500
Elofson	Miami	Account Rep	3/16/92	$47,500
Gillenson	Miami	Account Rep	3/16/92	$55,000

(a) Employees by Location and Name within Location

Employees Earning Between $40,000 and $60,000

Name	Location	Title	Hire Date	Salary
Milgrom	Boston	Manager	11/24/91	$57,500
Gillenson	Miami	Account Rep	3/16/92	$55,000
Adamson	Chicago	Manager	11/24/93	$52,000
Manin	Boston	Account Rep	10/31/89	$49,500
Johnson	Chicago	Account Rep	3/16/92	$47,500
Elofson	Miami	Account Rep	3/16/92	$47,500
Rubin	Boston	Account Rep	10/31/92	$45,000
James	Chicago	Account Rep	3/16/92	$42,500
Charles	Boston	Account Rep	11/24/93	$40,000

(b) Employees Earning between $40,000 and $60,000

Summary Statistics	
Total Salary for Account Reps:	$430.500
Average Salary for Account Reps:	$47,833
Maximum Salary for Account Reps:	$65,000
Minimum Salary for Account Reps:	$38,500
Number of Account Reps:	9

(c) Account Rep Summary Data

FIGURE 5.5   Data versus Information

CITY, STATE, AND ZIP CODE—ONE FIELD OR THREE?

The answer depends on whether the fields are referenced as a unit or individually. However, given the almost universal need to sort or select on zip code, it is almost invariably defined as a separate field. An individual's last name, first name, and middle initial are defined as individual fields for the same reason.

AutoFilter Command

A **filtered list** displays a subset of records that meet specific criteria. It is created by the **AutoFilter command,** which temporarily hides those records (rows) that do not meet the criteria. The hidden records are *not* deleted; they are simply not displayed.

Figure 5.6a shows the employee list as it exists at the end of the first hands-on exercise. Figure 5.6b displays a filtered version of the list in which only the Atlanta employees (in rows 2, 4, 6, and 15) are visible. The remaining employees are still in the worksheet but are not shown.

Execution of the AutoFilter command places drop-down arrows next to each column label (field name). Clicking a drop-down arrow produces a list of the unique values for that field, enabling you to establish the criteria for the filtered list. Thus, to display the Atlanta employees, click the drop-down arrow for Location, then click Atlanta.

A filter condition can be imposed on multiple columns as shown in Figure 5.6c. The filtered list in Figure 5.6c contains just the Atlanta employees. Clicking the arrow next to Title, then clicking Manager, will filter the list further to display the employees who work in Atlanta *and* who have Manager as a title. Only one employee meets both conditions as shown in Figure 5.6d. The drop-down arrows next to Location and Title are displayed in blue to indicate that a filter is in effect for these columns.

The AutoFilter command has additional options as can be seen from the drop-down list boxes in Figures 5.6a and 5.6c. *All* removes existing criteria in the column and effectively "unfilters" the list. *Custom* enables you to use the relational operators (=, >, <, >=, <=, or <>) within the criteria. *Blanks* or *Nonblanks* select the records missing or containing data in the specified column.

	A	B	C	D	E	
1	Name	Location	Title	Hire Date	Salary	
2	Adams	(All)	Trainee	11/24/93	$19,500	Drop-down arrows are next
3	Adamson	(Custom...)	Manager	11/24/93	$52,000	to each field name
		Atlanta				
4	Brown	Boston	Trainee	11/24/93	$18,500	
5	Charles	Chicago	Account Rep	11/24/93	$40,000	
		Miami				
6	Coulter	(Blanks)	Manager	3/16/92	$100,000	
7	Elofson	(NonBlanks)	Account Rep	3/16/92	$47,500	
8	Gillenson	Miami	Account Rep	3/16/92	$55,000	Click here to display unique
9	James	Chicago	Account Rep	3/16/92	$42,500	values in Location field
10	Johnson	Chicago	Account Rep	3/16/92	$47,500	
11	Manin	Boston	Account Rep	10/31/89	$49,500	
12	Marder	Chicago	Account Rep	10/31/90	$38,500	
13	Milgrom	Boston	Manager	10/31/91	$57,500	
14	Rubin	Boston	Account Rep	10/31/92	$45,000	
15	Smith	Atlanta	Account Rep	10/31/93	$65,000	

(a) Unfiltered List

	A	B	C	D	E	
1	Name	Location	Title	Hire Date	Salary	
2	Adams	Atlanta	Trainee	11/24/93	$19,500	
4	Brown	Atlanta	Trainee	11/24/93	$18,500	
6	Coulter	Atlanta	Manager	3/16/92	$100,000	
15	Smith	Atlanta	Account Rep	10/31/93	$65,000	

(b) Filtered List (Atlanta employees)

FIGURE 5.6 Filter Command

Figure 5.6e shows the list under a custom filter condition, which selects all employees whose salaries are greater than $40,000. (The filter condition for Atlanta Managers that existed in Figure 3.6d was removed prior to imposing the custom filter.)

Click here to display unique values in Title field

	A	B	C	D	E
1	Name ↓	Locatio ↓	Title ↓	Hire Date ↓	Salary ↓
2	Adams	Atlanta	(All)	11/24/93	$19,500
4	Brown	Atlanta	(Custom...)	11/24/93	$18,500
			Account Rep		
6	Coulter	Atlanta	Manager	3/16/92	$100,000
15	Smith	Atlanta	Trainee	10/31/93	$65,000
16			(Blanks)		
17			(NonBlanks)		

(c) Imposing a Second Condition

	A	B	C	D	E
1	Name ↓	Locatio ↓	Title ↓	Hire Date ↓	Salary ↓
6	Coulter	Atlanta	Manager	3/16/92	$100,000

(d) Filtered List (Atlanta Managers)

	A	B	C	D	E
1	Name ↓	Locatio ↓	Title ↓	Hire Date ↓	Salary ↓
3	Adamson	Chicago	Manager	11/24/93	$52,000
6	Coulter	Atlanta	Manager	3/16/92	$100,000
7	Elofson	Miami	Account Rep	3/16/92	$47,500
8	Gillenson	Miami	Account Rep	3/16/92	$55,000
9	James	Chicago	Account Rep	3/16/92	$42,500
10	Johnson	Chicago	Account Rep	3/16/92	$47,500
11	Manin	Boston	Account Rep	10/31/89	$49,500
13	Milgrom	Boston	Manager	10/31/91	$57,500
14	Rubin	Boston	Account Rep	10/31/92	$45,000
15	Smith	Atlanta	Account Rep	10/31/93	$65,000

(e) Custom Filter (salary > $40,000)

FIGURE 5.6 Filter Command (continued)

Advanced Filter Command

The **Advanced Filter command** extends the capabilities of the AutoFilter command in two important ways. It enables you to develop more complex criteria than are possible with the AutoFilter Command. It also enables you to copy the selected records to a separate area in the worksheet. The Advanced Filter command is illustrated in detail in the hands-on exercise that follows shortly.

Criteria Range

A **criteria range** is used with both the Advanced Filter command and the database functions that are discussed in the next section. It is defined independently of the list on which it operates, and it exists as a separate area in the worksheet. A criteria range must be at least two rows deep and one column wide.

The simplest criteria range consists of two rows and as many columns as there are fields in the list. The first row contains the field names as they appear in the list. The second row holds the value(s) you are looking for. The criteria range in Figure 5.7a selects the employees who work in Atlanta.

Multiple values in the same row are connected by an AND and imply that the selected records meet *all* of the specified criteria. The criteria range in Figure 5.7b identifies the Account Reps in Atlanta; that is, it selects any record in which the location field is Atlanta *and* the title field is Account Rep.

Values entered in multiple rows are connected by an OR in which the selected records satisfy *any* of the indicated criteria. The criteria range in Figure 5.7c will identify employees who work in Atlanta *or* whose title is Account Rep.

Name	Location	Title	Hire Date	Salary
	Atlanta			

(a) Employees Who Work in Atlanta

Name	Location	Title	Hire Date	Salary
	Atlanta	Account Rep		

Multiple values in same row

(b) Account Reps in Atlanta (AND condition)

Name	Location	Title	Hire Date	Salary
	Atlanta			
		Account Rep		

Values entered in multiple rows

(c) Employees Who Work in Atlanta or Who Are Account Reps (OR condition)

Name	Location	Title	Hire Date	Salary
			<1/1/93	

(d) Employees Hired before Jan 1, 1993

Name	Location	Title	Hire Date	Salary
				>$40,000

(e) Employees Who Earn More than $40,000

Name	Location	Title	Hire Date	Salary	Salary
				>$40,000	<$60,000

Lower and upper boundaries established for salary field

(f) Employees Who Earn More than $40,000 but Less than $60,000

Name	Location	Title	Hire Date	Salary
	=			

(g) Employees without a Location Entry

Returns all records with no entry in Location

Name	Location	Title	Hire Date	Salary

Returns all records

(h) All Employees (a blank row)

FIGURE 5.7 The Criteria Range

Relational operators such as the greater than or less than sign may be used with date or numeric fields to return records within a designated range. The criteria range in Figure 5.7d selects the employees hired before January 1, 1993. The criteria range in Figure 5.7e returns employees whose salaries are more than $40,000.

An upper and lower boundary may be established for the same field by repeating the field name within the criteria range. This was done in Figure 5.7f, which returns all records in which the salary is more than $40,000 but less than $60,000.

The equal and unequal signs select records with empty and nonempty fields, respectively. An equal sign with nothing after it will return all records without an entry in the designated field; for example, the criteria range in Figure 5.7g selects any record that is missing a value for the location field. An unequal sign ($<>$) with nothing after it will select all records with any nonblank entry.

An empty row in the criteria range returns *every* record in the list as shown in Figure 5.7h. All criteria are *case insensitive* and return records with any combination of upper and lowercase letters that match the entry.

THE IMPLIED WILD CARD

Any text entry within a criteria range is treated as though it were followed by the asterisk **wild card**; that is, New is the same as New*. Both entries will return New York, New Jersey, or any series of characters starting with New. To match a text entry exactly, begin with an equal sign, enter a quotation mark followed by another equal sign, the entry you are looking for, and the closing quotation mark—for example, ="=New" to return only the entries that say New.

Name Define Command

The **Name Define command** in the Insert menu equates a mnemonic name such as *employee_list* to a cell or cell range such as A1:E15, then enables you to use that name to reference the cell(s) in all subsequent commands. A name can be up to 255 characters in length, but must begin with a letter or an underscore. It can include upper- or lowercase letters, numbers, periods, and underscore characters.

Once defined, names adjust automatically for insertions and/or deletions within the range. If in the previous example, you were to delete row 4, the definition of *employee_list* would change to A1:E14. And, in similar fashion, if you were to add a new column between columns B and C, the range would change to A1:F14.

A name can be used in any formula or function instead of a cell address—for example, =SUM(SALES) instead of =SUM(M1:M10), where the name SALES has been defined as cells M1 through M10. It can also be used with database functions.

THE GO TO COMMAND

Names are frequently used in conjunction with the Go To command. Pull down the Edit menu and click Go To (or click the F5 key) to display a dialog box containing the names that have been defined within the workbook. Double click a name to move directly to the first cell in the associated range and simultaneously select the entire range.

Database Functions

The *database functions* DSUM, DAVERAGE, DMAX, DMIN, and DCOUNT operate on *selected* records in a list. The functions are illustrated in Figure 5.8 in conjunction with the employee list. The database functions parallel the statistical functions presented in Chapter 3 (SUM, AVERAGE, MAX, MIN, and COUNT) except that they affect only records that satisfy the established criteria.

The summary statistics in Figure 5.8 are based on the salaries of the managers in the list, rather than all employees. Each database function includes the criteria range in cells A17:E18 as an argument, and thus limits the selected employees to managers.

The *DAVERAGE function* returns the average salary for just the managers. The *DMAX* and *DMIN functions* display the maximum and minimum salaries for the managers. The *DSUM function* computes the total salary for all the managers, while the *DCOUNT function* indicates the number of managers.

Each database function has three arguments: the list on which it is to operate, the field to be processed, and the criteria range. Consider, for example, the DAVERAGE function as shown below:

=DAVERAGE(list,"field",criteria)

                     The criteria range can be entered as a cell range (such as A17:E18) or as a name assigned to a cell range (e.g., Criteria).

          The field name is enclosed in quotes—for example, "salary."

    The list can be entered as a cell range (such as A1:E15) or as a name assigned to a cell range (e.g., Database).

	A	B	C	D	E
1	**Name**	**Location**	**Title**	**Hire Date**	**Salary**
2	Adams	Atlanta	Trainee	11/24/93	$19,500
3	Brown	Atlanta	Trainee	11/24/93	$18,500
4	Coulter	Atlanta	Manager	3/16/92	$100,000
5	Smith	Atlanta	Account Rep	10/31/93	$65,000
6	Charles	Boston	Account Rep	11/24/93	$40,000
7	Manin	Boston	Account Rep	10/31/89	$49,500
8	Milgrom	Boston	Manager	10/31/91	$57,500
9	Rubin	Boston	Account Rep	10/31/92	$45,000
10	Adamson	Chicago	Manager	11/24/93	$52,000
11	James	Chicago	Account Rep	3/16/92	$42,500
12	Johnson	Chicago	Account Rep	3/16/92	$47,500
13	Marder	Chicago	Account Rep	10/31/90	$38,500
14	Elofson	Miami	Account Rep	3/16/92	$47,500
15	Gillenson	Miami	Account Rep	3/16/92	$55,000
16					
17	**Name**	**Location**	**Title**	**Hire Date**	**Salary**
18			Manager		
19					
20					
21			Summary Statistics		
22	Average Salary:				$69,833
23	Maximum Salary:				$100,000
24	Minimum Salary:				$52,000
25	Total Salary:				$209,500
26	Number of Employees:				3

Criteria range is A17:E18

FIGURE 5.8 Database Functions and the Data Extract Command

The criteria range may be reentered at any time, in which case the values of the database functions are automatically recalculated. In other words, if you were to change the entry in cell C18 to Trainee, the database functions would be calculated for trainees rather than managers.

FORMAT THE DATABASE

Formatting has no effect on the success or failure of database commands, so you can format the entries in a list to any extent you like. Select currency format where appropriate, change fonts, use borders or shading, or any other formatting option. Remember, however, that the accuracy of the data is much more important than its appearance.

HANDS-ON EXERCISE 2:

Data versus Information

Objective To sort a list on multiple keys; to demonstrate the AutoFilter and Advanced Filter commands; to define a named range; to use the DSUM, DAVERAGE, DMAX, DMIN, and DCOUNT functions.

Step 1: Sort the database
- ➤ Load Excel. Reset the TipWizard.
- ➤ Open the **EMPLOYE2.XLS** workbook created in the previous exercise.
- ➤ Click a single cell anywhere in the employee list. Pull down the **Data menu.** Click **Sort** to produce the dialog box in Figure 5.9a.
- ➤ Click the arrow in the **Sort By** list box. Click **Location** as the primary key.
- ➤ Click the arrow in the first **Then By** list box. Click **Name** as the secondary key.
- ➤ Be sure the **Header Row** option button is checked. Verify that **Ascending** is specified as the sequence for both the primary and secondary keys.
- ➤ Click **OK** to sort the file and return to the worksheet. The employees are listed by location and alphabetically within location.
- ➤ Save the workbook.

TWO KEYS—TWO CLICKS

The Ascending (Descending) Sort icon on the Standard toolbar sorts on a single key, but you can click either icon multiple times to sort on multiple keys. The trick is to do it in the right order; sort on the least significant field first, then work your way up to the most significant. To sort a list by location and by name within location, sort by name first (the secondary key), then sort by location (the primary key).

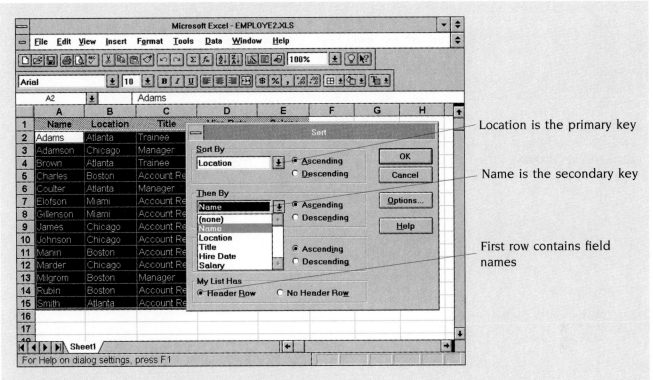

Location is the primary key

Name is the secondary key

First row contains field names

(a) The Data Sort Command (step 1)

FIGURE 5.9 Hands-on Exercise 2

Step 2: The AutoFilter command
➤ Click a single cell anywhere within the list. Pull down the **Data menu.** Click **Filter.** Click **AutoFilter** from the resulting cascade menu to produce the equivalent of a drop-down list box for each field name.
➤ Click the arrow next to **Title** to produce the list of titles shown in Figure 5.9b. Click **Account Rep.**
➤ The display changes to show only those employees who meet the filter condition. The worksheet is unchanged, but only those rows containing Account Reps are visible. The row numbers for the visible records are blue. The drop-down arrow for Title is also blue, indicating that it is part of the filter condition.

KEYBOARD SHORTCUTS

The keyboard is faster than the mouse if your hands are already on the keyboard and you know the menu shortcuts. Press the Alt key plus the underlined letter to pull down the menu—for example, Alt+D to pull down the Data menu; then type the underlined letter in the desired command—for example, F for Filter. In other words, Alt+D, then the letter F executes the Data Filter command.

Step 3: The Custom AutoFilter command
➤ Click the arrow next to **Salary** to display the list of salaries. Click **Custom** to produce the dialog box in Figure 5.9c.

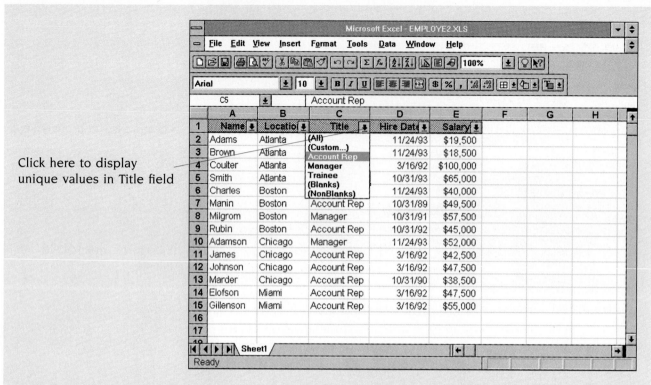

Click here to display
unique values in Title field

(b) The AutoFilter Command (step 2)

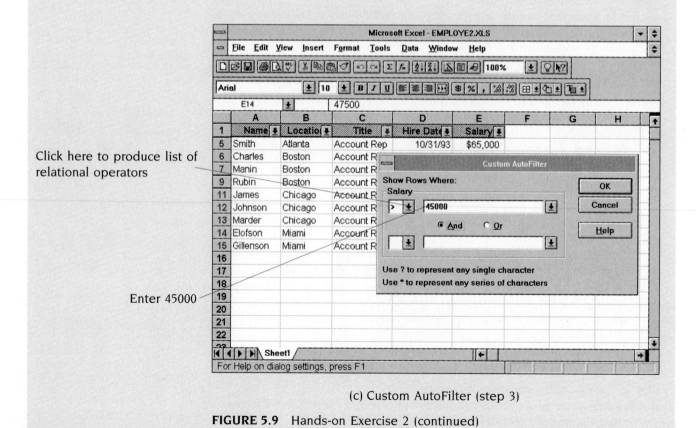

Click here to produce list of
relational operators

Enter 45000

(c) Custom AutoFilter (step 3)

FIGURE 5.9 Hands-on Exercise 2 (continued)

- Click the arrow in the leftmost drop-down list box for **Salary.** Click the **greater than** sign.
- Click in the text box for the salary amount. Type **45000.** Click **OK.**
- The list changes to display only those employees whose title is Account Rep *and* who earn more than $45,000.
- Pull down the **Data menu.** Click **Filter.** Click **AutoFilter** to remove the arrows next to the field names and cancel the filter condition. All of the records in the list are again visible.

WILD CARDS

Excel recognizes the question mark and asterisk as wild cards in the specification of criteria. A question mark stands for a single character in the exact position; for example, B?ll returns Ball, Bell, Bill, Boll, and Bull. An asterisk stands for any number of characters; e.g., *son will find Johnson, Anderson, and Elofson. (Excel uses the asterisk differently from DOS in that the Excel asterisk precedes a character string instead of following it.)

Step 4: The Advanced Filter command
- The field names in the criteria range must be spelled exactly the same way as in the associated list. The best way to ensure that the names are identical is to copy the entries from one range to the other.
  — Click and drag to select cells **A1 through E1.**
  — Click the **Copy icon** on the Standard toolbar. A marquee appears around the selected cells.
  — Click in cell **A17.** Click the **Paste icon** on the Standard toolbar to complete the copy operation. Press **Esc** to cancel the marquee.

DRAG-AND-DROP TO NONADJACENT RANGES

You can use the mouse to copy selected cells to a *nonadjacent* range provided the source and destination ranges are the same size and shape. Select the cells to be copied, point to any border of the selected cells (the mouse pointer changes to an arrow), then press and hold the Ctrl key (a plus sign appears) as you drag the selection to its destination. Release the mouse to complete the operation. Follow the same procedure, without pressing the Ctrl key, to move rather than copy the selected cells to a nonadjacent range.

- Click in cell **C18.** Type **Manager.** (Be sure you spell it correctly.)
- Click a single cell anywhere within the employee list. Pull down the **Data menu.** Click **Filter.** Click **Advanced Filter** from the resulting cascade menu to produce the dialog box in Figure 5.9d.
- Click in the **Criteria Range text box** within the Advanced Filter dialog box. Click in cell **A17** in the worksheet and drag the mouse to cell E18. Release the mouse. A marquee appears around these cells in the worksheet, and the corresponding cell reference is entered in the dialog box.
- Click **OK.** The display changes to show just the managers; that is, only rows 4, 8, and 10 are visible.

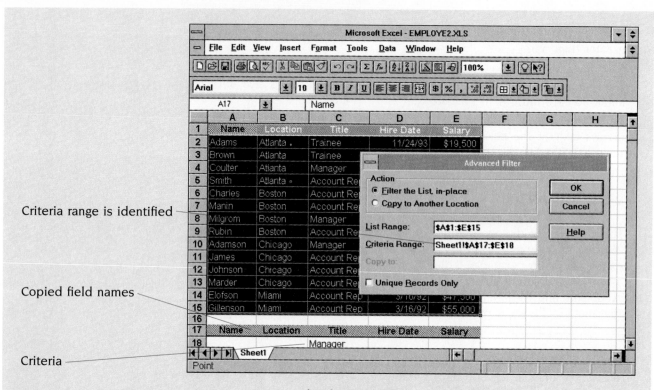

Criteria range is identified

Copied field names

Criteria

(d) Advanced Filter Command (step 4)

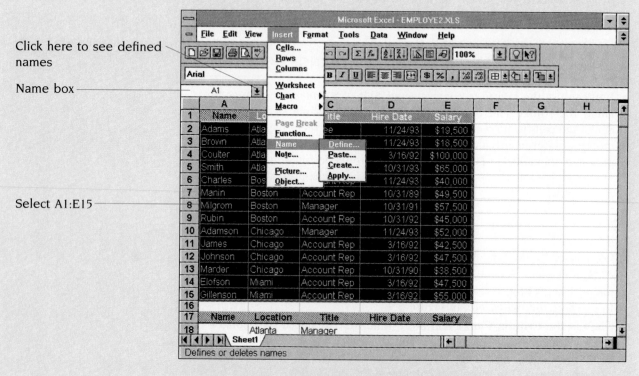

Click here to see defined names

Name box

Select A1:E15

(e) Name Define Command (step 5)

FIGURE 5.9 Hands-on Exercise 2 (continued)

- Click in cell **B18.** Type **Atlanta.** Press **enter.**
- Pull down the **Data menu.** Click **Filter.** Click **Advanced Filter.** The Advanced Filter dialog box already has the cell references for the List and Criteria ranges.
- Click **OK.** The display changes to show just the manager in Atlanta; that is, only row 4 is visible.
- Pull down the **Data menu.** Click **Filter.** Click **Show All** to remove the filter condition. The entire list is visible.

Step 5: The Name Define command
- Click and drag to select cells **A1 through E15** as shown in Figure 5.9e.
- Pull down the **Insert menu.** Click **Name.** Click **Define.** Type **Database** in the Define Name dialog box. Click **OK.**
- Pull down the **Edit menu** and click **Go To** (or press the **F5 key**) to display the Go To dialog box. There are two names in the box: Database, which you just defined, and Criteria, which was defined automatically when you specified the criteria range in step 4.
- Double click **Criteria** to select the criteria range (cells A17 through E18). Click elsewhere in the worksheet to deselect the cells.
- Save the workbook.

THE NAME BOX

Use the *Name box* to select a cell or named range by clicking in the box and then typing the appropriate entry. You can also click the arrow next to the Name box to select a named range from a drop-down list. And finally, you can use the Name box to define a named range, by first selecting the cells in the worksheet to which the name is to apply, then clicking in the box and entering the range name.

Step 6: Database functions (the Function Wizard)
- Click in cell **A21.** Type **Summary Statistics.** Select cells **A21 through E21,** then click the **Center Across columns** icon on the Formatting toolbar to center the heading over the selected cells.
- Enter the labels for cells **A22 through A26** as shown in Figure 5.9f.
- Click in cell **B18.** Press the **Del key.** The criteria range is now set to select only managers.
- Click in cell **E22.** Click the **Function Wizard icon** on the Standard toolbar to produce the dialog box in Figure 5.9f.
- Select **Database** in the Function Category list box. Click **DAVERAGE,** then click the **Next command button** to move to step 2 of the Function Wizard.

Step 7: The DAVERAGE function
- Click the **database text box** in the Function Wizard dialog box of Figure 5.9g. Type **Database** (the range name defined in step 5), which contains the employee list.

Function wizard tool

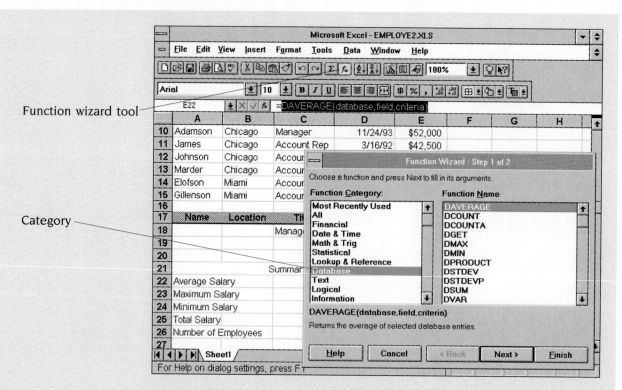

(f) Function Wizard (step 6)

Function

Computed value

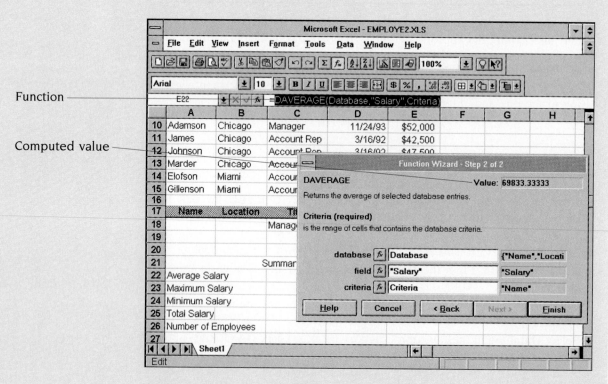

(g) DAVERAGE Function (step 7)

FIGURE 5.9   Hands-on Exercise 2 (continued)

- Click the **field text box.** Type **Salary,** which is the field name within the employee list.
- Click the **criteria text box.** Type **Criteria** (the range name defined during the Advanced Filter operation). The Function Wizard displays the computed value of 69833.33333.
- Click the **Finish command button** to enter the DAVERAGE function into the worksheet.
- Save the workbook.

DATABASE FUNCTIONS

Database functions should always be placed above or below the list to which they refer. They should never be placed to the left or right as the rows containing those entries may be hidden when a filter condition is in effect.

Step 8: The DMAX, DMIN, DSUM, and DCOUNT functions
- Enter the DMAX, DMIN, DSUM, and DCOUNT functions in cells E23 through E26, respectively. You can use the Function Wizard to enter each function individually, *or* you can copy the DAVERAGE function and edit appropriately:
  — Click in cell **E22.** Drag the **fill handle** to cells E23 through E26 to copy the DAVERAGE function to these cells.
  — Double click in cell **E23** to edit the contents of this cell, then click within the displayed formula to substitute **DMAX** for DAVERAGE. Press **enter** when you have completed the change.
  — **Double click** in the remaining cells and edit them appropriately. Figure 5.9h shows how double clicking a cell displays the cell contents, enabling you to edit within the cell itself rather than on the formula bar.
- The computed values (except for the DCOUNT function) are shown in Figure 5.9h.
- Select cells **E22 through E25,** then use the currency and decimal place icons on the Formatting toolbar to change to currency format with no decimals.
- Save the workbook.

Step 9: Change the criteria
- Click in the **Name Box.** Type **B18** and press **enter** to make cell B18 the active cell. Type **Chicago** to change the criteria to Chicago managers. Press **enter.**
- The values displayed by the DAVERAGE, DMIN, DMAX, and DSUM functions change to $52,000, reflecting the one employee (Adamson) who meets the current criteria (a manager in Chicago). The value displayed by the DCOUNT function changes to one to indicate one employee.
- Click in cell **C18.** Press the **Del key.**
- The average salary changes to $45,125, reflecting all employees in Chicago.
- Click in cell **B18.** Press the **Del key.**

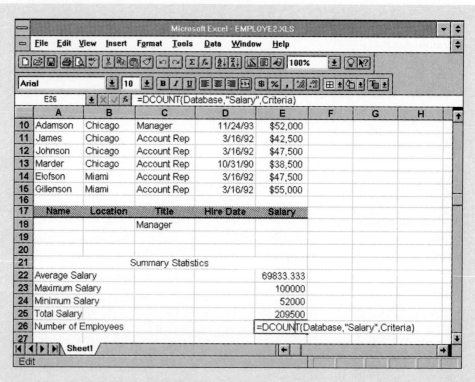

(h) DMAX, DMIN, DSUM, and DCOUNT Functions (step 8)

FIGURE 5.9   Hands-on Exercise 2 (continued)

> The criteria range is now empty. The DAVERAGE function displays $48,429, which is the average salary of all employees in the database.
> Click in cell **C18.** Type **Manager** and press the **enter key.** The average salary is $69,833, the average salary for all managers.

CLEAR THE CRITERIA RANGE

Clear the existing values within the criteria range before you enter new values, especially when the selection criteria are based on different fields. If, for example, you are changing from managers in any location (Title = Manager), to all employees in Chicago (Location = Chicago), you must clear the title field, or else you will get the employees who are managers and work in Chicago.

Step 10: Print the worksheet
> Save the worksheet.
> To print the entire worksheet, click the **Print icon** on the Standard toolbar.
> To print only a portion of the worksheet (e.g., just the summary statistics), select the cells you wish to print, pull down the **File menu,** and click **Print.** Click the **Selection option button.** Click **OK** to print the selected cells.

The **Subtotals command** in the Data menu computes subtotals based on data groups in a selected field. It also computes a grand total. The totals may be displayed with or without the detail lines as shown in Figure 5.10. Figure 5.10a displays the employee list as well as the totals. Figure 5.10b displays only the totals.

Execution of the Subtotals command inserts a subtotal row into the list whenever the value of the selected field (location in this example) changes from row to row. In Figure 5.10a the subtotal for the Atlanta employees is inserted into the list as we go from the last employee in Atlanta to the first employee in Boston. In similar fashion, the subtotal for Boston is inserted into the list as we go from the last employee in Boston to the first employee in Chicago. It is absolutely critical, therefore, that the list be in sequence according to the field on which the subtotals are based (location in this example) *prior* to executing the Subtotals command.

	A	B	C	D	E
1	**Name**	**Location**	**Title**	**Hire Date**	**Salary**
2	Smith	Atlanta	Account Rep	10/31/93	$65,000
3	Coulter	Atlanta	Manager	3/16/92	$100,000
4	Adams	Atlanta	Trainee	11/24/93	$19,500
5	Brown	Atlanta	Trainee	11/24/93	$18,500
6		**Atlanta Total**			$203,000
7	Charles	Boston	Account Rep	11/24/93	$40,000
8	Manin	Boston	Account Rep	10/31/89	$49,500
9	Rubin	Boston	Account Rep	10/31/92	$45,000
10	Milgrom	Boston	Manager	10/31/91	$57,500
11		**Boston Total**			$192,000
12	James	Chicago	Account Rep	3/16/92	$42,500
13	Johnson	Chicago	Account Rep	3/16/92	$47,500
14	Marder	Chicago	Account Rep	10/31/90	$38,500
15	Adamson	Chicago	Manager	11/24/93	$52,000
16		**Chicago Total**			$180,500
17	Elofson	Miami	Account Rep	3/16/92	$47,500
18	Gillenson	Miami	Account Rep	3/16/92	$55,000
19		**Miami Total**			$102,500
20		**Grand Total**			$678,000

(a) Detail Lines

	A	B	C	D	E
1	**Name**	**Location**	**Title**	**Hire Date**	**Salary**
6		**Atlanta Total**			$203,000
11		**Boston Total**			$192,000
16		**Chicago Total**			$180,500
19		**Miami Total**			$102,500
20		**Grand Total**			$678,000

(b) Summary Lines (Sum function)

FIGURE 5.10   The Subtotals Command

The Subtotals command does much more than its name implies in that you are not restricted to the summation function. Figure 5.10c, for example, displays averages (rather than totals) for the employees in each location. You can also obtain the maximum or minimum salary in each location, or the number of employees in each location, as described in the hands-on exercise that follows shortly.

The Subtotals command may be applied to a filtered list, in which case only values from the selected employees are included in the computed totals. Subtotals are removed from a worksheet by re-executing the Subtotals command and clicking the Remove All command button.

	A	B	C	D	E
1	**Name**	**Location**	**Title**	**Hire Date**	**Salary**
6		**Atlanta Average**			$50,750
11		**Boston Average**			$48,000
16		**Chicago Average**			$45,125
19		**Miami Average**			$51,250
20		**Grand Average**			$48,429

(c) Summary Lines (Average function)

FIGURE 5.10 The Subtotals Command (continued)

PIVOT TABLES

A *pivot table* extends the capability of individual database functions by presenting the data in summary form. It divides the records in a list into categories, then computes summary statistics for those categories.

The pivot table in Figure 5.11a displays the number of employees in each location according to job title. The column headings are the unique values in the Location field for employees in the associated list. The row labels are the unique values of the Title field. The values in the table show the number of employees in each Title-Location combination.

Figure 5.11b uses the identical categories (title and location) but computes the total salaries instead of the number of employees. Both pivot tables are based on the employee list we have been using throughout the chapter.

Count of Salary	Location				
Title	Atlanta	Boston	Chicago	Miami	Grand Total
Account Rep	1	3	3	2	9
Manager	1	1	1	0	3
Trainee	2	0	0	0	2
Grand Total	4	4	4	2	14

(a) Number of Employees for Each Job Title at Each Location

Sum of Salary	Location				
Title	Atlanta	Boston	Chicago	Miami	Grand Total
Account Rep	$65,000	$134,500	$128,500	$102,500	$430,500
Manager	$100,000	$57,500	$52,000	$0	$209,500
Trainee	$38,000	$0	$0	$0	$38,000
Grand Total	$203,000	$192,000	$180,500	$102,500	$678,000

(b) Total Salaries for Each Job Title at Each Location

FIGURE 5.11 Pivot Tables

A pivot table is created using the **PivotTable Wizard,** which prompts you for the information to develop the pivot table. You supply the field names for the row and column headings (title and location in our example) and the field on which the computation is based (salary). You also supply the means of computation (count in Figure 5.11a and sum in Figure 5.11b). The PivotTable Wizard does the rest. It creates the pivot table in its own worksheet and places it in the same workbook as the list on which it is based.

Once it has been created, you can add or remove categories within a pivot table by dragging the field names within the PivotTable Wizard. You could, for example, change the orientation of the tables in Figure 5.11 by switching the row and column headings. You could also add an additional field (e.g., an employee's sex) by dragging that field name onto the table. You can also modify the worksheet on which the pivot table is based (by adding, changing, or deleting employee records), then refresh the pivot table to reflect the changes made to the worksheet.

HANDS-ON EXERCISE 3:

Subtotals and Pivot Tables

Objective To display and modify subtotals within a list; to use the PivotTable Wizard to create and modify a pivot table.

Step 1: Open the EMPLOYE2 workbook
➤ Open the **EMPLOYE2** workbook from the previous exercise.
➤ Click and drag to select cells **A17 through E26.** Press the **right mouse button** to display a shortcut menu. Click **Clear Contents** to erase the criteria and summary statistics from the worksheet.
➤ Pull down the **File menu.** Click **Save As.** Save the workbook as **EMPLOYE3.XLS.**
➤ Press **Ctrl+Home** to move to cell A1. Click anywhere in **column C,** the column containing the employee titles.
➤ Click the **Sort Ascending icon** on the Standard toolbar. The employees should be arranged according to title.

Step 2: Insert a field
➤ Point to the column heading for column D, which presently contains the date of hire. Press the **right mouse button** to display a shortcut menu. Click **Insert** to insert a new column.
➤ Click in cell **D1.** Type **Sex** (the field name). Press the **down arrow key** to move to cell **D2.** Type **M.**
➤ Add the remaining entries in column D to match those in Figure 5.12a.
➤ Drag the border between the column headings for columns D and E to the left to make column D narrower.
➤ Click and drag to select cells **D1 through D15.** Click the **Centering icon** on the Formatting toolbar.
➤ Click outside the selected cells to deselect the range.

Step 3: Subtotals
➤ Pull down the **Data menu.** Click **Subtotals** to produce the Subtotal dialog box in Figure 5.12a.

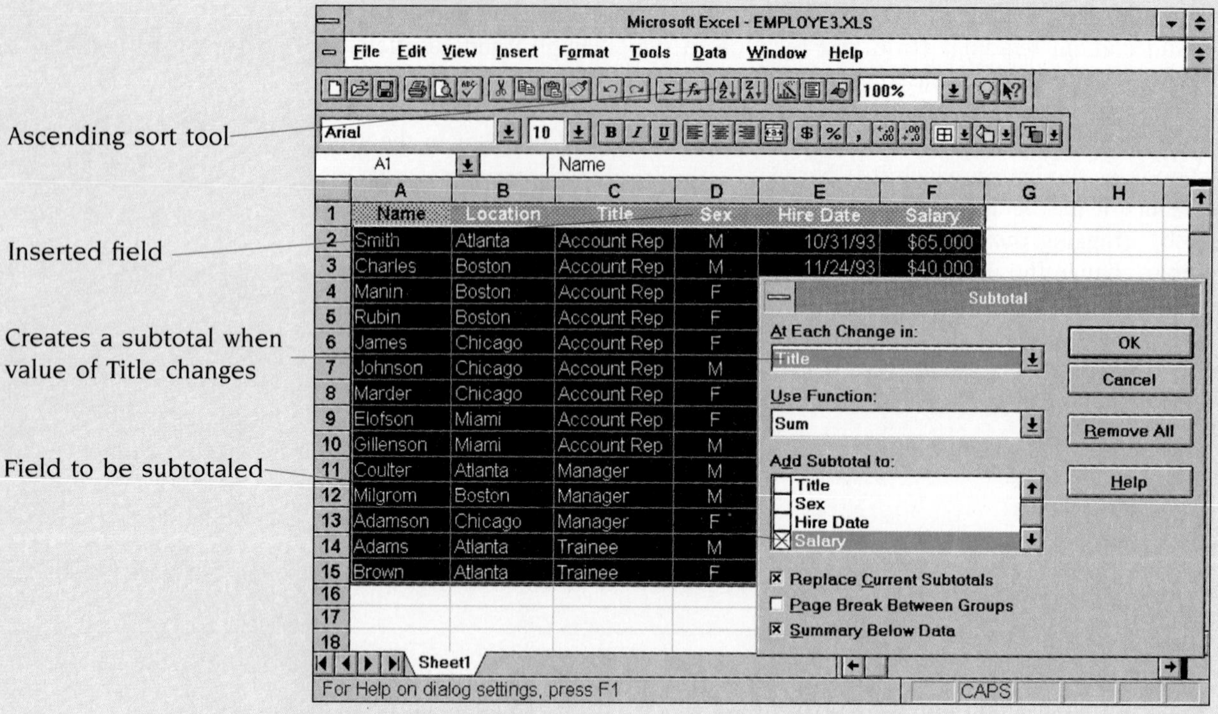
Ascending sort tool
Inserted field
Creates a subtotal when value of Title changes
Field to be subtotaled
Microsoft Excel - EMPLOYE3.XLS
File Edit View Insert Format Tools Data Window Help
Subtotal
At Each Change in:
Title
Use Function:
Sum
Add Subtotal to:
Title
Sex
Hire Date
Salary
OK
Cancel
Remove All
Help
Replace Current Subtotals
Page Break Between Groups
Summary Below Data
Sheet1
For Help on dialog settings, press F1

(a) Subtotal Command (step 3)

FIGURE 5.12 Hands-on Exercise 3

- Click the arrow in the **At Each Change in** list box. Click **Title** to create a subtotal whenever there is a change in title.
- Set the other options to match the dialog box in Figure 5.12a. Click **OK** to create the subtotals.

Step 4: Examine the subtotals

- Your worksheet should display subtotals as shown in Figure 5.12b.
- Click in cell **F11,** the cell containing the subtotal for Account Reps. The formula bar displays =SUBTOTAL(9,F2:F10), which computes the sum for cells F2 through F10. (The number 9 within the SUBTOTAL function indicates a sum.)
- Click in cell **F15,** the cell containing the subtotal for Managers. The formula bar displays =SUBTOTAL(9,F12:F14), which computes the sum for cells F12 through F14.

THE SUBTOTAL FUNCTION

The SUBTOTAL function can be entered explicitly into a worksheet or implicitly (and more easily) through the Subtotal command in the Data menu. The function has two arguments: a function number to indicate the type of computation, and the associated cell range. A function number of 9 indicates a sum; thus the entry =SUBTOTAL(9,E2:E10) computes the sum for cells E2 through E10. Pull down the Help menu and search on the SUBTOTAL function for additional information.

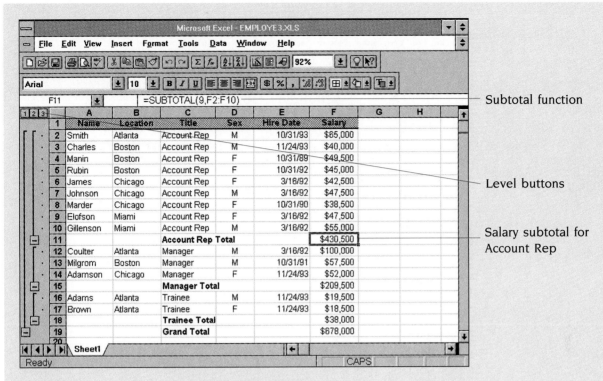

Subtotal function

Level buttons

Salary subtotal for Account Rep

(b) Subtotals (step 4)

FIGURE 5.12   Hands-on Exercise 3 (continued)

Step 5: Detail lines versus summary totals

➤ Click the **level 2 button** (under the Name box) to suppress the detail lines. The list collapses to display the subtotals and grand total as shown in Figure 5.12c.

➤ Click the **level 1 button** to suppress the subtotals. The list collapses further to display only the grand total.

➤ Click the **level 3 button** to restore the detail lines and subtotals. The list expands to display the employee records, subtotals, and grand total.

➤ Save the workbook. Click the **Print icon** on the Standard toolbar if you wish to print the list with the subtotals.

Step 6: The PivotTable Wizard

➤ You must clear all subtotals in order to create a pivot table. Click anywhere within the employee list or subtotals. Pull down the **Data menu.** Click **Subtotals.** Click the **Remove All command button.**

➤ Pull down the **Data menu.** Click **PivotTable** to produce step 1 of the Pivot-Table Wizard as shown in Figure 5.12d. The option button indicates the pivot table will be created from data in a Microsoft Excel List or Database.

➤ Click the **Next Command button** to move to step 2 of the PivotTable Wizard. You will see a dialog box where **Database** (the name assigned to the employee list in exercise 2) has already been entered in the Range text box.

➤ Click the **Next command button** to move to step 3, where you create the actual pivot table.

Step 7: The PivotTable Wizard (continued)

➤ Click the **Title field button** and drag it to the row area.

Print tool

Click here to suppress
detail lines

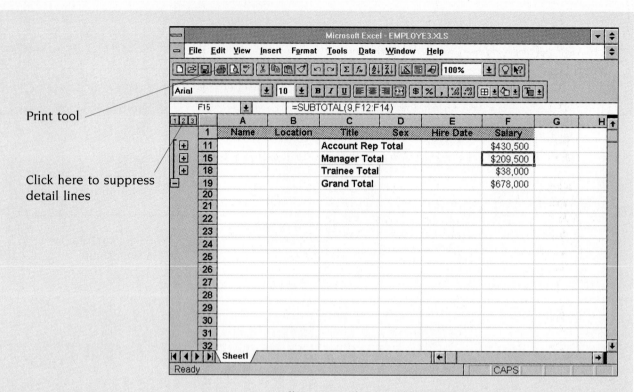

(c) Collapsing and Expanding Subtotals (step 5)

Click here to move to
step 2

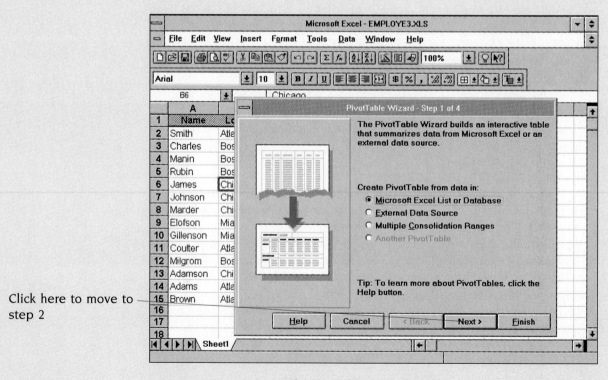

(d) PivotTable Wizard (step 6)

FIGURE 5.12   Hands-on Exercise 3 (continued)

➤ Click the **Location field button** and drag it to the column area.

➤ Click the **Salary field button** and drag it to the data area.

➤ The dialog box on your monitor should match Figure 5.12e. Click the **Next command button** to move to step 4, the final step in the PivotTable Wizard. The check boxes for all four options should be selected.

➤ Click the **Finish command button** to exit the PivotTable Wizard. The pivot table is placed in its own worksheet as shown in Figure 5.12f.

➤ Click the **Save icon** on the Standard toolbar to save the workbook.

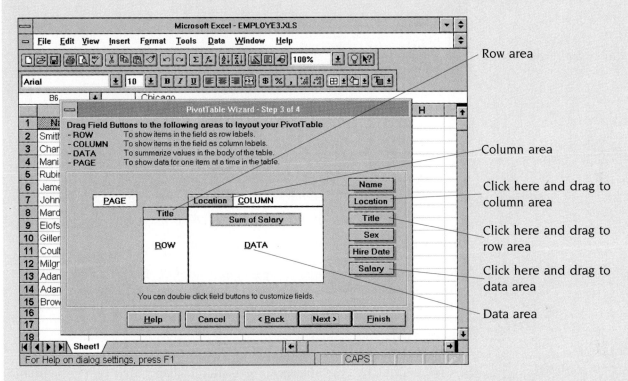

(e) PivotTable Wizard (step 7)

FIGURE 5.12 Hands-on Exercise 3 (continued)

Step 8: Worksheet tabs

➤ The pivot table is in its own worksheet. Point to the **Sheet2 tab** and click the **right mouse button** to display a shortcut menu. Click **Rename** to produce the Rename Sheet dialog box. Type **Pivot Table** as the new name of the tab. Click **OK.**

➤ Point to the **Sheet1 tab** and click the **right mouse button** to display a shortcut menu. Click **Rename** to produce the Rename Sheet dialog box. Type **Employee List** as the new name. Click **OK.**

➤ Click the **Pivot Table tab** to return to the worksheet containing the pivot table.

➤ Save the workbook.

Step 9: Modify the pivot table

➤ Click anywhere within the pivot table. Click the **Pivot Table Field icon** on the Query and Pivot toolbar to display the PivotTable Field dialog box shown in Figure 5.12f.

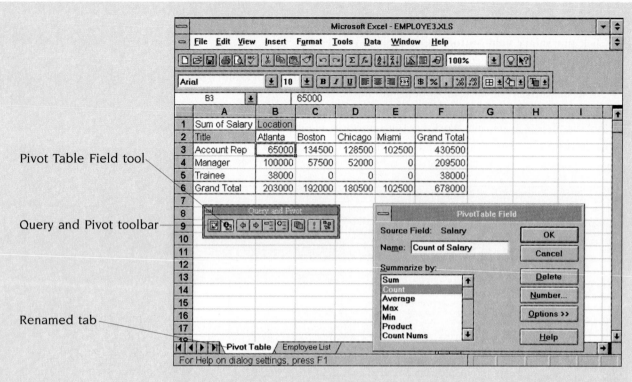

(f) Pivot Table (step 9)

FIGURE 5.12 Hands-on Exercise 3 (continued)

➤ Click **Count** in the Summarize By list box. Click **OK.** The pivot table changes to display the number of employees for each location–title combination. Note that there are two Account Reps and no Managers or Trainees in Miami.

Step 10: Modify the employee list
➤ Click the **Employee List tab** to return to the employee worksheet.
➤ Click in cell **C10.** Type **Manager.** Press **enter** to change Gillenson's title from Account Rep to Manager. Note that Gillenson works in Miami.

Step 11: Refresh the pivot table
➤ Click the **Pivot Table tab** to return to the pivot table. There are still two Account Reps and no Managers or Trainees in Miami because Gillenson's change in title is not yet reflected in the pivot table.
➤ Click the **Refresh Data icon** on the Query and Pivot toolbar to update the pivot table as shown in Figure 5.12g. Miami now has one Manager and one Account Rep, which reflects the change made to the worksheet in step 10.
➤ Save the workbook.

Step 12: Add a field to the pivot table
➤ Click the **PivotTable Wizard icon** on the Query and Pivot toolbar.
➤ Drag the **Sex field button** to the row area immediately beneath the Title field button as shown in Figure 5.12h. The pivot table has been modified to include the number of male and female employees in each job title in each location.
➤ Click the **Finish command button.**

Step 13: Pivot the table
➤ Click the **PivotTable Wizard icon** on the Query and Pivot toolbar.

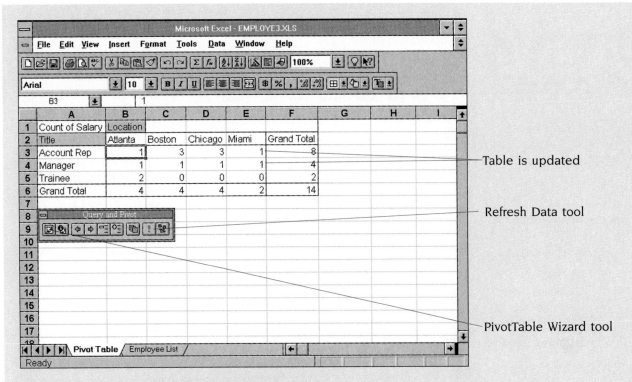

(g) Modified Pivot Table (step 11)

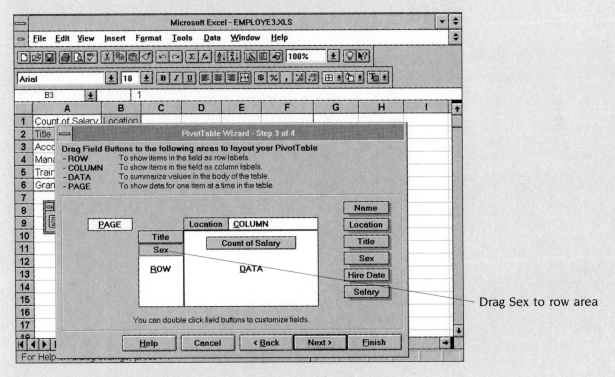

(h) Adding a New Field to the Pivot Table (step 12)

FIGURE 5.12   Hands-on Exercise 3 (continued)

➤ Drag the **Sex field button** to the column area beside the Location field button.
➤ Drag the **Location field button** to the row area under the Title field button.
   The dialog box for the PivotTable Wizard should match Figure 5.12i.

➤ Click the **Finish command button.** The pivot table has been modified as shown in Figure 5.12j.

Drag Sex to column area

Drag Location to row area

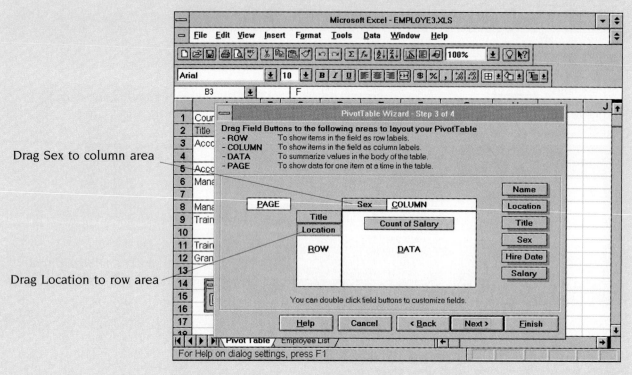

(i) Pivoting the Table (step 13)

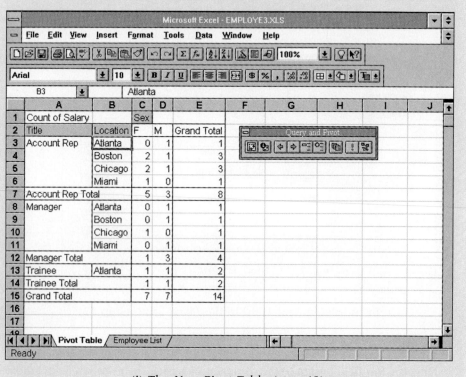

(j) The New Pivot Table (step 13)

FIGURE 5.12 Hands-on Exercise 3 (continued)

Step 14: Print the pivot table
➤ Pull down the **Print menu.** Click **Selected Sheet** to print only the pivot table.
➤ Click **OK**.
➤ Exit Excel. Exit Windows.

SUMMARY

A list is an area in a worksheet that contains rows of similar data. The first row contains the column headings (field names), and each additional row contains a record. A data form provides an easy way to add to, edit, and delete a list's records.

Data and information are not synonymous. Data refers to a fact or facts about a specific record such as an employee's name, title, or salary. Information is data that has been rearranged into a form perceived as useful by the recipient.

A filtered list displays only those records that meet specific criteria. Filtering is implemented through AutoFilter or the Advanced Filter command.

The Sort command arranges a list according to the value of one or more keys. Each key may be in ascending or descending sequence.

The database functions (DSUM, DAVERAGE, DMAX, DMIN, and DCOUNT) have three arguments: the associated list, the field name, and the criteria range. The simplest criteria range consists of two rows and as many fields as there are in the list.

The Subtotals command inserts subtotals (based on a variety of functions) into a list. A list should be sorted prior to execution of the Subtotals command.

A pivot table summarizes data from an existing list according to one or more fields within the list. The PivotTable Wizard creates a pivot table its own worksheet.

 Key Words and Concepts

Advanced Filter command	Field	PivotTable Wizard
Ascending sequence	Field name	Primary key
AutoFilter command	File	Record
Criteria range	File design	Secondary key
Data	File maintenance	Sort command
Data form	Filtered list	Subtotals command
Database	Form command	SUBTOTAL function
Database functions	Information	Tertiary key
DAVERAGE function	Insert Columns command	Wild card
DCOUNT function	Insert Rows command	
Delete command	Key	
Descending sequence	List	
DMAX function	Name box	
DMIN function	Name Define command	
DSUM function	Pivot table	

1. Which of the following describes the implementation of data management in Excel?
   (a) The rows in a list correspond to records in a file
   (b) The columns in a list correspond to fields in a record
   (c) Both (a) and (b)
   (d) Neither (a) nor (b)

2. Which of the following is suggested for the placement of a list within a worksheet?
   (a) There should be at least one blank row between the list and the other entries in the worksheet
   (b) There should be at least one blank column between the list and the other entries in the worksheet
   (c) Both (a) and (b)
   (d) Neither (a) nor (b)

3. Which of the following is suggested for the placement of database functions within a worksheet?
   (a) Above or below the list with at least one blank row separating the database functions from the list to which they refer
   (b) To the left or right of the list with at least one blank column separating the database functions from the list to which they refer
   (c) Both (a) and (b)
   (d) Neither (a) nor (b)

4. Assume that cells A21:B22 have been defined as the criteria range, that cells A21 and B21 contain the field names City and Title, respectively, and that cells A22 and B22 contain New York and Manager. The selected records will consist of:
   (a) All employees in New York regardless of title
   (b) All managers regardless of the city
   (c) Only the managers in New York
   (d) All employees in New York (regardless of title) *or* all managers (regardless of city)

5. Assume that cells A21:B23 have been defined as the criteria range, that cells A21 and B21 contain the field names City and Title, respectively, and that cells A22 and B23 contain New York and Manager, respectively. The selected records will consist of:
   (a) All employees in New York regardless of title
   (b) All managers regardless of the city
   (c) Only the managers in New York
   (d) All employees in New York (regardless of title) *or* all managers (regardless of city)

6. If employees are to be listed so that all employees in the same city appear together in alphabetical order by the employee's last name,
   (a) City and last name are both considered to be the primary key
   (b) City and last name are both considered to be the secondary key
   (c) City is the primary key and last name is the secondary key
   (d) Last name is the primary key and city is the secondary key

7. Which of the following can be used to delete a record from a list?
   (a) The Edit Delete command
   (b) The Data Form command
   (c) Both (a) and (b)
   (d) Neither (a) nor (b)

8. Which of the following is true about the DAVERAGE function?
   (a) It has a single argument
   (b) It can be entered into a worksheet using the Function Wizard
   (c) Both (a) and (b)
   (d) Neither (a) nor (b)

9. The Name box can be used to:
   (a) Define a range name
   (b) Select the range
   (c) Both (a) and (b)
   (d) Neither (a) nor (b)

10. Which of the following can be used to distinguish the first row in a list (the field names) from the remaining entries (the data)?
    (a) Insert a blank row between the first row and the remaining rows
    (b) Insert a row of dashes between the first row and the remaining rows
    (c) Either (a) or (b)
    (d) Neither (a) nor (b)

11. The AutoFilter command:
    (a) Permanently deletes records from the associated list
    (b) Requires the specification of a criteria range elsewhere in the worksheet
    (c) Either (a) or (b)
    (d) Neither (a) nor (b)

12. Which of the following is true of the Sort command?
    (a) The primary key must be in ascending sequence
    (b) The secondary key must be in descending sequence
    (c) Both (a) and (b)
    (d) Neither (a) nor (b)

13. A social security number is often used to identify a specific employee rather than the employee's name because:
    (a) The social security number is numeric, whereas the name is not
    (b) The social security number is unique, whereas the name is not
    (c) The social security number is a shorter field consisting of only nine digits, whereas the name contains many more characters
    (d) All of the above

14. Which of the following best describes the relationship between the Sort and Subtotal commands?
    (a) The Sort command should be executed before the Subtotals command
    (b) The Subtotals command should be executed before the Sort command
    (c) The commands can be executed in either sequence
    (d) There is no relationship because the commands have nothing to do with one another

15. A pivot table is:

(a) Created in a separate workbook from the associated list

(b) Automatically updated whenever the underlying list changes

(c) Both (a) and (b)

(d) Neither (a) nor (b)

ANSWERS

1. c	**9.** c
2. c	**10.** d
3. a	**11.** d
4. c	**12.** d
5. d	**13.** b
6. c	**14.** a
7. c	**15.** d
8. b	

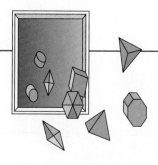

EXPLORING EXCEL

1. Use Figure 5.13 to match each action with its result; a given action may be used more than once or not at all.

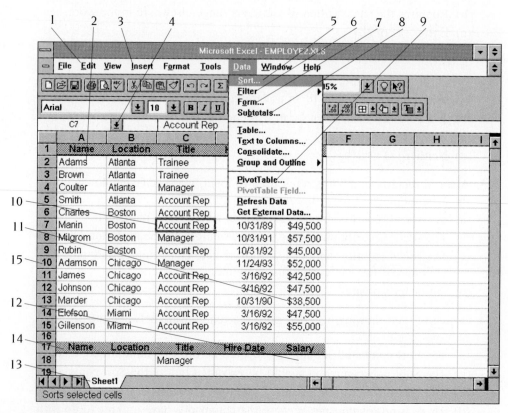

FIGURE 5.13 Screen for Problem 1

Action	Result
a. Click at 14, drag to 12, click at 3	___ Create a pivot table
	___ Select a range name
b. Click at 5	___ Add a record by using a data form
c. Click at 9	___ Create salary subtotals for each location
d. Click at 7	
e. Click at 15, click at 1	___ Hide records not meeting the current criteria
f. Click at 10 and enter the new data	___ Sort the list
g. Click at 6	___ Rename the active worksheet tab
h. Click at 4	___ Delete Adamson's record
i. Click at 8	___ Enter a new title for Manin
j. Click at 13, click right mouse button	___ Assign a name to the criteria range

2. Careful attention must be given to designing a list, or else the resulting system will not perform as desired. Consider the following:
   a. An individual's age may be calculated from his or her birth date, which in turn can be stored as a field within a record. An alternate technique would be to store age directly in the record and thereby avoid the calculation. Which field, that is, age or birth date, would you use? Why?
   b. Social security number is typically chosen as a record key instead of a person's name. What attribute does the social security number possess that makes it the superior choice?
   c. Zip code is normally stored as a separate field to save money at the post office in connection with a mass mailing. Why?
   d. An individual's name is normally divided into two (or three) fields corresponding to the last name and first name (and middle initial). Why is this done; that is, what would be wrong with using a single field consisting of the first name, middle initial, and last name, in that order?

3. Show the criteria range and associated entries to produce the following reports using the employee list presented in the chapter.
   a. All Trainees
   b. All Trainees in Chicago
   c. Employees who are Managers or Trainees
   d. Managers in Chicago or Trainees in Atlanta
   e. Employees hired before January 1, 1992, earning less than $50,000
   f. Employees missing a title or a location
   g. All employees in the company

4. Troubleshooting: The informational messages in Figure 5.14 appeared (or could have appeared) in response to commands that were executed in the various hands-on exercises in the chapter. Indicate the command that was executed prior to each message and the appropriate response.

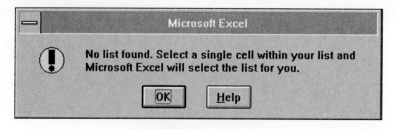

(a) Informational Message 1

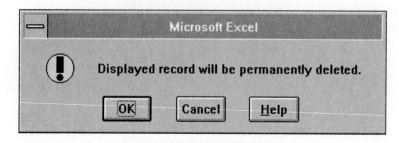

(b) Informational Message 2

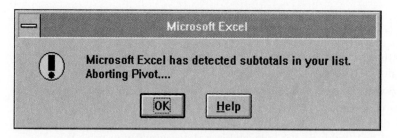

(c) Informational Message 3

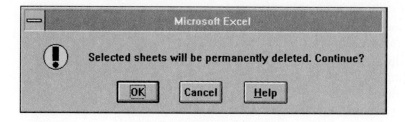

(d) Informational Message 4

FIGURE 5.14   Informational Messages for Problem 4

5. Figure 5.15 is a revised version of the employee list that was used throughout the chapter. A field has been added for an employee's previous salary as well as two additional fields for computations based on the previous salary.

   a. In which order are the employees listed? What is the primary key? Is the sequence ascending or descending?

   b. What formula (function) should be entered in cell G2 to compute the amount of the increase for employees who actually have an increase; that is, the increase for employees without a previous salary (i.e., new hires) is zero. (The zero values have been suppressed by pulling down the Tools menu, clicking Options, clicking the View tab, and removing the check in the Zero Values check box.)

	A	B	C	D	E	F	G	H
1	**Name**	**Location**	**Title**	**Hire Date**	**Salary**	**Previous Salary**	**Increase**	**Percentage**
2	Johnson	Chicago	Account Rep	3/16/92	$47,500	$40,000	$7,500	18.75%
3	Rubin	Boston	Account Rep	10/31/92	$45,000	$40,000	$5,000	12.50%
4	Coulter	Atlanta	Manager	3/16/92	$100,000	$90,000	$10,000	11.11%
5	Manin	Boston	Account Rep	10/31/89	$49,500	$45,000	$4,500	10.00%
6	Marder	Chicago	Account Rep	10/31/90	$38,500	$35,000	$3,500	10.00%
7	Elofson	Miami	Account Rep	3/16/92	$47,500	$45,000	$2,500	5.56%
8	Gillenson	Miami	Account Rep	3/16/92	$55,000	$52,500	$2,500	4.76%
9	Milgrom	Boston	Manager	10/31/91	$57,500	$55,000	$2,500	4.55%
10	James	Chicago	Account Rep	3/16/92	$42,500	$41,000	$1,500	3.66%
11	Adams	Atlanta	Trainee	11/24/93	$19,500			
12	Brown	Atlanta	Trainee	11/24/93	$18,500			
13	Smith	Atlanta	Account Rep	10/31/93	$65,000			
14	Charles	Boston	Account Rep	11/24/93	$40,000			
15	Adamson	Chicago	Manager	11/24/93	$52,000			
16								
17	**Name**	**Location**	**Title**	**Hire Date**	**Salary**	**Previous Salary**	**Increase**	**Percentage**
18							>0	
19								
20								
21						Evaluation of Salary Increase		
22						Average Increase	$4,389	8.99%
23						Maximum Increase	$10,000	18.75%
24						Minimum Increase	$1,500	3.66%
25						Number of Employees	9	9

FIGURE 5.15 Spreadsheet for Problem 5

c. What formula (function) should be entered in cell H2 to compute the percentage increase for those employees who have had an increase?

d. What is the criteria range? What would be the effect of removing the >0 entry from cell G18?

e. What is the entry in cell G22? in cell H22?

f. Retrieve the PROB0505.XLS workbook from the data disk, which is a partially completed version of Figure 5.15. The file contains the data in column F, but you will have to complete the entries in columns G and H, and define various ranges needed for the database commands and functions. When you are finished, type your name and title (compensation analyst) in cells A22 and A23, then print the worksheet and submit it to your instructor.

6. Open the worksheet in Figure 5.16, which is found on the data disk in the PROB0506.XLS workbook.

a. Delete the record for Julie Rubin, who has dropped out of school.

b. Change the data in Rick Fegin's record to show 193 quality points.

c. Use the Data Form command to add a transfer student, Jimmy Flynn, majoring in Engineering. Jimmy has completed 65 credits and has 200 quality points. Use the Tab key to move from one field to the next within the data form; be sure to enter the data in the appropriate text boxes. Do not enter Jimmy's GPA as it will be computed automatically.

d. Sort the list so that the students are listed in alphabetical order. Specify last name and first name as the primary and secondary key, respectively.

e. Does the sort you just performed explain why the last name and first name were defined as separate fields within the list? Would the students still be in alphabetical order if you had defined the name as a single field con-

	A	B	C	D	E	F
1	**Academic Advisor**					
2						
3	**Last Name**	**First Name**	**Major**	**Quality Points**	**Credits**	**GPA**
4	Moldof	Alan	Engineering	60	20	3.00
5	Stutz	Joel	Engineering	180	75	2.40
6	Rubin	Julie	Liberal Arts	140	65	2.15
7	Milgrom	Richard	Liberal Arts	400	117	3.42
8	Grauer	Jessica	Liberal Arts	96	28	3.43
9	Moldof	Adam	Business	160	84	1.90
10	Grauer	Benjamin	Business	190	61	3.11
11	Rudolph	Eleanor	Liberal Arts	185	95	1.95
12	Ford	Judd	Engineering	206	72	2.86
13	Fegin	Rick	Communications	190	64	2.97
14	Flynn	Sean	Business	90	47	1.91
15	Coulter	Maryann	Liberal Arts	135	54	2.50
16						
17						
18	**The Dean's List**					
19	**Last Name**	**First Name**	**Major**	**Quality Points**	**Credits**	**GPA**
20						>3.00
21						
22	**Last Name**	**First Name**	**Major**	**Quality Points**	**Credits**	**GPA**
23						
24						
25						
26						
27						
28						
29	**Academic Probation**					
30	**Last Name**	**First Name**	**Major**	**Quality Points**	**Credits**	**GPA**
31						<2.00
32						
33	**Last Name**	**First Name**	**Major**	**Quality Points**	**Credits**	**GPA**
34						
35						
36						
37						
38						
39						
40						
41						

FIGURE 5.16   Spreadsheet for Problem 6

sisting of the first name followed by the last name and you used the combined name as the primary key?

f. Save the workbook.

g. Create the Dean's List by using the Advanced Filter command to copy the qualified students to cells A22 through A27. Use A19:F20 as the criteria range for the Advanced Filter command.

h. Create the list of students on academic probation by using the Advanced Filter command to copy the selected students to cells A33 through A40. Use A30:F31 as the criteria range for this Advanced Filter command.

i. Add your name as the academic advisor in cell C1. Print the worksheet with both lists of students and submit it to your instructor.

7. Object Linking and Embedding: The compound document in Figure 5.17 consists of a memo created in Word for Windows 6.0 and the pivot table created in the third hands-on exercise. The document was created in such a way that any change in the worksheet will be automatically reflected in the memo.

a. Copy the pivot table to the clipboard:

➤ Open the EMPLOYE3.XLS workbook created in the third hands-on exercise.

➤ Modify the pivot table that is currently in the workbook so that it matches the table in Figure 5.17.

➤ Select the pivot table. Pull down the Edit menu. Click Copy to copy the pivot table to the Windows clipboard.

Soleil Shoes

Italy, London, Madrid

Dear John,

Enclosed please find the salary analysis you requested last Friday. I have broken down the salaries by title and location.

Sum of Salary	Location				
Title	Atlanta	Boston	Chicago	Miami	Grand Total
Account Rep	$65,000	$134,500	$128,500	$47,500	$375,500
Manager	$100,000	$57,500	$52,000	$55,000	$264,500
Trainee	$38,000	$0	$0	$0	$38,000
Grand Total	$203,000	$192,000	$180,500	$102,500	$678,000

I noticed that the manager in Atlanta is paid disproportionately well compared to his counterparts in the other cities. Let me know if you need any other information.

Bob

FIGURE 5.17 Compound Document for Problem 7

b. Open Word for Windows:

➤ Press and hold the Alt key, while you press and release the Tab key repeatedly to cycle through the open applications. Release the Alt key when you see Program Manager displayed in a box in the middle of your screen.

➤ Open Word for Windows by double clicking its program icon. Type the salutation and first two lines of the memo as shown in Figure 5.17.

c. Link the pivot table to the word processing document:

➤ Pull down the Edit menu, click Paste Special, and choose Microsoft Excel 5.0 Worksheet Object from the open list. Click the Paste Link option button, then click OK.

➤ The pivot table should appear within the memo as shown in Figure 5.17.

d. Change the underlying worksheet data:

> ➤ Use Alt+Tab to return to Excel. Press the Esc key to remove the marquee around the pivot table.
> ➤ Click the Employee List tab to return to the worksheet containing the employee list.
> ➤ Click in cell F12 and enter 75000 to change Milgrom's salary.
> ➤ Click the Pivot Table tab to return to the worksheet containing the pivot table. Click anywhere in the pivot table. Click the Refresh icon on the Query and Pivot toolbar to recalculate the pivot table. The pivot table changes to reflect Milgrom's new salary as does the overall total for both Manager and Boston.

e. Return to the Word document:

> ➤ Use Alt+Tab to return to the word processing document.
> ➤ The pivot table within the document has been automatically updated to include Milgrom's new salary.
> ➤ Complete the memo and save the document. Exit Word. Exit Excel. Exit Windows.

Case Studies

The United States of America

What is the total population of the United States? What is its area? Can you name the 13 original states or the last five states admitted to the Union? Do you know the 10 states with the highest population or the five largest states in terms of area? Which states have the highest population density (people per square mile)?

The answers to these and other questions are readily available, provided you can analyze the data in the USADBASE.XLS workbook that is available on the data disk. This assignment is completely open-ended and requires only that you print out the extracted data in a report on the United States database. Format the report so that it is attractive and informative.

The Super Bowl

How many times has the NFC won the Super Bowl? When was the last time the AFC won? What was the largest margin of victory? What was the closest game? What is the most points scored by two teams in one game? How many times have the Miami Dolphins appeared? How many times did they win? Use the data in the SUPERBWL workbook to prepare a trivia sheet on the Super Bowl, then incorporate your analysis into a letter addressed to NBC Sports. Convince them that you are a super fan and that you merit two tickets to next year's game.

Personnel Management

You have been hired as the Personnel Director for a medium-sized firm (500 employees) and are expected to implement a system to track employee compensation. You want to be able to calculate the age of every employee as well as the length of service. You want to know each employee's most recent performance evaluation. You want to calculate the amount of the most recent salary increase, in dollars as well as a percentage of the previous salary. You also want to know how long the employee had to wait for that increase—that is, how much time elapsed between the beginning of present and previous salary.

Design a worksheet capable of providing this information. Enter test data for at least five employees to check the accuracy of your formulas. Format the worksheet so that it is attractive and easy to read.

Equal Employment Opportunity

Are you paying your employees fairly? Is there any difference between the salaries paid to men and women? between minorities and nonminorities? between minorities of one ethnic background and those of another ethnic background? Use the EEO.XLS workbook to analyze the data for the listed employees. Are there any other factors not included in the database that might be reasonably expected to influence an employee's compensation? Write up your findings in the form of a memo to the Vice President for Human Resources.

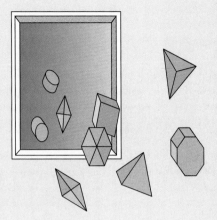

Appendix A:
Toolbars

M icrosoft Excel 5.0 offers thirteen predefined toolbars to provide access to commonly used commands. The toolbars are displayed in Figure A.1 and are listed here for convenience:

  Auditing
  Chart
  Drawing
  Formatting
  Forms
  Full Screen
  Microsoft
  Query and Pivot
  Standard
  Stop Recording
  TipWizard
  Visual Basic
  Workgroup

The Standard and Formatting toolbars are displayed by default and appear immediately below the Menu Bar. The other toolbars can be displayed as needed or, in some cases, may appear automatically when you access their corresponding feature (e.g., the Chart toolbar or the Query and Pivot toolbar).

The icons on the toolbars are intended to be indicative of their function. For example, clicking on the printer icon (fourth from the left on the Standard toolbar) executes the Print command. If you are unsure of the purpose of any icon, point to it, and a Tool Tip will appear that displays its name.

You can display multiple toolbars at one time, move them to new locations on the screen, customize their appearance, or suppress their display.

➤ To display or hide a toolbar, pull down the View menu and click the Toolbars command. Select (deselect) the toolbar(s) that you want to display (hide). The selected toolbar(s) will be displayed in the same position as when last displayed.

You may also point to any toolbar and click with the right mouse button to bring up a shortcut menu, after which you can select the toolbars to be displayed (hidden).

➤ To change the size of the tools, display them in monochrome rather than color, or suppress the display of the Tool Tips, pull down the View menu, click Toolbars and then select/deselect the appropriate check box.

➤ Toolbars may either be docked (along the edge of the window) or left floating (in their own window). A toolbar moved to the edge of the window will dock along that edge. A toolbar moved anywhere else in the window will float in its own window. Docked toolbars are one tool wide (high), whereas floating toolbars can be resized by clicking and dragging a border/corner as you would any window.

— To move a docked toolbar, click anywhere in the gray background area and drag the toolbar to its new location.

— To move a floating toolbar, drag its title bar to its new location.

➤ To customize one or more toolbars, display the toolbars on the screen. Then pull down the View menu, click Toolbars, and click the Customize command button. Alternatively, you can click on any toolbar with the right mouse button and select Customize from the shortcut menu.

— To move a tool, drag the tool to its new location on that toolbar or any other displayed toolbar.

— To copy a tool, press the Ctrl key as you drag the tool to its new location on that toolbar or any other displayed toolbar.

— To delete a tool, drag the tool off of the toolbar and release the mouse button.

— To add a tool, select the category from the Categories list box and then drag the tool to the desired location on the toolbar. (To see a description of a tool's function prior to adding it to a toolbar, click the tool in the Customize dialog box and read the displayed description.)

— To restore a predefined toolbar to its default appearance, pull down the View menu, click Toolbars, select the desired toolbar, and click the Reset command button.

➤ The Borders, Color, and Font Color buttons on the Formatting toolbar, the Chart Type button on the Chart toolbar, and the Pattern button on the Drawing toolbar also function as movable tear-off palettes. Display the desired palette by clicking the associated down arrow, then drag the palette onto the worksheet in order to make it more accessible as you work. Double click its control-menu box to close the palette.

➤ To create your own toolbar, pull down the View menu and click Toolbars. Alternatively, you can click on any toolbar with the right mouse button and then select Toolbars from the shortcut menu.

— Enter a name for the toolbar in the dialog box that follows. The name can be any length and can contain spaces.

— Click the New command button.

— The new toolbar will appear at the top left of the screen. Initially, it will be big enough to hold only one tool. Add, move, and delete tools, following the same procedures as outlined above. The toolbar will automatically size itself as new tools are added and deleted.

— To delete a custom toolbar, pull down the View menu, click Toolbars, select the custom toolbar to be deleted. Click the Delete command button. Click Yes to confirm the deletion.

Auditing Toolbar

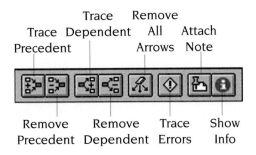

Chart Toolbar

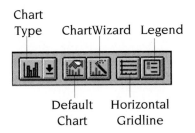

Drawing Toolbar

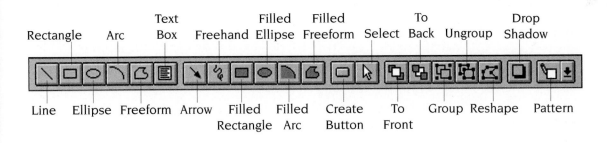

Formatting Toolbar

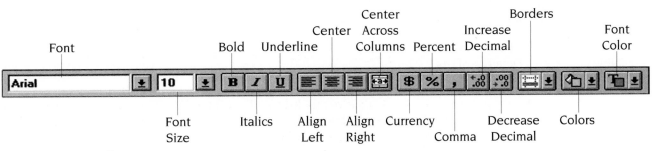

FIGURE A.1 Toolbars

Forms Toolbar

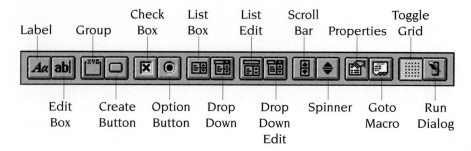

Label Group Check Box List Box List Edit Scroll Bar Properties Toggle Grid

Edit Box Create Button Option Button Drop Down Drop Down Edit Spinner Goto Macro Run Dialog

Full Screen Toolbar

Full Screen

Microsoft Toolbar

Word Access Project Mail

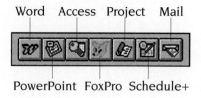

PowerPoint FoxPro Schedule+

Query and Pivot Toolbar

Pivot Table Wizard Ungroup Hide Detail Show Pages

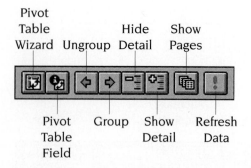

Pivot Table Field Group Show Detail Refresh Data

FIGURE A.1 Toolbars (continued)

Standard Toolbar

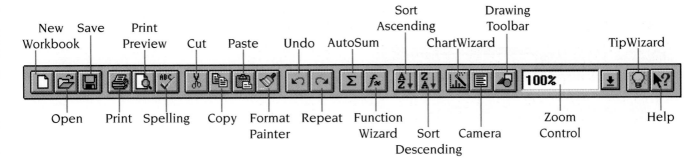

Stop Recording Toolbar

TipWizard Toolbar

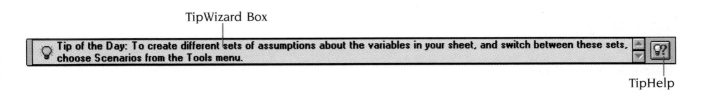

Visual Basic Toolbar

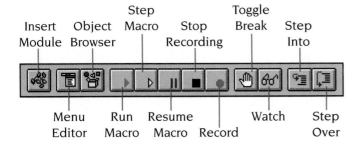

FIGURE A.1   Toolbars (continued)

Workgroup Toolbar

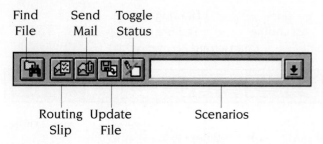

FIGURE A.1 Toolbars (continued)

Index

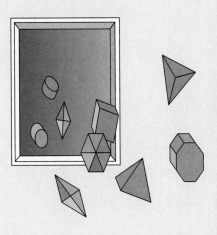